D0856942

Robert Steele deserves our admiration and our focused attention for bringing the idea of open source information to the fore. His passion to serve the nation by developing this new approach to better understanding the conditions and circumstances we are faced with daily - is exemplary. Steele's advocacy and efforts have led the way toward an enlightened and informed public. We all owe him a debt of gratitude for the sacrifices he has made to drag us - kicking and screaming - into the modern information age.

Patrick Hughes, LTGEN, USA (Ret)

THE SMART NATION ACT:
Public Intelligence in the Public Interest

**Foreword by Congressman Rob Simmons (R-CT-02)
Sponsor, The Smart Nation Act**

Robert David Steele (Vivas)
MA, MPA, NWC, USMC, CIA, OSS

**OSS International Press
Oakton, Virginia**

This book and others in the series are available at quantity discounts for group or class distribution. Books come 20 to the box. Please communicate with the publisher.

OSS International Press is the book-publishing arm of OSS.Net, Inc., publisher of *Proceedings of the Global Information Forum* (annual), *OSS Notices* (occasional series), and the ten-book series *ON INTELLIGENCE*. Visit www.oss.net.

Published by OSS International Press (OSS)   September 2006
Post Office Box 369
Oakton, Virginia 22124 USA
(703) 242-1700 Facsimile (703) 242-1711
Email oss@oss.net, Web: www.oss.net

Cover graphic: The view of Africa, Antarctica, the Indian and Atlantic Oceana from 23,000 miles out in space as the last Apollo flight coasted to the moon, December 1972. Original photo credit NASA 1989. Available in sticker form as item Apollo 17(E). Correspond with EarthSeals, POB 8000, Berkeley, CA 94707 USA. The orange square around the globe represents the Earth at a tipping point in relation to the ten threats.

Printed and bound in the United States of America

9 8 7 6 5 4 3 2

───────────────────────────────

LIBRARY OF CONGRESS CATALOGING-IN-PUBLICATION DATA

Steele, Robert David, 1952-
    THE SMART NATION ACT: Public Intelligence in the Public Interest/ Robert David Steele
    p.   cm.
Includes bibliographical references and index.
ISBN 978-0-9715661-3-2 (alk. paper)
1. Intelligence service.. 2. Military intelligence.. 3. Law enforcement intelligence.
    4. Business intelligence. 5. Internet. 6. Organizational change. 7. Strategic
    planning. 8. Leadership. 9. Information Technology. 11. Economic forecasting.
    12. Business forecasting. 13. Knowledge, theory of. 14. Power (Social
    sciences). 15. Information science—social aspects. 16. Competition. 17.
    National security—management of. 18. Political planning. 19. Gaming &
    Scenarios. 20. Decision-support.
I.   Title.
JK468.I6S74 2006
327.1273—dc21   00-029284

New Players

We are entering a period of turbulence and innovation. Here is an illustration of where we think the world is going regardless of what the three branches of the Federal government decide to do or not do. This book puts forward ideas for creating a "Smart Nation" in which the Federal level is both fully informed about global reality, and able to provide to all statehouses, schoolhouses, chambers of commerce, and social clubs, a very strong and sustained exposure to global reality.

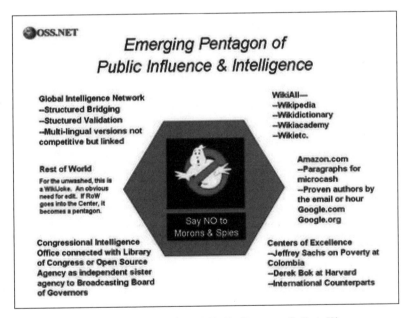

Emerging Pentagon of Public Influence & Intelligence

The American public now has the same power to do good that networked terrorists have to do bad. It will be up to Congress to decide whether or not to nurture this emerging pentagon of public influence & intelligence. *St.*

i

THE SMART NATION ACT: Public Intelligence in the Public Interest

THE SMART NATION ACT: Public Intelligence in the Public Interest

Table of Contents

Foreword

In the mid-1990s, it was my honor to command the 434th Military Intelligence Detachment (MID), a U.S. Army Reserve unit associated with Yale University and located in New Haven, Connecticut. Our unit wrote the first handbook for Open Source Intelligence (OSINT) for the U.S. Army. In 1994, our unit was honored with the Golden Candle Award presented by Open Source Solutions in recognition of its "unusual dedication and persistence … in preparing a primer, *Open Source Intelligence Resources for the Military Intelligence Officer*, which is of value to all joint and coalition personnel." The following year the Reserve Officers Association gave the 434th MID its "Outstanding USAR Small Unit Award" for 1995-1996, due in no small part because of its contributions to OSINT.

In 1997 General Peter Schoomaker, USA then Commander-in-Chief of the U.S. Special Operations Command (USSOCOM), was briefed on OSINT, understood its value, and ordered the creation of an OSINT support cell within the Special Operations Command Joint Intelligence Center (SOCJIC). Today that small unit, for a negligible amount of money, is responsible for satisfying 40% of the all-source intelligence requirements generated by all elements of USSOCOM.

In 2000, General William F. Kernan, USA, then serving as both the ranking flag officer of the Joint Forces Command (USJFCOM) and as the Supreme Allied Commander, Atlantic (SACLANT), agreed to a suggestion by Brigadier General James Cox of Canada, then the Deputy J-2 at Supreme Headquarters, Allied Powers Europe (SHAPE), validated by General Kernan's Deputy at the Atlantic Command, Admiral Sir James Perwone of the United Kingdom, and commissioned three study guides for the North Atlantic Treaty Organization (NATO): the *NATO Open Source Intelligence Handbook*, the *NATO Open Source Intelligence Reader*, and (NATO) *Intelligence Exploitation of the Internet*. All three of these documents remain valid and useful today.

In the years between 1994 and today, over 40 countries have developed some form of OSINT Center or Cell, most of them for military use. The United

1

States, however, was slow to focus on OSINT across the board, and on 11 September 2001, we were attacked on our homeland by a terrorist group whose intentions had been amply documented in both secret and open sources.

What we have learned since 9/11 is that Information Operations (IO) is the primary means of both understanding and of stabilizing the world. Belief systems in all languages, and an understanding of those belief systems in the context of their own history in their own language, their own sermons today in their own language, are the absolutely essential foundation for national security and national competitiveness in the age of globalization.

OSINT is an integral supporting element of IO. Robert Steele has done more than any other person to promote the effective use of OSINT in support of policy, acquisition, operations, logistics, and all-source intelligence, and with this book—his fourth book—he brings to Congress and the public carefully developed arguments and supporting documentation for the Smart Nation Act. The Open Source Solution refers to both OSINT and to open source software.[1]

As I reflect on all that I have learned since being Staff Director to Senator Barry Goldwater (R-AZ), then Chairman of the Senate Select Committee on Intelligence (SSCI); as an Army officer; and as a Congressman with responsibilities on both the House Armed Services Committee and as Chairman of the Subcommittee on Intelligence, Information Sharing, and Terrorism Risk Assessment of the House Homeland Security Committee, I find myself seeing four areas where we can improve our Nation's prospects for the future:

First, it is clear, as this book suggests and as Dr. Cambone has demanded, that we must be able to access all information in all languages, all the time. Secret intelligence is a fraction of what we need to know to defend America, collaborate with allies, and enhance the prosperity of all countries. It is no longer enough to have spies and diplomats—we are engaged in a 100-year six-front Global War, and nothing less than universal information coverage will

---

[1] Open Source Software, sometime called Free/Open Source Software, is not necessarily free of price, but rather free of the cumbersome restrictions that come with proprietary software. Open Source Software is not only very inexpensive in comparison with proprietary solutions, it is more secure, allows for faster better cheaper sharing of all forms of information, and is infinitely improvable by all.

meet our needs. Nor can we limit ourselves to online information. We must be able to access historical and cultural documents, and all off-line information.

Second, it is clear to me that information sharing rather than secrecy must be the most important mind-set to be fostered as we go forward. Information must be shared in secure reasonable ways across all boundaries. Multi-national, multi-agency, multi-disciplinary, multi-domain information sharing—what the Swedes call M4IS—is the wave of the future.

Third, since 80% of what we need to know is controlled or accessible only to non-governmental organizations or private sector parties, most of whom have no wish to be associated with covert intelligence organizations, it is clear to me that the Nation needs to create a national Open Source Agency.

Fourth and finally, we must recognize that the traditional information technology approach, in which unlimited amounts of taxpayer dollars are applied to proprietary, unilateral, expensive systems operating in isolation from one another, is neither affordable nor sensible.

- External to the Republic, we must interact and share information with non-governmental organizations, universities, and foreign governments and their sub-state elements, all with limited budgets.

- Internal to the Republic, we must dramatically improve the ability of state, local, and tribal governments to make sense of all of the information available to them, while also making it possible for them to interact with our federal government and other parties using the best available *affordable* digital technologies.

For these two reasons, open source software must join open source information as a foundation for global information sharing and IO.

The Smart Nation Act, originally conceptualized by the author in 1994, and then included as Chapter 15 of his first book, *ON INTELLIGENCE: Spies and Secrecy in an Open World,* a book honored with a Foreword by Senator David Boren (D- OK), retired and past Chairman of the Senate Select

Committee on Intelligence, has been re-directed in three important ways by recent circumstances, including the introduction by Congressman Jeff Flake (R-AZ-06) and Congressman Adam Schiff (D-CA-29) of the Intelligence Oversight Act demanding intelligence sharing for all Committees.

First and most importantly, the Act, originally developed to create an Open Source Agency within the U.S. Intelligence Community, now distinguishes between the protection and enhancement of open source intelligence in support of secret intelligence, and the need to have the primary national open source information collection and sharing capability *outside* the U.S. Intelligence Community, as a sister agency to the Broadcasting Board of Governors (BBG).[2]

Second, inspired by the bi-partisan leadership of Congressmen Flake and Schiff, the Act has been modified to add two capabilities supportive of Congressional oversight of both intelligence and all jurisdictions:

- The first, as called for by the Intelligence Oversight Act, provides for each Congressional committee to have a sub-committee of at least two individuals, two *Members*, who shall have access to classified information relevant to their jurisdictions.

- The second, inspired by the need of Congress for tailored intelligence across each jurisdiction, creates a Congressional Public Intelligence Office that has absolutely no access to secret sources and methods, in order to provide Congress, and the public, with the best available open source intelligence on all important topics across all jurisdictions. This will be our public baseline.

Congress may wish to integrate elements of the Smart Nation Act into the Intelligence Oversight Act, or move in other directions, but at least all of these needs and proposed solutions are now before the public, not just Members.

---

[2] This important intellectual contribution is from Dr. Joseph Markowitz, the only Director of the Community Open Source Program Office (COSPO), before it was shut down by individuals who did not appreciate the value of open sources of information.

- It creates the long-needed Community Intelligence Centers and state-wide county-level networks for collecting, evaluating, and acting on the "bottom-up" dots that have no place to go today—the Federal level has been in the past unresponsive and ineffective at the state, local, and tribal level. This capability includes very innovative 119 and 114 numbers for citizens to alert each other via cell phone in an emergency, or report suspicions without over-burdening the 911 system. The Centers, relying on low-cost open source software equally available to Statehouses, schools, and Chambers of Commerce, will also allow us to deliver, at no further cost to the tax-payer, all of the open source information collected about the world, down to the municiple level—this will not only enhance our national security, it will enhance our educational system and our business competitiveness in a globalized environment.

- It creates a national virtual translation network that allows all organizations to leverage their own employees, to share employee language translation and cultural understanding capabilities among varied organizations, and to default to commercially-provided expert human translators when none is otherwise available. This not only solves the increasingly urgent need for being able to receive 911 calls in all languages, but it also affords both Members and state, local, and tribal authorities a ready means of interacting with constituents, especially elderly constituents, whose life circumstances have not allowed them to learn English. It can also support our troops in the field, with a global reach-back capability that is now affordable on a 24/7 basis in all languages.

- Finally, it moves open source software to the forefront of the Homeland Security information sharing environment. Building on STRONG ANGEL III, which has pioneered open source software capabilities that can be delivered free to non-governmental organizations as well as state, local, and tribal governments, this extraordinary suite of advanced analytic, collaborative work, and information sharing within a commercially secure environment, breaks down all of the barriers that have prevented the varying levels and types of government and non-government organizations from near-real-time distributed collaboration and inter-agency analytics.

I have worked very hard during my three terms in Congress to date, both to serve the needs of my constituents that count on me to represent them, and to enhance the capabilities that contribute to both the well-being of our Armed Forces in the field and in harms way, and to the depth and breadth of our Homeland Security, including the all-important security of our ports and territorial waters.

I defer to the Chairmen of the varied Committees of Congress and to the broader body of Members who will have an opportunity to adopt some or all of the provisions of the Smart Nation Act. Simply by putting this Act forward for consideration, here and now in September 2006, I believe that the author has rendered a useful national service. The time is ripe to engage in a national discussion of these issues.

This book is an invitation to think about how public intelligence might contribute to sound public policy in the public interest. I urge the reader to take it to heart and to mind. God Bless America!

Second District, Connecticut
Colonel, USAR, RET

Preface

This book is being published and released on 9-11 2006. It is about what Congress can do today for America, without delay—pass a Smart Nation Act.

In my view, with the non-partisan anti-incumbent mood sweeping across the country, each Member has a unique opportunity to reflect on what went wrong, not only with 9-11 but with the rush to war on Iraq that now clearly appears to have been based on bald lies from the Executive to Congress, the public, and the United Nations. Five years since 9-11, we are no safer, and indeed poorer. Secret intelligence failed us, not only because we did not have enough of it, current and accurate, but because secret intelligence can be ignored.

It is my earnest hope that the Members will consider the Intelligence Oversight Act being sponsored by Congressman Jeff Flake (R-AZ-06) and Congressman Adam Schiff (D-CA-29) as an opportunity. Together with initiatives that may emerge from the Senate side, and with the informed assistance of Congressman Rob Simmons (R-CT-02), the one Member who has focused on Open Source Intelligence (OSINT) across his three terms, it is possible for the Members to pass a short Public Intelligence Act, or as I have been calling it since 1994, the Smart Nation Act. Whether in this session, or the future, America needs this.

If Congress returns home, having established a Congressional Public Intelligence Office (CPIO), sub-committees for intelligence in each jurisdiction, an *independent* Open Source Agency to support the Director of National Intelligence, the rest of the Executive, the CPIO as well as the other Congressional agencies, with the Government Accountability Office (GAO) being especially meritorious and in need of public intelligence support, then Congress can go home with its head high, and tell our public that we were all fooled, but never again. The Smart Nation Act restores informed democracy, and gives Congress and the public a baseline for reducing and evaluating secret intelligence as a tool for manipulating public policy. We need this Act. *St.*

7

Part I:
Climbing the Policy Curve

The illustration below shows where we are today in relation to the beginning of the fight to establish public intelligence, in 1988, when the founders of the Marine Corps Intelligence Center (today a Command), discovered that 80-90% of what they needed to create policy, acquisition, operations, and logistics intelligence, was not secret, not online, not in English, and not known to anyone in the National Capital Area. That is still the case today, and nothing of substance is being done about it. Congress must mandate a solution—an open source information solution meeting the needs of every jurisdiction.

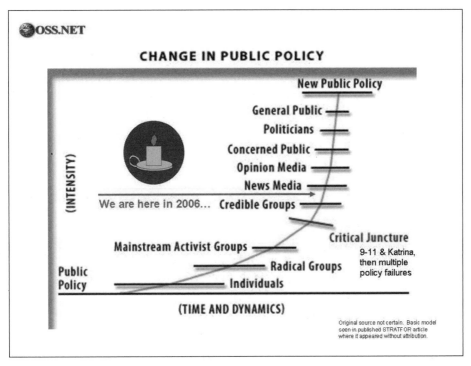

Figure 1: Time Dynamics for Public Policy Change

This first section is tailored to meet the needs of Members for a fast read.

Chapter 1: "Smart Nation Act" High-Level Documentation (2006)

In this section, a simple summary of key elements of a proposed Act are offered for consideration, along with an itemization of how public intelligence is vital to each of the major Congressional jurisdictions, an executive decision briefing routed to the Office of Management and Budget (OMB), and a capabilities and budget summary for full funding in five years. Several drafts of the Smart Nation Act are available electronically. The first one was written in 1994, and published as Chapter 15 in *ON INTELLIGENCE: Spies and Secrecy in an Open World* (AFCEA, 2000), with a Foreword by Senator David Boren (D-OK), today the President of the University of Oklahoma.

Chapter 2: "Reinventing Intelligence," in Forbes.com (2006)

The business community has been increasingly interested in commercial intelligence, and it was a real honor to be selected by Forbes.com to write the short piece on "Reinventing Intelligence." The companion piece on "Reinventing Education" was written by Derek Bok, President Emeritus of Harvard University and author of the book *The State of the Nation*. For the first time, this article explains to the informed reader the insanity of spending $60 billion a year on the 10-20% we can steal, and virtually nothing at all on the other 80-90% in 183 languages we do not speak.

Chapter 3: "The New Craft of Intelligence," in Time.com (2003)

The respect accorded to the notion that America required an Open Source Agency stemmed in large part from the untiring efforts of a handful of U.S. military officers, most of them associated with the U.S. Special Operations Command or the U.S. Army, among whom Col (now Congressman) Rob Simmons was most influential. This short piece was the first nationally-disseminated statement calling for national open source capabilities.

Chapter 4: Creating a Smart Nation (1996)

This chapter first appeared in *Government Information Quarterly* in 1996, having been written in 1995. It was the first government-wide articulation of the need for a National Information Strategy that recognized the role of public intelligence in the public interest. The Smart Nation Act can make this happen.

10

Chapter 1:
"Smart Nation Act"

Elements of the Act Proposed for Discussion

- Protects and enhances role of the Assistant Deputy Director of National Intelligence for Open Sources (ADDNI/OS) by legislatively mandating an **Open Source Intelligence Program** (OSIP) under the complete control of the Director of National Intelligence, directing that no less than 1% of the total National Foreign Intelligence Program (NFIB) be allocated to the collection, processing, and analysis of open sources of information in all languages, which are essential to the mission of the secret intelligence community. To the extent acceptable to the DNI and the ADDNI/OS, recommends that most raw unclassified information be delivered to a central federal processing facility to be located in **Southwest Virginia** and near the digitization facility across the border in **West Virginia**, to avoid duplicative collection by others.

- Creates **Congressional Public Intelligence Office (CPIO)** in close alliance with the Library of Congress and in direct support of each Committee as well as CRS, CBO, and GAO. This office, to be located on the campus of the University of **Maryland**, will be focused on helping Congress understand the strategic future costs of decisions and budget allocations today, across all Congressional jurisdictions, while producing **tailored Open Source Intelligence (OSINT) for Congress that may also be shared with the public in order to heighten public understanding of global threats validated by the respective Committees**. The CPIO shall not have access to classified information, and shall be supported with raw and processed OSINT by the Open Source Agency (OSA).

- Creates two-person **intelligence sub-committees** within each Committee to receive secret intelligence relevant to each jurisdiction, as sought by

11

Representatives Flake (R-AZ-06) and Schiff (D-CA-29). Only Members will be provided with classified intelligence relevant to their jurisdictions.

- Creates an **Open Source Agency (OSA),** as a sister-agency to the Broadcasting Board of Governors (BBG), with the same arms-length independence that Congress wisely mandated to assure journalist independence, but in this case, to assure the integrity of public intelligence. Consequently, public intelligence can support public diplomacy without taint from the secret world, while making all information within the Open Source Information Network (OSIN) immediately available to the U.S. Intelligence Community by channeling the information, pre-tagged to Intelink standards, to the NIPR and SIPR nets. The small Headquarters could be constructed on the **South-Central Campus**, adjacent to the **U.S. Institute of Peace (USIP)**, which could serve as a partner in global **information peacekeeping**, and easily accessible to the employees of the **Department of State** and the **National Intelligence Council** as well as others to be based on this campus to be completed and occupied by all parties no later than 1 January 2008.

- Broadens the mandate of the **Broadcasting Board of Governors (BBG)** with non-reimbursable funding from the OSA to create an Internet dissemination capability that offers **free universal access to all unclassified information** acquired by the OSA, with a robust man-machine translation capability that offers **free online education in at least 31 major languages** as an important new foundation for public diplomacy and information peacekeeping.

- Within the Department of State, establishes, with non-reimbursable funds assigned to Defense Support to Public Diplomacy, an **Office of Information Sharing Treaties and Agreements** to negotiate no-cost information sharing treaties with Nations, and agreements with non-governmental and private sector organizations including universities world-wide, and establish standards facilitating both sharing and semantic web sense-making across all languages.

- Within the Department of Defense, establishes an independent **Open Source Field Activity** with nodes in **Florida** (USSOCOM), **Colorado** (USNORTHCOM) and **Connecticut** (Groton Submarine Base with a

12

training activity at the U.S. Coast Guard Academy when dormitories are available). This technical processing and advanced analytic capability, in partnership with the OSIP under the DNI and the OSIN under the OSA, will be responsible for meeting all DoD needs for OSINT, and for porting all OSIF from the OSA to the high-side of Intelink. It will provide OSINT training for multinational, multiagency, multidisciplinary, multidomain cadres as a service of common concern.

- Creates **fifty state-based Community Intelligence Centers** to be manned by the National Guard, and broad networks that permit citizens to report threats (119) and suspicions (114), while also leveraging a global translation network (below) that can do all languages for the 911 system (and the new 119 and 114 systems) across the Nation. This solves the current lack of a place for bottom-up dots to be collected and analyzed, while providing a channel for distributing global information to all schoolhouses and chambers of commerce as a means of enhancing our national security and global competitiveness at the local level.

- Expands the concept of the National Virtual Translation Center by establishing a **National Virtual Translation Network (NVTN)** using commercial open source software now available, to allow all jurisdictions to handle both 911 calls in all languages, and to do critical translations for immigrant constituencies of Congress, as well as 24/7 live remote interactive translation for diplomats and warriors in the field. This open source software system can leverage existing employees, and default to commercial as needed.

Congressional Jurisdictions' Benefits of Public Intelligence

Agriculture

Commercial imagery radically improves land productivity by lowering cost of watering and fertilization. Water is going away—our most urgent public intelligence priority is to study water deficits, and begin implementing conservation and alternative practices that restore the aquifers and secure fresh water for the future.

Appropriations

Cost of goods intelligence has been used by business world to establish best prices, best practices, major oversight role. Public intelligence can identify up to $500 billion a year more in federal revenue.

Armed Forces—Armed Services

Only open source intelligence can meet USDI's need for 24/7 universal coverage in all languages at neighborhood level while also being shared with coalition partners and non-governmental organizations as called for by the Defense Science Board in its report on *Transitions to and From Hostilities* (now implemented in DoD Directive 3000.cc). Open sources in all languages, in near-real-time, are also essential in providing context and tip-off for Strategic Communication and Defense Support to Public Diplomacy.

Banking

Global financial stability easily monitored by open sources, and public intelligence can help the formal banking system understand the *halawa* and other offline banking systems.

Budget

"Reality-based budgeting" is inevitable. Best to have Congress tie public intelligence to public budget. This initiative is explicitly responsive to the alarms being sounded by the Comptroller General of the United States. At some point in the near future WikiCalc is going to allow citizens to see, in dramatically visualized terms, how inappropriate our national spending is, and what the future really looks like in terms of deficit, debt, and unfunded future deficiencies. "It's not policy until it's in the budget." Policy reform starts with a budget that provides for the future.

Commerce, Education, Energy—Energy & Commerce

Thomas Jefferson said "A Nation's best defense is an educated citizenry." The new rules for the networked economy demand a range of changes in laws and customs, as well as energy conservation and alternatives, all powered by a massive increase in public intelligence and information sharing. Education and copyright are in conflict with reality today—online learning, constant learning, free universal access to all knowledge, are what will power both a revitalization of America, and the stabilization of the poor and conflicted around the world.

Environment

Changes that used to take 10,000 years now take 3 years. Real-time science is essential. Earth Science initiative can be radically expanded to create near real time simulations and serious games, help make the public case for accelerating our adaptation to global warming, modifying harmful actions.

Ethics

The "cheating culture" can be studied and remediated.

Finance—Financial Services

There are three kinds of money: financial instruments, intangible value in knowledge, and goods. Public intelligence can provide a more accurate understanding of both the formal economy, and the barter and illicit economies.

Foreign Relations—International Relations

Department of State wants to be an end-user of intelligence, not a collector, but they have abdicated their role as the primary agency for collecting, interpreting, translating, and disseminating unclassified knowledge relevant to our foreign policy and trade. An Open Source Agency as a sister agency to the Broadcasting Board of Governors is a perfect way to avoid espionage taint while collecting and creating public intelligence to support public diplomacy and what General Al Gray called "peaceful preventive measures, what I call "information peacekeeping."

15

Government Reform

Open Source Intelligence can support government reform by creating and applying metrics for measuring performance and return on investment of the taxpayer dollar. For example, $4 million, on a one-time basis, found $79 million a year in crop insurance fraud, and eliminated it. In another example, two researchers using openly available Department of Commerce, identified $50 billion a year in import-export tax fraud (underpricing goods going out, overpricing goods coming in).

Health

Infectious disease is the #2 international threat and the single real-world threat to the Nation as a whole. A great deal more can be done by the Global Public Health Intelligence Network, aided by a structured government focus on public intelligence.

Homeland Security

We urgently need a nation-wide network of commercially secure networks and bottom-up Community Intelligence Centers to collect the localized dots and disseminate real-world public intelligence—only the citizens stopped one plane on 9/11. Also 24/7 human translators. Senator Boren and David Gergen have both called for the internationalization of education—the best security comes from an educated citizenry in touch with global reality. These same networks that collect bottom-up dots can communicate to every statehouse, schoolhouse, and chamber of commerce, at no additional cost to the taxpayer, the open source information being obtained for federal purposes.

Judiciary

Public intelligence can produce, at very low cost, actionable and shareable intelligence on bankruptcy, civil liberties, status of the courts, quality and utility of government information, interstate compacts, status of crimes and claims, status and cost of prisons, emerging new standards in copyright, patent, and trademark, and highly useful information on protecting and enhancing U.S. trade and commerce in the face of unlawful restraints and monopolies.

16

Resources

Public intelligence will dramatically impact on both natural and financial resources. A nation-wide intelligence study on water, with public intelligence and compelling visualizations online, will mobilize all parties so we do not make the same mistake with water that we made in ignoring the Peak Oil hearings in 1974-1979. Every resource in America can be protected and enhanced by applying open source intelligence methods to produce understandable public intelligence.

Science

We're losing the science race. A national public intelligence network will save us, in part by energizing education, making multi-lingual sources available in English through man-machine translation, helping measure the progress of others (Latin America, for example is going off the charts).

Transportation

Public intelligence can cut energy consumption, emissions, and costs in half.

Ways and Means

Public intelligence can find $500 billion a year more in federal revenue.

As a general observation, while respecting the role of the Congressional Research Service, and the value of the Library of Congress, there is no Congressional jurisdiction, including Caucuses, that could not benefit from tailored Open Source Intelligence (OSINT). The Congressional Public Intelligence Office (CPIO), working closely with all Congressional offices including the General Accountability Office (GAO) can produce tailored intelligence, including counterintelligence on fraud, waste, and abuse in the Executive, using only legal and ethical open sources of information in all languages.

MEMO FOR SENIOR STAFF, OMB
Starting Point for Inter-Agency Discussion

Subject: Open Source Intelligence and Government Operations

1. Background. Six trends bear on intelligence support to international security management:

   • continued lack of secret intelligence support to most Executive departments and agencies

   • increase in the number and the influence of non-state actors as well as small states;

   • increase of complex emergencies (refugees, food scarcity, plagues, water scarcity, *inter alia*), combined with ethnic conflict, transnational narco-terrorism, other non-traditional threats;

   • limited applicability of secret sources & methods for lower-tier issues, especially for those areas now largely "dark" under the existing system: Africa, South America, and Central Asia;

   • increase in relevant information available openly in over 33 main, 150 other languages.

   • new demand by Congressional Committees for intelligence sharing where it pertains to their jurisdictions (e.g. Armed Services, Foreign Affairs, Homeland Security, Justice)

2. What Is Open Source Intelligence (OSINT)? OSINT goes beyond normal staff work to combine the proven process of intelligence (requirements definition, collection management, source discovery and validation, multi-source fusion, compelling presentation) with the *purchase* of international open sources of information and complex related services. "Open sources" go well beyond the Internet (3 billion pages of substance and rising) or premium online services to include "gray literature" (limited edition publications including dissertations and local directories from around the world); specialized market research, private investigative, and other information broker services; direct hire of world-class experts on any topic

18

"one day at a time;" and geospatial information services including micro-satellites on demand, one-meter commercial imagery on demand, and Russian tactical combat charts at the 1:50,000 level or better (including current 1:10,000 scale city and port maps). OSINT, unlike staff work or academic research, creates overt *intelligence* that is responsive to policy, acquisition, operational, and logistics needs.

3. <u>Who Is Doing What Today?</u> Although the departments should be the primary collectors and exploiters of open sources, the over-all U.S. Government bureaucracy, including all elements of the Department of Defense, has neglected external non-digital unclassified information. The Department of State has no funds for the purchase of local knowledge. The Central Intelligence Agency has "promoted" the Foreign Broadcast Information Service to an Open Source Center and given it $20M a year for a Large Scale Internet Exploitation pilot, but does not offer support outside the CIA. None of the elements of the U.S. Government have credible concepts, doctrine, training, manning, or funding for OSINT in support of policy, acquisition, operations, or logistics. There are no structured processes for the collection, translation, digitization, and analysis of Chinese, Russian, Arabic, North Korean, Farsi, Urdu, or other "hard" languages, including the indigenous languages of the non-Arabic Muslim world. Experts estimate that foreign information available in English contains less than a third of the information relevant to U.S. national security needs, and only a fraction of that is available online. Of our $60 billion a year spent on various aspects of national and military intelligence, less than $250 million is spent on open source information procurement and exploitation. The Aspin-Brown Commission on the future of the U.S. Intelligence Community found that U.S. capabilities to exploit open sources are "severely deficient" and should be a "top priority for funding." The Hart-Rudman Commission on national security similarly concluded that OSINT requires additional emphasis. On 27 February 2003 Dr. Stephen Cambone, responding to a question from Senator John Warner (R-VA), in testimony to the Senate Armed Services Commission, that "Open source information can be enormously valuable. And I think the short answer is no, we don't put enough of our resources against that." The 9-11 Commission called for an Open Source Agency on page 413, without comment.

4. <u>Benefits</u>. Benefits of a national Open Source Agency as a sister agency to the Broadcasting Board of Governors (hence, public intelligence in support of public diplomacy, and no limits to sharing across Executive, Congress, public, and abroad)

- provision of an *insurance policy* for intelligence coverage of Third World security issues, and especially in regions of the world where classified capabilities have not been and are not likely to be focused in any depth in the near future (Central Asia, Africa, Americas, non-Arab Muslim crescent);

- increase in the timeliness, coverage, and political-military utility of overtly available information directly to operators, logisticians, acquisition managers, and all-source intelligence professionals (both disciplinary collectors and all-source analysts);

- increase in open source information sharing across the departments and with private sector academics, investigative specialists, and business managers with foreign area access and knowledge;

- foundation for web-based OSINT exchanges with allies, other nations, and non-state actors including relief agencies and religious organizations with strong local networks.

- foundation for broader and more effective public diplomacy and strategic communication programs, including the internationalization of education in the USA as called for by both Senator David Boren and Mr. David Gergen, among others.

- foundation for intelligence support to Congressional Committees, both to better inform them, and to sharply reduce their need for secret intelligence briefings.

5. <u>Competing Proposals</u>

- The Assistant Deputy Director of National Intelligence for Open Source (ADDNI/OS) and the Open Source Center (OSC) within the Central Intelligence Agency, seek to have the OSC upgraded to agency status and report to the Director of National Intelligence. They seek to build this new agency around the existing OSC, which is itself a poorly-funded and poorly managed cosmetic renaming of the Foreign Broadcast Information Service (FBIS). This proposal would focus on supporting the Intelligence Community, not the rest of the government.

- Dr. Joseph Markowitz, the only person who has served as Director of the Community Open Source Program Office (COSPO) before it was closed down by the Deputy Director of Central Intelligence for Community Management, recommends that the new Open Source Agency be under diplomatic auspices rather than espionage auspices, in order to better support both public diplomacy, and defense strategic communications and information sharing with non-governmental organizations participating in stabilization and reconstruction operations. Mr. Robert Steele, called the "father of open source intelligence" by Congressman Rob Simmons (R-CT-02), points out that 90% of the information we wish to obtain access to is controlled by organizations and individuals that want nothing to do with U.S. Intelligence. He also recommends a diplomatic Office of Information Sharing Treaties and Agreements as a vehicle for maximizing global information sharing on the ten threats identified by the High Level Threat Panel of the United Nations: poverty, infectious disease, environmental degradation, inter-state conflict, civil war, genocide, other atrocities, proliferation, terrorism, and transnational crime. This proposal would emphasize support to the intelligence community, to defense, and to homeland security, while meeting the needs of all jurisdictions for decision support: unclassified intelligence tailored to the needs of each client.

6. <u>Cost</u>. Two studies, one sponsored by the Director of Central Intelligence ("Challenges of Global Coverage, July 1997) and one by the Undersecretary of Defense for Intelligence ("Defense Open Source Program, March 2006) see a major national program as meriting $1.5 billion (DCI) to $2 billion a year at Full Operating Capability (FOC), and inclusive of commercial source imagery acquisition and other geospatial information acquisition. This is essentially $10 million per year for each of 150 lower-tier countries and topics not covered by classified intelligence but strongly associated with global instability. $250M per year would be an appropriate level to start, with $75M directly responsive to DoD needs, $45M responsive to non-DoD national security needs, $5M earmarked for trade & commerce, and $2.5M earmarked for each of the 50 states or

commonwealths to create unclassified community intelligence networks. At FOC, $1.5B per year would focus on external reality (all information, all languages, all the time), and $1.5B would fund 50 $30 million a year community intelligence and information sharing networks reaching out to every schoolhouse, chamber of commerce, statehouse, and so on.

7. <u>References</u>. The most important current reference is DoD Directive 3000.cc, which implements the recommendations of the Defense Science Board summer study on *Transitions to and from Hostilities*. That study, drafted in part by Dr. Markowitz, found that DoD cannot do transitions to and from hostilities without comprehensive information sharing among US Government inter-agency elements, coalition partner inter-agency elements, and non-governmental organizations; and that open sources of information are the cheapest, fastest, and best means of establishing common understandings of threats and solutions. The North Atlantic Treaty Organization (NATO) has taken a strong interest in OSINT because of the challenge it faces in integrating and working with the Partnership for Peace and Mediterranean Dialog nations. Under the authority of General William Kernan in his capacity as Supreme Allied Commander Atlantic, NATO has published three documents, each close to 100 pages, and all available for no-cost download from www.oss.net under Archives, then References: *NATO Open Source Intelligence Handbook* (SACLANT, November 2001); *NATO Open Source Intelligence Reader* (SACLANT, February 2002); *Intelligence Exploitation of the Internet* (SACLANT, October 2002)

8. <u>Legislation in Play</u>. There are two bills on the House side that are in play. The first, from Congressman Simmons (R-CT-02) has a mark and is supportive of full discussion of the broader solution if combined with the second, from Congressman Jeff Flake (R-AZ-06) and Congressman Adam Schiff (D-CA-26). This initiative, the Intelligence Oversight Act, seeks to demand intelligence sharing across the varied Committees previously shut off from secret intelligence by the Intelligence Committee. Senator Bill Nelson (D-FL) and other Senators are being approached by Mr. Steele to obtain a Senate bill that proposes the broader solution under diplomatic auspices. Mr. Steele's views are summed up in the attached letter to the Secretary of State. State may ignore this issue—OMB may wish to nurture.

9. <u>Recommendation</u>. That Dr. Markowitz and Mr. Steele be invited to participate in a senior staff roundtable at OMB.

PARTIAL TEXT OF LETTER TO SECRETARY OF STATE 29 July 2006

MEMO FOR THE HONORABLE CONDOLEZZA RICE

Madam Secretary,

The attached letter went to all but a handful of the Ambassadors posted to the United States of America, in both Washington, D.C. and New York City. It is my hope that you will note with interest the possibility that Congress might create a national Open Source (Intelligence) Agency, and that you will place the full weight of your office behind the more reasonable of the two competing proposals, to wit, that it be completely independent of the secret intelligence community, and a sister agency to the Broadcasting Board of Governors. This agency could help revitalize diplomacy world-wide.

I respectfully note that Congress created the Broadcasting Board of Governors and its special arms-length relationship with the Department of State in order to ensure the journalistic integrity of the international broadcasting programs that are so vital to Public Diplomacy. This serves the American people well by nurturing openness, transparency, and regard for the truth—truth that can be shared with all publics.

Similarly, Madam Secretary, it is essential that Open Source Intelligence (OSINT), also known as Public Intelligence and in some circles as Collective Intelligence, be nurtured by the Department of State and protected from two fatal flaws in the competing proposal, to wit, placing this agency under the Director of National Intelligence, and building it around the Foreign Broadcast Information Service, a group of well-intentioned people who have been incapacitated by their indoctrination into the culture of the Central Intelligence Agency, their parent organization, with all of its hostility toward sharing information and its paranoia over direct contacts with foreigners.

[Last paragraph not shown.]

Notional Spending Plan for $3B at FOC
National Open Source Agency (OSA)

Although I recommend that Year 1 be limited to $250M as originally proposed to OMB and SASC, this is how $3 billion a year can be spent very effectively (realizing that we would create a requirements process and field requests and suggestions that would be handled within the margin of error of the below plan):

At Full Operational Capability: $1.5 Billion a year ($10 million a year for each of 150 lower tier countries and instability topics) focused on global Open Source Collection, Processing, Analysis, and Dissemination in Support of each Executive Agency and Department not receiving secret intelligence support, and in support of the Congressional Public Intelligence Office as appropriate; and $1.5 Billion a year ($30 million a year for each of the 50 states) to create a national Public Intelligence Network including bottom up 119 and 114 numbers, and a global online translation system in the primar5y 33 languages with augmentation for US deficiencies in the other 150 languages relevant to global stabilization and reconstruction.

These funds would be distinct from the funds now available to the Director of National Intelligence, who would retain control of all personnel and funds now assigned to the cognizance of the Assistant Deputy Director of National Intelligence (ADDNI/OS). These funds would cover the establishment and maintenance of:

- Congressional Public Intelligence Office (CPIO)
- Sub-Committees on Intelligence for each Congressional jurisdiction
- Open Source Agency as sister agency to Broadcasting Board of Governors
- Digital Marshall Plan to provide free universal access to knowledge (BBG)
- Office of Information Sharing Treaties and Agreements (State)
- Independent Field Activity (Defense, in Tampa)
- 50 state-based community intelligence centers and networks
- National Virtual Translation Network, 911, 119, 114 support, and global

Within the national agency, the following specific capabilities would be created as services of common concern subject to OMB and GSA oversight and collaboration, and with a full embrace of GAO advice and scrutiny.

Digital History Project
    Expert Scouts
    In-Country Collection
    Digitization
    Translation
    Visualization
    Expert Annotation

NGO Data Warehouse and Network
    Generic Desktop Software Package
    Field Digitization
    Meta-Standards
    Training (distance, mobile, on-site)

Virtual Intelligence Community
    Weekly Reports
    Distance Learning
    Expert Forums (Multi-Level Security)
    Virtual Library
    Global Rolodex (Multi-level and compartmented access)
    Global Calendar (Multi-level and compartmented access)
    Virtual Budget (Multi-level and compartmented access)
    Virtual Requirements Coordination (Multi-level and compartmented access)
    Virtual Help Desk (Multi-lingual, both government and private sector)

Training Program (first on OSINT, then on topics, have at least 7 teams)
    Distance Learning
    Mobile Training Teams
    OSINT Academy at US Coast Guard when dormitories vacant

Future Intelligence Collaborative Environment
    Generic STRONG ANGEL Information Sharing & Analysis Network
    Generic Source Subscription Package "Gold License" with audit trail
    Generic Global Spider/Bot Package
    Online Translation & Networking Services

Regional Open Source Intelligence Centers and Networks
  Generic Center C4I Package,
    Regional Multi-Lingual Scout, Source, Digitization, Translation, Authentication, Networks
  Regional Subject Matter Expert Work (both Published and Unpublished)

International Trade and Chamber of Commerce Network
  Global Regulatory Scanning & Expert Network
  Global Taxation Scanning & Expert Network
  Global Transportation Scanning & Expert Network
  Global Risk Scanning & Expert Network
  Global Corporate Agent Services on Demand

Digital Marshall Plan
  Project to Leverage Abandoned DoD Satellites for Residual Capabilities
  Project to Install T-3 Connectivity into Provinces of every African Country
  Project to install Internet Cafes in any town in Africa where permissions are available

University of the Republic (multiple locations, free online distance learning in all languages as new part of public diplomacy)
  Seven Tribes College (Entry-Level)
  Seven Tribes Institute (Mid-Career)
  Seven Tribes University (Senior School)
  Seven Tribes Council (Master's Forum)

NOTE: The Regional OSINT Centers could be identical to the 50 Community Intelligence Centers proposed for each of the 50 states & commonwealths of the USA. At FOC, $1.5B has been proposed for the OSA (external-focus), with an additional $1.5B for the state centers & networks. It is our professional estimate that the $3B a year investment will attract $30B a year in free useful end-user information digitized, tagged, and shared at no additional expense to the U.S. taxpayer, apart from the impact on increasing federal revenues.

*"Information ***costs*** money, intelligence ***makes*** money."*

Robert Steele

Chapter 2:
"Reinventing Intelligence"

Blank Slate

Open Source Intelligence

Robert David Steele 04.18.06, 6:00 PM ET

Robert David Steele

<u>Open Source Intelligence</u>

<u>How   Bad   Is   U.S.
Intelligence?</u>

Poll: <u>What was the biggest
U.S. intelligence failure?</u>

FULL COVERAGE >

NEW YORK -

On Sept. 11, 2001, four airplanes were hijacked by terrorists who intended to crash them into a series of high-profile U.S. targets. Two crashed into the twin towers of the World Trade Center. The third collided with the Pentagon. But passengers on the fourth plane were alerted to the crisis while still in the air. They fought back, and the plane went down in rural Pennsylvania, sparing its intended target, the U.S. Capitol.

In other words, the only hijacked airplane that failed to hit its target on Sept. 11 was the one where informed citizens were able to take direct action. It gave proof that our national security establishment is broken. A $500 billion per year defense department and a $50 billion per year secret intelligence community failed where a few brave citizens armed only with cell phones succeeded.

This tragic event illustrates the way we must reinvent our national intelligence system. The threats we face don't lend themselves to pre-planned, centrally controlled government direction. Only a nation in which each citizen is both a collector and consumer of intelligence, able to share information adequately and in real time, will survive the tribulations to come.

Today, U.S. "intelligence" is upside down and inside out. It is upside down because it relies on satellites in outer space rather than human eyes on the ground. It is inside out because it tries to divine intelligence unilaterally, without first asking anyone else what information they might provide.

Despite high-profile intelligence failures such as Sept. 11, a series of directors of Central Intelligence have failed to significantly change the way we collect and process information. They simply have not gotten it through their heads that intelligence is about knowing enough to make smart decisions at all levels, on all subjects, not just about stealing very expensive secrets on a handful of what they call "hard targets"--China, Iran, Russia and a few others.

Fortunately, the idea of "collective intelligence" is gaining acceptance--at least outside of government circles.

In short, collective intelligence relies on the combined brain power of large groups of people. We see it at work when political parties choose a candidate or create policy platforms. We see it on the Internet, when groups of strangers solve problems and edit collaborative encyclopedia entries. We even see it in the behavior of ants, which are capable of maintaining complicated nests and executing huge military raids, tasks far beyond the intellectual abilities of any one ant.

We also saw collective intelligence at work in the wake of the 2004 tsunami that ravaged South Asia. After the waters receded, international citizens with cell phones and cameras started sending photos and text messages back to their friends at home. All over the world, volunteers jumped in to set up bulletin boards on the status of survivors, helping families reunite or check on loved ones. A hundred citizens on the ground, with eyes on target and cell phones in hand, proved themselves far more useful than one spy could ever be.

How can we use this to reform intelligence? I suggest we create a national Open Source Agency. Half of the money earmarked for the agency would go toward traditional intelligence work. The other half would provide for 50 state-wide Citizen Intelligence Networks, including a 24/7 watch center, where citizens can both obtain and input information.

We could establish new emergency intelligence phone numbers--think 119 instead of 911--allowing any housewife, cab driver or delivery boy to contribute to our national security. All they have to do is be alert, and if they see something, take a cell phone photograph and send it in with a text message. If three different people notice the same suspicious person taking photographs of a nuclear plant, for instance, it could be hugely important. The system could even evolve to automatically mobilize emergency workers or warn citizens. Imagine if after people alerted the network about a roadside car bomb, it automatically sent text messages to every phone in the immediate area, warning people to stay away.

When you think about how the system will change, it may be helpful to picture national intelligence as a baseball game. In the old days, government bureaucrats accustomed to unlimited budgets and secret methods would try to win a game simply by bribing a player (Clandestine Intelligence), putting a "bug" in the dug-out (Signals Intelligence), trying to "sniff" the direction and speed of the ball (Measurements & Signatures Intelligence), or taking a satellite picture of the field every three days (Imagery Intelligence).

This approach is no longer appropriate. In our new era, everyone, including any terrorist, has the option of using open sources of information that are equal or superior to secret sources. The new craft of intelligence requires all the players to function as part of a team, and asks them to win however they can. It uses the collective wisdom of all the participants. It encourages the crowd to participate. Open source intelligence harnesses what *everyone* sees and knows. It changes the rules of the game.

We must study, digitize, translate and learn from the history of all nations and peoples and lands. We must share the cost of collecting and understanding all information in all languages with knowledgeable individuals from all nations, not just our own. We must harness the distributed intelligence of the entire nation, such that everyone might participate. We will still need spies and secrecy, but improved use of public intelligence will allow them to focus more narrowly.

"A nation's best defense is an educated citizenry." Thomas Jefferson said that. Not only was he right when he said it, but today, his words must lead us to realize the importance of public intelligence.

Robert David Steele is a retired Marine Corps Reserve infantry and intelligence officer who served four years active duty and the remainder in the Individual Ready Reserve. After joining the CIA in 1979, he served three back-to-back tours in Latin America as a clandestine case officer, including one tour as one of the first officers focused full time on terrorism. He is the author of three books about intelligence and the chief executive of OSS.net .

Blank Slate
U.S. Intelligence: How Bad Is It?
Robert David Steele 04.18.06, 6:00 PM ET

How inept is our secret national intelligence bureaucracy? Here is an example: In August 1995, at the request of the Aspin-Brown Commission, which wanted to test secret against open sources, I called five private-sector information providers and asked them to provide the commission, overnight, with as much information as possible about the civil-war-torn nation of Burundi. After one working day, they provided the following:

* From Oxford Analytica, 20 two-page executive reports on the political-military implications of Burundi, Rwanda, and the attendant genocide, for the United States, the United Nations and Africa in general.
* From Jane's Information Group, concise tribal orders of battle created over the weekend and one-paragraph summaries of every article they had ever published on that conflict.
* From East View Cartographic, a complete list of all immediately available Russian military maps with contour lines at very fine levels of detail (today the U.S. still lacks such printed maps for 90% of the world--if computers fail due to bullet holes or moisture or sand, our troops literally go blind).
* From Lexis-Nexis, a list of top journalists who cover Burundi, all immediately available for a detailed debriefing.
* From the Institute of Scientific Information, a list of the top academics in the world on all aspects of the conflict, the tribes and the conditions, each immediately available for debriefing.
* From Spot Image, complete commercial imagery for all of Burundi, less than three years old, cloud free, at a very detailed level of resolution.
Meanwhile, the U.S. intelligence community had one of those bland little schoolroom maps of the country with no detail, and a regional economic study with severely flawed premises.

Chapter 3:
"The New Craft of Intelligence"

TIME

The New Craft of Intelligence
Making the Most of Open Private Sector Knowledge
By Robert David Steele

Despite the fact that U.S. taxpayers have been paying more than $30 billion a year for a national intelligence and counterintelligence community to protect it from both traditional state-based threats and unconventional non-state actors, the events of 9-11 demonstrated our inability to detect and prevent bold asymmetric attacks that used our own airliners as precision missiles. Armed with new concepts, money, and suicidal pilots, Osama bin Laden has cost us at least $20 billion in damages.

The problem with spies is they only know secrets

Unfortunately, our spies and our satellites have lost touch with reality, for they collect less than 10% of the relevant information that we must digest to understand the complex multi-cultural world that is now capable of producing very wealthy and suicidal terrorists. We need a "new craft of intelligence" that can access and digest the broad historical, cultural, and current events knowledge that is available openly in over twenty-nine languages — by exploiting these open sources we can create open source intelligence, or OSINT, suitable for informing our public as well as our state, local, and tribal authorities and our international partners, as to the threats to our nation.

What are open sources? Open sources go well beyond the Internet (3 billion pages of substance and rising) and premium online services (ten times what is on the Internet, with value-added) to include "gray literature" (limited edition publications including dissertations and local directories from around the

31

world); specialized market research, private investigations, and other information broker services; and geo-spatial information services including commercial imagery and Russian military maps for all countries of the world (the U.S. does not have military maps for 90% of the world.) Open sources include experts on any subject, in any language. Shocking as it may seem, our intelligence community does not routinely strive to identify the top people in the world (not just Americans) on the various topics of concern — from terrorism to the environment to human trafficking to corruption to disease and public health — with the result that our analysis tends to be shallow and incestuous, relying on the same consultants again and again.

Where's the action?

Why is this not obvious, and, more importantly, why is it not being acted upon? Although the bipartisan Aspin-Brown Commission on intelligence reform (reporting in March 1996) found that our intelligence community is "severely deficient" in its access to open sources of information, and also found that the various departments and agencies of government have failed to fulfill their responsibilities for collecting, processing, and analyzing open source information relevant to their missions, nothing has been done to implement the Commission's recommendations for reform. The Commission specifically stated that OSINT should be a top priority for funding within our $30 billion a year intelligence budget, and that it should be a top priority for the attention of the Director of Central Intelligence.

☐ The DCI then serving, John Deutch, and the DCI now serving, George Tenet, chose to ignore virtually all of the recommendations of this bipartisan Commission.

☐ The Department of State, which is statutorily responsible for the collection of open source information abroad, has abdicated this responsibility and has no funds and no process in place for responsibly collecting relevant information from all the countries where we have taxpayer-funded Embassies.

☐ Just recently, the Department of Defense, about to spend billions and billions of dollars on new satellites that we do not need, closed down the open source information portion of the General Defense Intelligence Program, claiming they lacked sufficient funds and that open source intelligence is not a priority.

☐ The various other departments rely almost exclusively on "free" information that is given to them by parties with their own agenda to pursue.

☐ There are no structured processes for the collection, translation, and analysis of Islamic, Chinese, Russian, Arab, Japanese, Korean, or other foreign language materials.

☐ There is no central coordinating authority for ensuring that open sources acquired or translated by one part of the government are readily available by all the other parts, nor is there a government-wide open source intelligence requirements and acquisition authority.

The rewards of open source intelligence

There are immediate benefits to both national security and national prosperity of creating a government-wide open source intelligence program — preferably *not* managed by the intelligence specialists, who have repeatedly demonstrated their complete disdain for open sources of information. Those benefits would include the provision of an insurance policy for intelligence coverage of Third World security issues; an immediate increase in the timeliness, coverage and political utility of overtly available information; an immediate increase in open source information sharing across the departments and with the private sector; and finally, the provision of a foundation for a web-based OSINT exchange with allies, other nations and international groups.

I believe that a government-wide open source intelligence executive authority should be established, and a budget authorized and appropriated, to fulfill the following open source intelligence support objectives, and I have advocated this approach since 1992. The goals: to improve diplomatic understanding of foreign perceptions and conditions ($45M); to improve military and law enforcement understanding of emerging and existing threats ($75M) and to improve commerce and treasury understanding of international economic environment ($5M). I have already established that this proposal is acceptable to key Congressional leaders and to the political leadership in the Office of Management and Budget (OMB), but to my enduring dismay, have been unable to break through the staff barriers to any Cabinet leader in government willing and able to take on this function on behalf of the people of the United States of

America — Colin Powell is my first choice for the post. My second choice is the creation of a small new agency.

I would venture two common-sense observations that we must communicate to our government: 1) we cannot afford to ignore the rest of the world; and 2) we need a government-wide open source program right now. In close coordination with the most authoritative experts and retired intelligence and defense leaders available, I've created a list of initiatives to achieve these objectives, which appears below. If you think this makes sense, I hope you will write to your Senators and Representatives in Congress. The common sense of the people must come into play on this matter.

Recommended Open Source Initiatives

☐ Digital History Project ($5M) to digitize and translate key Islamic, Chinese, and other foreign language historical, political, economic, cultural, social, and technical materials.

☐ Non-Governmental Organization Data Warehouse ($10M) to provide free storage and network access to the various international organizations whose "local knowledge" is vital to U.S. understanding.

☐ Global Coverage Distance Learning and Expert Forum Network ($10M) that will establish open ethical boards of review for all countries and topics, including distance learning and expert forums.

☐ Generic Open Source Training Initiative ($10M) to create both distance learning modules accessible by our state, local, and tribal, armed forces and diplomatic personnel and our public.

☐ Public Information Sharing and Collaboration Toolkit ($10M) comprised of a generic set of industry standards and related tools for desktop level exploitation and analysis of digital foreign information.

☐ Regional Open Source Information Networks for Africa, Asia, Europe, and Latin America ($40M) , each with an open source collection and processing center in partnership with local governments who will provide regional language skills and access to gray literature and local experts.

☐ International Trade and Chamber of Commerce Network ($5M) to establish a web-based network maximizing access by U.S. businesses to foreign economic, regulatory and taxation information.

☐ Digital Marshall Plan ($20M) to provide direct assistance and subsidies to extend the Internet to every corner of the world (including rural areas in America) via wireless delivery means.

☐ University of the Republic & Global Outreach Program ($15M) that will bring together and educate "cohorts" of mid-career subject-matter experts from state, local, and tribal governments, the federal government, and the business, academic and media communities, as well as foreign professionals.

About the Author
Robert David Steele is a 25-year veteran of the U.S. national security community. He has been a clandestine case officer in three foreign countries, helped program funds for imagery satellites, carried out tactical operations in support of strategic signals intelligence programs and founded the Marine Corps Intelligence Center (now Command). He and his small company have been featured in Year in Computers (2000) and the writings of Alvin Toffler, among others. His first book, "On Intelligence: Spies and Secrecy in an Open World," sold out in the weeks after 9-11, has just been re-issued. His forthcoming book, "The New Craft of Intelligence: Personal, Public, & Political (Citizen's Action Handbook for Fighting Terrorism, Genocide, Disease, Toxic Bombs, & Ignorance)", will be available in late April 2002. Steele is the founder of Open Source Solutions, Inc., which sponsors an annual conference for intelligence professionals from all walks of life and all countries of the world.

Chapter 4:
Creating a Smart Nation:
Strategy, Policy, Intelligence, and
Information

In an age characterized by distributed information, where a majority of the expertise is in the private sector, the concept of "central intelligence is an oxymoron. The greatest threat to both national security and national economic competitiveness is ignorance—uninformed decision-making. Intelligence communities are slowly discovering that they should not send a spy where a schoolchild can go, and that spies are not harnessing the vast distributed intelligence of the private sector. Unfortunately, the culture of intelligence in most countries believes that its uniqueness rests on secrets rather than thinking—on producing secrets rather than informing policy. To survive in the 21st century, every nation must become a smart nation" and engage all of its citizens—every citizen must be a collector, producer, and consumer of intelligence—and thus, create the Virtual Intelligence Community. To integrate and make the best use of both open-source intelligence and traditional classified intelligence, each nation must establish a National Information Strategy, which addresses connectivity, content, coordination, and computational security .[3]

This chapter outlines both the requirement for, and a recommended approach to the creation of a National Information Strategy. Despite the fact that we have leaders in both the administration and the legislature who understand the

---

[3] An earlier version of this material appeared in *Government Information Quarterly*, Volume 13, Number 2, pp 151-173 (Summer 1996).

critical importance of information as the foundation for both national security and national competitiveness at ' dawn of the 21st century, our leadership has failed to articulate a strategy and a policy which integrates national intelligence (spies, satellites), government information, and private-sector information objectives and resources

In the Age of Information, the absence of a National Information Strategy is tantamount to abdication and surrender—the equivalent of having failed to field an army in World War II, or having failed—to establish a nuclear deterrent in the Cold War. This chapter is both an orientation for citizens and bureaucrats and a call to arms for both policymakers and legislators. It is a fundamental premise of this chapter that in the Age of Information, the most important role of government—at the Federal, state, or local level—will be the nurturing of the "information commons."[4]

National security will be largely a question of protecting information infrastructure, intellectual property, and the integrity of data. National competitiveness will be completely redefined: corporations and individuals are competitive in a global economy-and it is the role of nations to be "attractive" to investors. How nations manage their information commons will be a critical factor in determining "national attractiveness" for investment in the 21st century.[5]

This chapter addresses and defines the challenge of change; the information commons and information continuum; the theory and practice of intelligence in the Age of Information: the ethical, ecological, and evolutionary implications of this approach; the need to reinvent and integrate national intelligence (spies and satellites) into a larger network of distributed intelligence largely accessible to citizens; and, finally, the concrete elements which must comprise the National Information Strategy.

---

[4] Lee Felsenstein, then of the Interval Research Corporation, is the originator of the term information commons."

[5] I am indebted to Dr. Katrina Svensson, of Lund University. who brought to my attention the work on decision-support and information access as a key to national competitiveness.   Her views are consistent with those of Secretary of Labor Robert Reich, who defines "U.S. companies" as those that employ U.S. citizens and pay U.S. taxes See also Len Oxelheim, "Foreign Direct Investment and the Liberalization of Capital Movements in the Global Race for Foreign Direct Investment," *Prospects for the Future,* edited by Len Oxelheim (Berlin: *Springer-Veriag,* 1993).

THE CHALLENGE OF CHANGE

As we enter the 21st century, we arc faced with several dramatic challenges, confronted by order-of-magnitude changes that defy resolution under our existing paradigms and organizational or policy structures.

The most obvious challenge to government as a whole is the changing nature of the threat. Since the rise of the nation-state, with its citizenship, taxation, and standing armies, the most fundamental national security issue for governments has been the sanctity of its borders and the safety of its citizens and property abroad. Physical security maintained by threat of force was easy to understand and easy to implement. Today, we face a world in which transnational criminal gangs have more money, better computers. better information, and vastly more motivation to act and to act ruthlessly, than most states, Perhaps even more frightening, we face a world in which we are allowing technology and limited policy understanding to create very significant masses of displaced and alienated populations—including sizeable elements within our own borders; at the same time, we are ignoring our government's obligations to provide for home defense, for electronic civil defense, in the private sector.[6]

There is another important change requiring government diligence, and that is the change in the role of information as the "blood" of every enterprise, every endeavor. Three aspects of this change merit enumeration: first, each citizen, whether conscious of this fact or not, is increasingly dependent on accurate and

---

[6] "Hackers" are not the threat. As I have noted on many occasions, hackers are a national resource because they are forcing us to acknowledge that "the emperor is naked." Sherry Turkle in My *Second Self: Computers and the Human Spirit* (New York: Simon & Schuster, 1984) examines the origin of "hacking" at MIT and demonstrates conclusively that the backer ethic is identical to "right stuff" associated with the early astronauts--both push the edge of the envelope striving for excellence. The actual "threat" to our national information infrastructure begins with bad engineering and culminates primarily in authorized users doing unauthorized things. David Ioove, Karl Seger, and William Von Storch note in *Computer Crime: A Crime-Fighter's Handbook* (Sebastopol, CA: O'Reilly & Associates, 1995) that economic losses associated with computers are attributed as follows: 55% to human error and 20% to physical disruption such as natural disasters or power failure (one could say, poor computer design), 10% to dishonest employees; 9%t o disgruntled employees; 4%to viruses; and only 1-3% to outsider attacks.

timely information in order to be fully functional; second, the "information explosion," like a major climatic change, is making it difficult for citizens accustomed to slower times and simpler tools to adjust to the requirements of life in the fast lane of the information superhighway; and finally, most citizens, stockholders, and business managers do not realize that we have national telecommunications, power, and financial networks that have been designed without regard to security or survivability. It is not safe, today, to work and play in cyberspace, and we do not even have a body of law that requires communications and computing providers to assure their customers that their services and products are safe and reliable.[7]

In brief, we now have an information environment in which every citizen needs to be a collector, producer, and consumer of "intelligence," or decision-support; and at the same time, we have an extraordinarily complex and fragile information infrastructure which can be destroyed, disrupted, and corrupted by single individuals or small groups now capable of attacking our information infrastructure nodes through electronic means or simple physical destruction— and able to do so anonymously.

DEFINING THE "INFORMATION COMMONS"

The "information commons" can be viewed-as the public commons for grazing sheep was once viewed in old England-as a shared environment where information is available for public exploitation to the common good. There are three major information "industries" that must contribute their fair share to the commons if the commons is to be robust and useful

---

[7] The seminal work in this area is Winn Schwartau, I*nformation Warfare: Chaos on the Electronic Superhighway* (New York: Thunder Mouth Press. 1994). Thoughtful papers on the vulnerability of specific networks include Maj Gerald R Rust, "Taking Down Telecommunications" (School of Advanced Airpower Studies, 1993); Maj Thomas E. Griffith Jr., "Strategic Attack of National Electrical Systems" (School of Advanced Airpower Studies, October 1994); and H.D. Arnold, J. Hyukill, J.Keeney. and A Cameron, "Targeting Financial Systems a Center of Gravity: 'Low intensity' to 'No Intensity' Conflict," *Defense Analysis,* 10(2, 1994). S. One major U.S. government agency, extremely competent in computing, intercepted all communications and computing hardware and software reaching its loading docks for a period of one year. It found 500 separate viruses contained in shrink-wrapped products coming straight from the factory.

The first, relatively unknown to most citizens, is the U.S. intelligence community, traditionally associated with spies and satellites. In fact, between 40% and 80% of the raw data going into the final products of the intelligence community comes from "open sources"—from public information legally available.[8] Unfortunately, this S25 billion (today $60 billion) dollar-a-year community buries its open source acquisitions in the "cement overcoat" of classification, with the result that most of the useful public information acquired by the intelligence community at taxpayer expense is not, in fact, made available to the citizen-taxpayer.

The second, well known to most citizens as a massive bureaucracy which generates regulations and imposes taxation, is the government. The government is *not*, however, known for making information available to the public, and this is an extraordinary failure, for it turns out that not only is the government acquiring enormous stores of information at taxpayer expense on every imaginable topic, but the government also serves as a magnet for vast quantities of information that it receives "free" from other governments, from think-tanks, lobbyists, universities, and every other purveyor of a viewpoint desiring to influence the bureaucrats who comprise the government. In the Age of Information, governments must make the transition from the industrial model (vast bureaucracies attempting to deliver goods and services using a hierarchical structure to control resources) to the "Third Wave" model (small expert nodes nurturing distributed centers of information excellence).[9] There

---

[8] The Director of the Canadian Security Intelligence Service (CSIS), Ward Elcock has stated publicly that 80% of the inputs for finished intelligence products come from open sources; the Canadian service also makes it a point to publish unclassified intelligence reports. Although the U.S. intelligence community only acknowledges 40% as the official contribution of open sources, the former Director for Sciences & Technology has stated publicly that the figure is actually 70%. As a general rule, if a Service is competent in accessing open sources of information, which is not the case with the U.S. Intelligence Community, it should be able to answer 80% of its essential elements of information (EEI) using low-cost legal ethical sources and methods. This does, however, require interaction with foreigners who do not have security clearances, and it is this reality that tends to constrain secret agencies from making the best possible use of open sources of information in all languages.

[9] Although several authors, including Peter Drucker, have addressed reinvention and reengineering imperatives in relation to the information age, none have done more to help public undemanding than Alvin and Heidi Toffler with their books *PowerShift: Knowledge, Wealth and Violence at the Edge of the 21st Century* (New York: Bantam

are some significant capabilities within government intended to address this issue, including the National Technical Information Service (NTIS) in the Department of Commerce and the Defense Technical Information Center (DTIC) in the Department of Defense, but by and large government information is *out of control.* If the intelligence community is a S25-billion-a-year industry, then the U.S. government can safely be assumed to be at least a $250-billion-a-year industry strictly speaking of information alone.

The third "industry" capable of contributing to the information commons is the most important, the most diverse, and the most dynamic—it is the private sector. This has extraordinary implications for both governance and enterprise in the 21st Century, because of four characteristics of "knowledge battle" in the 21st century that governments must recognize if they are to do their part:

- First, 90-95% of knowledge is open, not secret—governments that continue to believe in secrecy as the paramount element of executive action will fail;

- Second, the center of gravity is in the civil sector—governments that continue to rely on their military and their police and exclude from consideration the role of private sector capabilities, will fail;

- Third, information today is *distributed*—governments that persist in relying upon "central intelligence" structures will fail; and

- Finally, information is multilingual—governments that do not invest in analysts and observers able to move easily in multilingual environments will fail.

If the intelligence community is a $25-billion-a-year industry, and the U.S. government is a $250-billion-a-year industry, the private sector can safely be assumed to be a $2.5-trilli9oin-a-year industry.[10]

1990) and *War and Peace.: Survival the Dawn of the 21st Century* (Boston MA: Little Brown, 1993).

[10] At the time this was originally drafted, 1995, the U.S. Intelligence Community budget had been cut back from $30 billion a year to $25 billion a year. Today (2006) it is

THE INFORMATION CONTINUUM

The "information continuum" for any nation is comprised of the nine major information-consuming and information-producing sectors of society: schools, universities, libraries, businesses, private investigators and information brokers, media, government, defense, and intelligence.

It is very important to understand three basic aspects of the information continuum:

- First, each organization within each sector pays for and controls both experts and data that could contribute to the information commons. Perhaps most importantly from the taxpayer and government point of view, these distributed centers of excellence are maintained at no cost to the government.

- Second, it is important to understand that what any one organization publishes for sale or for free, whether in hardcopy or electronically, represents less than 20%—often less than 10%—of what they are actually holding in their unstructured databases, email depositories, or in the tacit knowledge of their individual employees.

- Third, and her we begin to set the stage for why a National Information Strategy is essential, it is important for both citizens and bureaucrats to realize that across the information continuum there are "iron curtains" between sectors, "bamboo curtains" between organizations, and "plastic curtains" between individuals within organizations.

---

generally believed to be at $60 billion a year, with $8-10 billion of that being for the simple protection of secrets—the cost of storage and security, not the cost of acquisition or exploitation. The deficit is just over a half trillion a year, the debt is at $9 trillion, and we have $40 trillion in unfunded future obligations. The only person in the Nation that seems truly concerned is the Honorable David Walker, Comptroller General of the United States, and director of the Government Accountability Office (GAO).

The role of government in the 21st century is to provide incentives and to facilitate the sharing and exchange of information between the sectors, the organizations, and the individuals that comprise the national information continuum—and to work with other governments to create an international and transnational information commons.[11]

Schools and universities have expert faculty and willing student labor as well as significant electronic storage and processing facilities. They also tend to have multilingual populations that can do very fine data filtering and data entry work. Two examples are the Monterey Institute of International Studies (MIIS), which uses graduate students fluent in Russian, Korean, Vietnamese, and Arabic to maintain the world's best database on the proliferation of nuclear, chemical, and biological weapons; and Mercyhurst College, which uses undergraduate students to produce newsletters on narcotics trafficking and other trends of interest to law enforcement agencies.[12] Universities can also provide technical assistance and project assistance—one fine example of this capability, which provides direct support to local government agencies as well as small and medium-sized businesses, is the InfoMall developed by Syracuse University.

Libraries represent "distributed knowledge" in the best possible way and provide citizens with not only direct access but also with skilled librarians who can serve as intermediaries in global discovery and discrimination. Examples of unique contributions in the library arena include the University of Colorado, which created Uncover Reveal to distribute electronically the tables of contents of all journals it processes; the Special Libraries Association, which brings together corporate and association librarians; and the Library-Oriented List Service developed by Charles Bailey, Jr.[13]

---

[11] Since this was written in 1995 and published in 1996, the stated objective of some formidable public advocacy groups has become that of "free universal access to all knowledge." The author shares that objective for the simple reason that it is the fastest way to unleash the entrepreneurial productive capacity of the five billion poor. Cf. C. K. Prahalad, *The Fortune at the Bottom of the Pyramid* (Wharton, 2004).

[12] Robert Heibel, who received one of the twelve lifetime achievement awards in the field of Open Source Intelligence (OSINT) in 2006, was a decade ahead of his time. Today his program, still the best in the world, is being emulated by Johns Hopkins University and others, as the concept of legal intelligence as decision-support begins to prove its value in the business world.

Businesses not only hold significant amounts of data that they generate themselves, including customer preference data that could contribute to aggregate industry studies, but they also pay for great quantities of data, such as market surveys, which could after a short passage of time be eligible for sharing with smaller businesses and universities. One of the challenges facing nations that desire to be attractive to international investors is that of creating "information-rich" environments within which corporations can be globally competitive. One way of doing this is by developing information consortia and protocols for releasing into the information commons such data as might have already been exploited by the company that collected it or paid for it but which could now have a residual value for the larger community.[14]

Private investigators, information brokers, and commercial intelligence are addressed separately because they play a unique role in a global economy driven by information, in which information is—as Alvin and Heidi Toffler have noted—a substitute for wealth, violence, labor, and capital. The capabilities of organizations dedicated to finding and processing information can be extraordinary and worth every penny of investment. It is important to note that one of the most significant changes to occur in relation to government is that the "information explosion" and the free market economy have led to the establishment of private sector capabilities that are superior to traditional government collection and processing mechanisms, even the most secret and expensive programs. Examples of "best in class" commercial intelligence capabilities include the Institute of Scientific Information (ISI) with its *Science Citation Index* and *Social Science Citation Index* for identifying the top experts in the world on any topic; InfoSphere AB in Sweden, with a global network of legal and ethical experts and observers who work on a "just enough, just in

---

[13] Today, a decade later, two individuals stand out: Brewster Kahle, who has extended his Internet Archive to include digitization projects at major libraries around the world; and Larry Brilliant, who has become the Executive Director of Google.org, with a mission of applying information to global challenges. His first investment was in the Global Public Health Intelligence Network.

[14] During an annual conference of middle-aged hackers, popularly known as the Hackers or THINK Conference (started by Stewart Brand, today managed by Glenn Tenney) there was a discussion of what return on investment one received from volunteering information into the Internet. The *general* consensus was that for every piece of information that one contributed to the commons, 100 pieces were received in return, of which 10 were actually useful. This is a 10-to-1 noise to signal ratio, but it is also a 10-to-1 substantive return on investment.

time" basis; Deep Web Technologies, which has taken multilingual web exploitation to the next level; All World Languages, which can meet the needs for native language translation capabilities the government does not have; and East View Cartographic, which offers world-class Russian maps of the 90% of the world the USA decided not to map, at the military resolution level of 1:50,000 (1:10 meters) with contour lines.[15]

The utility of **media** information for policy, economic planning, military contingency planning, and law enforcement, is almost always severely underestimated. In fact, journalists—especially investigative journalists like David Kaplan of US News & World Report, or adventure journalists like Robert Young Pelton (host of Discovery Channel, "Come Back Alive") and Robert Kaplan or Ralph Peters—are extraordinarily talented, energetic, and well-connected individuals who produce very significant and accurate reports that can be integrated into finished reports on virtually any topic. It is also worth noting that most journalists publish only roughly 10% of what they know. James Baker, former Secretary of State, notes in his memoirs that "in terms of fine-turning our own work, staying abreast of the press comments was particularly important."[16] Colin Powell, in his own book, notes that when he was Military Assistant to then Sectary of Defense Casper Weinberger, he preferred the *Early Bird* with its compendium of newspaper stories to the "cream of overnight intelligence" which was delivered to the Secretary of Defense by a Central Intelligence Agency (CIA) courier each morning.[17] In a direct and practical example, the U.S. Southern Command, working with the Los Alamos National Laboratory, was able—at very low cost—to exploit Latin American investigative reporting such that tactical interdiction missions could be planned and executed based primarily on media reporting." This is not to say that media sources are superior to classified intelligence, only that they cannot

---

[15] Most of the companies mentioned in the original article have fallen by the wayside. The field is wide-open now, and most interestingly, as discussed by Yochai Benkler in *The Wealth of Networks: How Social Production Transforms Markets and Freedom* (Yale, 2006), and by *Business Week* in a cover story, "The Power of Us" (20 June 2006), individuals are finding that voluntary intellectual labor produces income and benefits no one ever imagined previously. Lego Corporation, in an example offered by Business Week, received 1,600 engineering hours free from loyal fanatic customers eager to help design new systems.

[16] James A. Baker, III, *The Politics of Diplomacy: Revolution, War & Peace. 199-1992* (New York: O.P. Putnam's Sow, 1995), p. 154.

[17] Colin Powell, *My American Journey* (Random House, 1995)., p. 293.

be discounted and are especially useful to those in the private sector and in much of government who do not have authorized access to classified information.[18]

Finally, we have **the government**, including state, local, and tribal governments and their information holdings, the Department of Defense, and the intelligence community. These are not examined in detail here. However, it bears mentioning that in the absence of a policy supportive of information archiving and public dissemination-and the means for implementing that policy —vast stores of information reaching the U.S. government, including information collected and processed by contractors to the U.S. government, are being "buried" each day, needlessly depriving the public of significant information resources. FirstGov, now going toward its third iteration, is promising, as are the distributed commercially-secure storage and retrieval capabilities of IBM's Blue Genie, the Googleplex, and the Internet Archive.

INTELLIGENCE IN THE AGE OF INFORMATION

Having explored in general terms the elements of the information commons and the information continuum, we now must focus on the specifics of intelligence in the Age of Information.[19] Among the core concepts that government and private sector information managers must adopt and promulgate are:
Espionage, whether by governments or corporations, is less cost-effective than intelligent exploitation of open sources. Unfortunately, most intelligence communities are trained, equipped, and organized to do secrets, and they are not well positioned to collect and integrate open sources-public information-into their analysis and production processes. This needs to be changed and is discussed further below.

---

[18] This exciting story, by the principal investigator at Los Alamo National Laboratory, is contained in James Holden-Rhode, *Sharing the Secrets: Open Sources and the War on Drugs* (Albuquerque: University of New Mexico Pre, 1994). The various laboratories of the Department of Energy are, in fact, the nation's most important open source asset, and very important examples of why we can no longer afford to compartment classified information apart from "rest of government" information.

[19] My keynote speech to the Association for Global Strategic Information (AGSI) contained many of these operational concepts and has been reprinted as "Access: The Theory and Practice of Competitor Intelligence," *Journal of AGSI* (July 1994). My most developed work in this area, is my white paper, "'Access: Theory and Practice of Intelligence in the Age of Information." (October 26, 993).

The customer and the environment are the best target for the application of intelligence methods (requirements analysis, collection management, analytical fusion, forecasting and visualization of information) *not* a competitor.

Decision-Support (intelligence) is the ultimate objective of all information processes. One must carefully distinguish between intelligence, which is the raw text, signal, or image; *information,* which is collated data of generic interest; and *intelligence,* which is information that has been tailored to support a specific decision by a specific pennon about a specific question at a specific time and place. Most government information and so-called intelligence products are so generic as to be relatively useless in directing action. Only when information serves as the foundation for *intelligence* can its cost be justified.

Distributed information is more valuable and yet less expensive than centralized information. The art of information governance in the 21st century will focus on harnessing distributed centers of excellence rather than on creating centralized repositories of information.

"Just in time" information collection and intelligence production is far less expensive and far more useful to the consumer of intelligence than 'just in case" collection and archiving.[20]

The value of information is a combination of its content, the context within which it is being used, and the timeliness with which it is obtained and exploited. This means that information which has been used by an organization declines in value when taken out of context and after time has passed. This, in turn, means that there is every reason for an organization to barter, share, or sell information (e.g., market research) once its "prime" value point has passed. This is especially important to an organization as a means of increasing it's acquisition of new information which-in its own context and time-has greater value than when it was lying fallow in the information commons.

The new paradigm for information acquisition is the 'diamond paradigm" in which the consumer, analyst, collector, and source are all able to communicate

---

[20] Paul Evan Peters, Executive Director of the Coalition for Networked Information, is the originator of this concept.

directly with one another. The old paradigm, the 'linear paradigm" in which the consumer went to the analyst who went to the collector who went to the source, and back up the chain it went, is not only too slow but is also unworkable when you have a fast-moving topic with many nuances that are difficult to communicate. Today and in the future, the information manager' greatest moment is going to be when a consumer can be put in direct touch with exactly the right source who can answer the question directly, at low cost. by creating new knowledge tailored to the needs of the consumer, at that exact moment.

The most important information resource is the employee. Every employee must be a collector, producer, *and consumer* of information and intelligence. This is called the "corporate hive"[21] model, and it is the foundation for creating a "smart nation." If every personnel description does not list as task number one: "collect and report information useful to the organization," and if organizations do not provide a vehicle and a protocol for sharing information among employees, then by definition the organization is "dumb."

Published knowledge is old knowledge. The art of intelligence in the 21st century will be less concerned with integrating old knowledge and more concerned with using published knowledge as **a** path to exactly the right source or sources that can create new knowledge tailored to a new situation, in real time.[22]

---

[21] Kevin Kelly, *Out of Control: The Rise of the Neo-Biological Civilization* (Reading, MA Addison-Wesley 1994), provide a brilliant exposition of why, in a very complex global system driven by information, organic self-healing and relatively autonomous elements must be accepted and nurtured. It is impossible to control complexity in a centralized preplanned fashion. Those concerned about the fragility of our information infrastructure would do well to read Kelly's work, a well as one predating him by 10 years, Charles Perrow's *Normal Accidents: Living with High-Risk Technologies (New York*: Basic Books, 1984). Simple systems have single points of failure fairly easy to diagnose. Complex systems have multiple points of failure that interact in unanticipated ways. Today we have a constellation of very complex information systems, all built by the lowest bidder and without regard to the dangers of authorized users doing unauthorized things.

[22] We keep forgetting that books were generally written as dissertations or started roughly 10 years before finally appearing in print; articles are generally 10 months or so old; and even newspaper stories are at least a day if not 3-10 days old. Within academic circles, it is well-known that if one is not receiving the drafts of works in progress and the pre-prints, it is simply not possible to be a serious competitor.

The threat (or the answer) changes depending on the level of analysis. The most fundamental flaw in both intelligence and information today is the failure to establish, for each question, the desired level of analysis. There are four levels of analysis: strategic, operational, tactical, and technical. These, in turn, are influenced by the three major contexts of inquiry: civil, military, and geographic.[23] A simple example from the military sphere will illustrate the importance of this issue. Examining the capability of a specific Middle Eastern country in the mission area of tank warfare, it was found that while the initial threat assessment (by someone unfamiliar with the levels-of-analysis approach) was very high because this country had a great many modem tanks, in fact the threat varied significantly depending on the level of analysis. Only at the technical level (lethality) was the threat high. At the tactical level (reliability), the threat was, in fact, very low because the crews were not trained and had poor morale, and the tanks were generally in storage and not being maintained.the operational level (availability), the threat increased to medium because there were large numbers of tanks widely scattered over the country. At the strategic level (sustainability), the threat dropped again to low because it would be almost impossible for this country to carry out extended tank warfare operations, even on its own terrain. This approach can and should be applied to every question for which intelligence—tailored information—is to be provided.

ETHICS, ECOLOGY, AND EVOLUTION

---

[23] At the strategic level, civil allies, geographic location, and military sustainability are critical At the operational level civil instability, geographic resources, and military availability At the tactical level, civil psychology, geographic atmosphere, and military reliability determine outcome. At the technical level, civil infrastructure, geographic atmosphere, and military lethality are the foundation for planning and employment. This is an original analysis model developed by the author while serving as the Deputy Director and Special Assistant (senior civilian) in the new Maine Corps Intelligence Center (today a Command) in Quantico, Virginia At the time, examining all products from the Central Intelligence Agency and the Defense Intolerance Agency then in hand, the author discovered that none of the products purported a specific decision and that none of the products was related to any specific level of analysis.. Everything was generic, topical, a "snapshot," virtually useless to a policymaker or commander. Little has changed since then, one reason why some policymakers feel they can define reality in ideological terms—and a major reason why we need an ethical *public* intelligence capability.

Our "Industrial Age" concept of intelligence and information has relied heavily on a centralized, top-down "command and control" model in which the question virtually determined the answer, and the compartmentation of knowledge—Its restriction to an elite few—has been a dominant feature of information operations. This chapter suggests that the true value of "intelligence" lies in its informative value, a value which increases with dissemination. The emphasis within our government, therefore, should be on optimizing our exploitation of open sources, increasing the exchange of information among the intelligence community, the rest of government, and the private sector, and producing unclassified intelligence. This could be called the "open books" approach to national intelligence.[24]

As we prepare to enter the 21gt century, we must ask ourselves some fundamental questions. How do we define national security? Who is the customer for national intelligence? What is our objective? There appears to be every reason to discard old concepts of national security and national intelligence and to focus on developing integrated nationwide information and intelligence networks, which recognize that national security depends on a solid economy and a stable environment; that the center of gravity for progress in the future is the citizen, not the bureaucrat; and that our objective must be to enable informed governance and informed citizenship, not simply to monitor conventional and nuclear threats.

I am convinced that the "ethics" of national intelligence requires a dramatic reduction in government secrecy as well as corporate secrecy. After 20 years an intelligence professional, I am certain that secrets are inherently pathological, undermining reasoned judgment and open discussion.[25] Secrets are also abused, used to protect bureaucratic interests rather than genuine

---

[24] *This* section draws on a full-length article, "E3i: Ethics, Ecology, Evolution, and Intelligence," published in the *Whole Earth Review* (Fall 1992).

[25] Although Alvin and Heidi Toffler h called me "the greatest enemy of secrecy" in the United States (in their book *War and Anti-War),* that s not quite correct. I am an enemy of unnecessary secrecy because it costs a great deal--not only in dollars but also n terms of lost opportunities. My complete views arc set forth in my "Testimony and Comments on Executive Order 12356, 'National Security Information.'" provided by invitation to the Presidential Inter-Agency Task Force on National Security Information, Department of Justice, June 9, 1993. believe that we should all be strong advocates of "no classification without justification."

equities. Consider the following statement by Rodney B. McDaniel, then Executive Secretary of the National Security Council:

> *Everybody who's a real practitioner, and I'm sure you're not all naive in this regard, realizes that there are two uses to which security classification is put: the legitimate desire to protect secrets, and protection of bureaucratic turf. As a practitioner of the real world, it's about 90% bureaucratic turf and 10% legitimate protection of secrets a far as I'm concerned[26].*

Thomas Jefferson once said: "A nation's best defense *is* an educated citizenry." I firmly believe that in the Age of Information, national intelligence— unclassified national intelligence—must be embedded in every decision, every process, and every organization. The "ethics" of openness needs to apply to the private sector as well as to the government. Universities should not be allowed to hold copyrights or patents if they are not able or willing to disseminate knowledge or commercialize technology. Corporations should not be allowed to monopolize patents solely to protect archaic production processes.

The environment in which we live, in which we hope to prosper and secure the common defense, is our most important intelligence target and our most neglected intelligence target. Our traditional intelligence community and our more conventional government information community both appear reluctant to take on the hard issues of honestly evaluating the larger context within which we export munitions, keep the price of gasoline under two dollars a gallon, permit unfettered gang warfare and exploitation within our immigrant communities, and so on. At what point are we going to establish an architecture for integrating Federal, state, and local data about the natural environment and for producing useful strategic analyses about specific political, economic, and cultural issues? The following paraphrased observation by Ellen Seidman, Special Assistant to the President on the National Economic Council, is instructive:

---

[26] He was speaking in 1990 to a group of government employees selected for increased responsibility and attending a Harvard Executive Program Cited in Thomas P. Coaklcy (ed.), *C'I: Issues of Command and Control* (National Defense University, 1991), p. 68.

CIA reports only focus on foreign economic conditions. They don't do domestic economic conditions and so I cannot get a strategic analysis that compares and contrasts strengths and weaknesses of the industries I am responsible for. On the other hand, Treasury, Commerce, and the Fed are terrible at the business of intelligence — they don't know how to produce intelligence.[27]

Taken in combination, what we do out of ignorance to our environment each day through our existing energy, trade, defense, housing, transportation, and education policies is far worse than a whole series of Chernobyls.

Finally, if the nation is to evolve, if it is to "harness the distributed intelligence of the Nation," as Vice President Al Gore has taken to saying in his many speeches on the National Information Infrastructure,[28] then we must come to grips with the fact that we are "losing our mind" as a nation and that education is the "boot camp" for national intelligence. We must revitalize our educational system, including corporate training and continuing education programs, and realize that openness is a powerful catalyst for bringing to bear the combined intelligence of every citizen and resident. Instead of "National Intelligence" (spies and satellites) bearing the burden for informing policy, we should rely upon "national intelligence" (smart people) and use our distributed network of educated scholars, workers, information brokers, journalists, civil servants, require a depth and breadth of commitment to information as a commodity; to information as a substitute for time, space, capital, and labor. Intelligence—applied information—is vital to both our defense and our prosperity.

Connectivity is but one of the four major elements of what must soon become a National Information Strategy.[29]

---

[27] Seidman was speaking to the Open Source Lunch Club on January 1, 1994. Her observations were subsequently reported in *OSS Notices* 94001 dated February 21, 1994.

[28] This phrase was borrowed from the author by Mike Nelson, aide to Al Gore.

[29] Among my many speeches and publications in this area, the following are especially pertinent: "National Intelligence Strategy: Needed initiatives," speech to the National Defense University Foundation National Industrial Security Association Symposium on The Global Information Explosion A Threat to National Security, May 16, 199S (with Alvin Toffler, Bo Cutter, Emmett Paige, Robert Johnson, and Bill Studeman); National Intelligence: The Community Tomorrow?.," speech to the Security Affairs Support

For those counseling the incremental approach, "connectivity today, content tomorrow," one must say: it will be too late. The fragility of our position in the world, in terms of brain drain, budget deficit, and electronic security, all require that we establish a four-point integrated program, as outlined below, immediately.

- ***Connectivity.*** Such a strategy should build upon the National Infrastructure as its technical foundation, but provide for three additional elements:

- ***Content.*** Existing government programs, under the auspices of a National Information Foundation within the White House, should provide incentives for all elements of the information continuum (K-12, universities, libraries, business, information brokers, media, government, defense, and intelligence) to put content online; only in this way can we establish a robust national "information commons" and give Robert Reich's symbolic analysts something other than a starvation diet It is vital that we establish a means of nurturing distributed centers of excellence throughout our nation in all topical areas, providing all sectors with incentives to place encyclopedic information into the 'information commons" and, thus, stimulating productivity. Just S billion a year invested in this program could yield enormous productivity and competitiveness gains across our entire private sector. Within government, we should dramatically accelerate NTIS involvement in structuring and digitizing information now in the possession of the government but not .-available to the public.

Association Spring Symposium, National Security Agency, April 20, 1995; Private Enterprise Intelligence: let's Potential Contribution to National Security." paper presented to the Canadian Intelligence Community Conference on Intelligence Analysis and Assessment, October 29, 1994; and "A Critical Evaluation of U.S. National Intelligence Capabilities" *International Journal of Intelligence and Counterintelligence* (Summer1993). I have also provided invited testimony to the Commission on Intelligence and the House Permanent Select Committee on Intelligence.

- *Coordination.* Using a body similar to those now orchestrating Nil technical issues. focus on resource management across government and private sector boundaries in both technical and nontechnical (content) arenas. There is no good reason why hundreds of major organizations should be wasting approximately $2 billion a year creating hundreds of variations of a basic multimedia analysis workstation. There is no good reason why hundreds of corporations and other organizations should be wasting enormous sums collecting and processing the same encyclopedic information about foreign countries, companies, and capabilities. Presidential leadership would make a difference and save the nation billions of dollars annually, not only within government but across the private sector.

- *Communications and Computer Security,* We have a house built over a sinkhole The vulnerabilities of our national telecommunications infrastructure to interruption of services as well as destruction, degradation, and theft of data are such that experts feel comfortable in predicting that—unless we are able to establish a major Presidential program in this arena—we will see a series of enormously costly electronic attacks on our major financial and industrial organizations, generally undertaken by individuals who stand to benefit financially from degraded or interrupted performance. The current generation of systems engineers was not raised in an environment where security was a necessary element of design. At every level, through every node, we are wide open-and in a networked environment, one open house contaminates the rest of the network.

Such an integrated program could be established using exiting resources. The cost savings from the elimination of redundant and counterproductive investments in information collection and information technology across government departments and into the private sector would also make a substantive difference against the deficit, while inspiring productivity increases that would address our future unfunded obligations now known to exist.[30]

CONCLUSION

We are a smart people today, but a dumb nation Our national security and our national attractiveness as a site for international investment which permit our citizens to prosper arc both at risk. We have no alternative but to completely redefine the role of government to emphasize its responsibility for the nurturing of our national information commons, and to redefine national intelligence so as to create a Virtual Intelligence Community in which every citizen is a collector, producer, and consumer of intelligence. To do this, we must have a National Information Strategy. The Smart Nation Act will give precisely the constellation of mixed public-Congressional-Executive capabilities needed to be the smartest, safest, most productive Nation in the Age of Information.

---

[30] One authority, Paul Strassmann, estimates that in information housekeeping costs alone $22 billion could be saved over seven years. This is apart from policy savings derived from improved intelligence support. Strausmann has been Director of Defense Information and Chief Information Offer of the Xerox Corporation and other major companies. His books, including *The Politics of Information Management. The Business Value of Computers, and Information PayOff,*and are all exceptional.

Part II:
Public Intelligence in the Public Interest

The illustration below depicts in very clear terms all that the secret intelligence community is not addressing with its $60 billion a year budget. There is of course a good reason why it is not applying the proven process of intelligence to open sources relevant to these ten global threats, twelve policy areas, and eight challengers—the secret world has long held that it is the policy agencies that are responsible for overt collection and analysis. Unfortunately the policy agencies do not know how to do Open Source Intelligence (OSINT), and neither do the elements of the Congress.

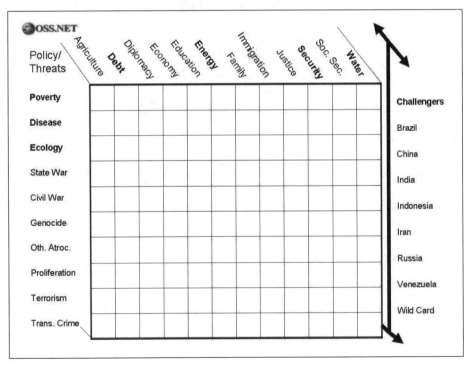

Figure 2: Public Intelligence & Policy Challenges

This second portion of the book provides a deeper look at why an independent Open Source Agency, outside the U.S. Intelligence Community but of course channeling all possible information to the secret agencies, is needed.

Chapter 5: Ten Threats, Twelve Policies, Eight Challengers

This chapter provides a strategic overview for Congress on why, in the era of globalization, extremism, and free Internet communications, it is essential to deal with the ten global threats as part of a strategic mosaic, ensuring that each of the twelve policies is in harmony with a national strategy set largely by Congress in relation to ways, means, and ends.   The eight challengers, including the Wild Card of extremist religions (ours as well as theirs) and evil belief systems, help to emphasize the shallowness of our strategic thinking.

Chapter 6: The Open Source Intelligence (OSINT) Story, 1988 to date

The modern OSINT story began in 1988 when the Marine Corps Intelligence Center (now a Command) discovered that 80-90% of what it needed to do policy, acquisition, operations, and logistics intelligence was not secret, not online, not in English, and not known to anyone in Washington, D.C. That is still the case today, but as this story outlines, over thousands of people from across 40 countries have been fighting the good fight since 1988. It falls to Congress now to give them a mandate and a foundation for the future.

Chapter 7: Intelligence Affairs: Evolution, Revolution, or Reaction?

Current intelligence reforms are "reactionary" and neither evolutionary or revolutionary. Secret intelligence has come to the end of its prime.

Chapter 8: Intelligence in Denial: The Need for Independence

Despite going from $30 billion to $60 billion a year, the secret intelligence world still thinks in terms of governments & states, not tribes & global threats.

Chapter 9: Open Source Intelligence: The Strategic Value to the Nation

This is the seminal chapter, forthcoming in *Strategic Intelligence* (Westport, CN: Praeger, 2007), under the editorial guidance of Dr. Loch Johnson.

Chapter 5:
Ten Threats, Twelve Policies, Eight Challengers

Ten Threats Demanding Information Sharing and Collaborative Inter-Agency Intelligence[31]

Poverty	Disease	Environmental Degradation	Inter-State Conflict	Civil War
Genocide	Other Atrocities	Proliferation	Terrorism	Transnational Crime

Twelve Policy Areas Demanding Public Intelligence to Restore Sensible Honest Government[32]

Agriculture	Debt	Diplomacy	Economy
Education	Energy	Family	Immigration
Justice	Security	Social Security	Water

Eight Challengers Who Will Overwhelm Us If We Do Not Restore Moral Informed Politics[33]

Brazil	China	India	Indonesia
Iran	Russia	Venezuela	Wild Card

---

[31] Per the High-Level Panel on Threats, Challenges and Change, *A more secure world: Our shared responsibility* (United Nations, 2004). The US focuses on #8 and #9 only. This is foolish—we must mobilize all parties to achieve balanced attention—and sign treaties and agreements to nurture the sharing of relevant open source information—to address all of these threats over time and to act wisely today on behalf of the future.

[32] As developed by author from a cross-section of historical "mandate for change" documents in US politics.

[33] As developed by author from global review of relevant books. Wild Card examples: South Africa or Turkey, and of course extremist religious ideologies that are intolerant.

Four Reforms Necessary to Re-Establish "America the Good"[34]

| Electoral | Intelligence | National Security | Budget |

Eight Tribes Whose Wisdom and Knowledge Must be Harnessed to Achieve Peace and Prosperity[35]

Government	Military	Law Enforcement	Business
Academia	Media	Non-Governmental	Civil Societies[36]

Eight Functionalities of the Open World Brain Empowering All Individuals, Especially the Poor[37]

Public Daily Brief	Distance Learning	Virtual Library	Open Forum
Global Calendar	Global Directory	Virtual Budget	Global Plot

On the pages that follow we provide a very modest first step in defining the strategic implications of each of the ten threats. The other elements are addressed by our Public Daily Briefs and Weekly Summaries at www.oss.net.

---

[34] These four reforms are discussed in more detail in a short document called: "In Search of a Leader, visible at http://www.citizens-party.org. .

[35] See the author's books, *THE NEW CRAFT OF INTELLIGENCE*, and also *INFORMATION OPERATIONS*. Online versions are available for open license (free) translation by any government or organization http://www.oss.net. See also the Co-Intelligence Institute and especially the "Eight Strands of Collective Intelligence" for a sense of the possibilities. The edited work on *PEACEKEEPING INTELLIGENCE* is also relevant.

[36] This includes religions and labor unions as well as the wide variety of normal citizens' advocacy groups.

[37] C.K. Prahalad establishes the possibilities in *The Fortune at the Bottom of the Pyramid*. TIME Magazine's issue of 29 May 2006 included "Cool Tools for the Third World" and there appears to be an emerging realization that empowering the poor with information and information tools is the fastest way to what some call "infinite wealth." Our next book, *INFORMATION PEACEKEEPING: Saving the World by Empowering the Poor*, integrates this vision and our own. A sense of the larger moral schema can be seen in the author's 1993 lecture on "God, Man, and Information." Some specific examples of citizen oversight made possible by Open Source Intelligence are at Appendix 2. A one-page listing of essential references on the history, context, practice, policy, and other aspects of OSINT can be readily utilized online at http://www.oss.net/BASIC. See also the books in the Appendix.

THREAT #1: POVERTY[38]

Give a man a fish and you feed him for a day. Teach him how to fish and you feed him for a lifetime. (attributed to. Lao Tzu)

Poverty in the developing world should not be confused with *emergencies*. Anyone can have a sudden need for food and shelter (New Orleans after *Katrina*). International programs against "poverty" go beyond this to building the capacity of a population to maintain and grow the means of self-sufficiency. If "real" aid is drilling wells, not bottled water, it is also about training locals to drill wells and maintain machinery. Action against poverty is now seen as a mix of **Aid**, **Trade**, **Investment**, **Migration**, **Environment**, **Security**, **Technology**. As well as shipping in bags of grain, it is more important to stop the war that will destroy the next crop, to invent appropriate technologies (the **cow-dung radio** in India), and to build local economies through investment and trade. *Migration* is contentious – accepting the unskilled and displaced counts as aid, but enticing every trained nurse in Ghana to London not only does not count as aid but is a negative step for Ghana. The US is 20th in the world for aid as a portion of GDP (0.14%). 72% of this is **tied aid** ("with strings") and much goes to less poor and totalitarian regimes. US aid is perceived to be largely directed by national interest, whereas some nations, such as **Denmark** (first in world ranking), seem motivated otherwise – if Danish secret agendas exist they are well hidden. But in the broadest view aid *is* about self-interest. In **Somalia**, failure to understand root problems and obsession with forming a nation in a preconceived image led to a decade of bronze-age governance. **Islamists** now seem the only hope for stable government, and a shining hope in Africa for **Taliban**-style regimes. What started as an aid problem ended as a political problem because the earlier efforts were unbearably tainted with politics.[39]
Near-Term

---

[38] Each of the ten threat forecasts in this section were developed by the very strong intellects of OSS Australia, the same individuals that corrected our Latin in 1994 when we first devised as the OSS motto, *E Veritate Potens*, "From Truth, Power." OSS Europe is responsible for the Internet link charts that are posted at http://www.oss.net.

[39] Many facts quoted are from Center for Global Development.[USA], http://www.cgdev.org.

Near-Term

For aid to be effective in the longer term – to be "real" – donors need to understand bottom-line causes. Some are geographical (systematic lack of water), many are social/political (enduring clan and tribal rivalries), many are simple perfidy (corrupt regimes and callous middle class elites). In each case the solution is dictated by the cause and is often obvious. Educating policy-makers in the underlying causes of each aid case goes a long way to making aid effective.

Mid-Term

Even blind incompetence is better than aid for doctrinaire or the wrong reasons. The *top-down* approach of the 1960's – fortify the rulers and elites and they will fix their countries – is discredited for good reason. It resulted in a sudden demand for Rolls Royce cars, weapons, all the while accelerating the deterioration of subsistence societies, and even in nations rich in natural resources, misdirecting the common wealth for the private gain of a few elites. Recipients should not have to convert to Jesus – or the Danish way of life – to eat. A recent notion – fix poverty **one village at a time** (bottom-up) – is the most rational approach with the best chance of success thus far.

Long-Term

Many Asian nations jumped from primitive telephone networks to ubiquitous internet and cellular networks. This technological *leap-frog* awaits developing nations. The West will be burdened with 2nd or 3rd generation modalities when poorest nation will suddenly have 4th generation technologies. In 10 years the West will be weighed down by old costly infrastructure (the London tube) and many "developing" nations will be growing from strength to strength driven by clean, green high-tech practices.

THREAT #2: INFECTUOUS DISEASE

Globalization and freedom of air travel allow a communicable human disease to travel from anywhere to anywhere else within 24 hours. Short of blood tests and lengthy quarantine of travelers there is little that can be done to prevent a carrier of a highly communicable, highly lethal disease walking the streets of a large population centre today. The use of disease as a new asymmetric tactic would make explosives seem primitive. Walking the path to martyrdom through densely populated cities infected with a well-chosen disease, a "dead man walking" could bring havoc – and fear. But if the "terrorists" don't do it, diseases assisted only by ignorance and negligence may get there first. Broadly speaking, diseases have three sources:

Protozoa – the tiniest of animals typically inhabiting water and other animals as parasites; the commonest example is **malaria**, threatening one-twelfth of the human population, caused by protozoans in the bite of an infected female *Anopheles* mosquito. Such diseases can be prevented by physical interdiction (DDT, mosquito nets) and medication treating or repairing the effects.

Bacteria – microscopic single celled organisms; life would not exist without bacteria in animal digestion, the nitrogen cycle and other essential processes. But some bacteria turn to the dark side – **tuberculosis** readily treatable if diagnosed early is caused by *Mycobacterium tuberculosis*; *Bacillus Anthracis* can form hardy air-borne *spores* and cause highly lethal **anthrax**. Common treatments are killing the bacteria before it infects or the use of the appropriate *antibiotic* after infection.

Viruses, the ultimate in simplicity and masters of self-preservation, are simply a *nucleic acid* (DNA or RNA) instruction-set covered by a protein sheath. They reproduce only by penetrating cells and using the cell's reproductive mechanism to replicate themselves. Variations in copying the code produces *mutations* of the virus. Examples are highly contagious, high lethality **Ebola** caused by an airborne virus spores and **H5N1** (avian influenza) that is highly communicable among some animals but noncommunicable (or weakly communicable) to humans. Such infections are commonly prevented or attenuated by injecting a *vaccine*, small doses of crippled or dead versions of the target virus, that teaches the body's immune system what to kill on sight.

That's the good news. *DDT* remains the most effective interdiction against **malaria** but it is banned in most developed nations because of the devastating persistent effect on the environment. Use of the wrong *antibiotic*, or misuse, or over-use creates – by *natural selection* – strains of bacteria that are *resistant* to many or all antibiotics. *Mutation* of *viruses* means that the vaccine administered today after three months development may be useless against a mutant version of the virus that appeared in the infected subject yesterday. Simple changes in the protein sheath will render it invisible to an immune

63

system trained by a vaccine to recognize other characteristics. The worst case is when a virus attacks the cells of the *immune system* itself – as with **HIV/AIDS**. These "second generation" dangers of infectious diseases are not just theoretical. A new strain of **tuberculosis** identified recently in **South Africa** is quickly fatal in HIV/AIDS patients and a disease once thought beaten may spread around the world anew. A mutation in the **H5N1** virus is theoretically possible any day and would make it highly communicable to humans. A range of vaccine-preventable diseases thought to be eliminated in developed countries such as *measles, mumps, whooping cough,* and *poliomyelitis* are making a reappearance – complacency has led to a drop-off in vaccination and many doctors have "forgotten" to look for these diseases in patients. Neglect of these vaccination programs poses the hazard of self-inflicted epidemics. The over-use and misuse of antibiotics over decades, particularly in the **US**, is acknowledged as a major contributor to new more dangerous strains of pathogens such as some *Staphylococci* that are found only in hospitals.

Apart from these dangers to ourselves, miscreants using asymmetric tactics can bring immense harm to populations by transporting uncommon but highly contagious pathogens to highly populated areas. Whether a pathogen is *weaponisable* is a buzz-word in this field; that is, can it be produced, packaged, transported and effectively deployed in potent, dispersed form. **Anthrax** in *spore* form is well-suited to this but a range of other pathogens can be presented in a matrix of lethality and deployability. There is little confidence that health infrastructures could cope beyond a few days or weeks against even a small but effective pathogen attack in a large population centre — the health services themselves will be the first victim, followed possibly by public order. Mortality will be a mere detail.

Near-Term

There is every indication that a public health investment would yield worthwhile benefits in doing the easily do-able — education of doctors and the population about vaccination, misuse of antibiotics, and early detection and treatment of diseases such as **tuberculosis**. Meanwhile, the security Community should continue to inventory the hazards from various pathogens – *lethality* vs. *communicability* vs. *availability* vs. *deployability* vs. *treatments* vs.

likelihood. A careful study may show that **anthrax** (and *VX*) is the least of worries.

Mid-Term

The abilities of the biological sciences around the world is as good as scientific discovery allows. The weakest link by far is government coordination in the mitigation of avoidable endemic diseases, foreknowledge of the logically possible types of pathogen attacks by miscreants, and planning for response in the event of such attacks. Planning and exercises around the world prompted by the perceived **H5N1** threat are encouraging but exercises and resource planning should accommodate a range of incubation periods and infection rates. Many variations will provide very bleak results.

Long-Term

Control of airspace, liquids on aircraft, quick temperature measurement of incoming travelers and other measures all mitigate against some forms of biological attack. One scenario worthy of exploring is a highly contagious, highly lethal (or debilitating) disease with a long incubation period and long period of contagion. Concealing a weapon of mass destruction in the cells of the body is simple, cheap, effective, and undetectable until vast numbers of people have been infected. Generally, the actors in this scenario need to be prepared to die but that might not be an impediment.

THREAT #3: ENVIRONMENTAL DEGRADATION

The Environment became a mainstream political issue only ten years after "environmentalist" was a pejorative term for fringe trouble-makers. Political environmentalism can be traced back more than ten years, to Rachel Carson's *Silent Spring* (1962) which after a long and bitter battle led to the restriction of DDT. Then the 1970s saw new terms such as "agent orange" in every newspaper and pictures on every television of wildlife habitats obliterated by oil spills. Public opinion shifted slightly. With the environment as a new factor – as lip-service or hard policy – environment debates were now not just academic. Profitability or oblivion suddenly depended on a percentage point in government emission/pollution standards. But even though the environment, like crime, is an issue there are no obvious *a priori* rules. At bottom there is always a Faustian test – a few billion in personal wealth today in exchange for the *chance* your grand-children will be homeless or be born limbless. Nothing is black or white. To further confuse things -- DDT remains one of the best weapons against the world's greater killer – malaria.

Clarify the Now

Most developed nations now factor environmental impacts into decision-making. Big-stakes cases hinge on contradictory evidence of each party's expert witnesses and judgments often depend on an intellectual coin-toss, manipulation of public opinion, or corrupted officials. Only the creation of disinterested expert jurisdictions removes important environmental issues from the dread grasp of short-term political vision. Also, only public education (or opinion leaders at least) can give a better grasp of *cost*. Discussion of cost in environmental debates is often deceitful, often on both sides.

Clarify the Future

Rachel Carson was called a liar and alarmist by opponents but history proved she was a prophet. The same problem remains today – early warnings are always so early that well-financed inertial mass of vested interests are able to discount and ridicule them. If early warnings on *tobacco* or *asbestos* had been investigated, no-one smoking today would have started smoking, no-one dying of asbestos would be dying. Because government does not see beyond five years or the next election, only statutory agencies that outlive governments can be trusted to observe the public environmental interest into the conceivable future..

Globalize the Public Interest

Initial excitement about globalization lost its innocence when nations realized that everyone really meant "my globalization: not yours". But the underlying premise of globalization – interconnectedness of all nations is inescapably true. Nations will realize that environmental problems in one sovereign state are also eventually a problem for all. The rapid destruction of the Amazon is not Brazil's problem but a factor of global climate. My Chernobyl is your

Chernobyl. Governments and their electorates will soon realize all nations are in the same boat.

THREAT #4: INTER-STATE CONFLICT

> *War is not an independent phenomenon, but the continuation of politics by different means.* Vom Kriege (1832), Carl von Clausewitz (1780-1831)

Although the US has not declared war since the World War II, it has been involved in several dozen war-like circumstances occasioning the death of soldiers and others. These range from the UN *Police Action* in **Korea** (1950+), to *Military Assistance* in **Vietnam** (1961–72), to *All Necessary Means* under UN Security Council Resolution 678 (**UNSCR 678**) in **Iraq** (1991), to the present **Iraq** liberation (2003+) based in **UNSCR 687**, the cease-fire conditions for the 1991 action. Because very few profit from war, it is often bad press to start one. This may explain few wars but very many *police actions*, *military operations*, *pre-emptive strikes* and *responses* to something the enemy did. Also – to use scurrilous logic -- if war is not declared it can not be lost, there can be no war crimes, no blame for starting a war (which is against international law), no obligation to obey rules of war, or rules for treatment of combatants, or rules for the protection of Cultural Property under the **Hague Convention** (1899, 1954).

Another practical reason for not calling a war a war is to circumvent constitutional and legal constraints on *Declaration of War*. In the US, only the Congress has power to "declare War". Whether this also means Congress alone has power to approve *war-like* actions has not been tested in the Supreme Court. Clausewitz says war is a complex interplay of a three elements – the goals of government, the sentiments of the population, and the intrinsic uncertainty of warfare itself. A war may start with popular support and then lose it; government imperatives may change during the war, an unbeatable army may be defeated by a trick, or the weather, or by the enemy general. This trinity of war – Government, Population, Military – seems to work well for any of the euphemisms for war and for other actions counter-posed to war such as *civil war* and *insurgency* where two or more political wills, populations, and armed groups are in conflict. But war is not going to get any easier. In future there may be fewer howitzers but a grinding globalize antipathy lasting decades, routine sabotage of home and foreign assets and infrastructure, and the occasional devastating 9/11 type of incident – the sort of continuing social unease that renders fielded forces, and some of Clausewitz, useless. The euphemism of politics has largely done away with War – we may now be in for a century or two of something worse.

Near-Term

Iraq (and **Somalia**) remind us there is also politics and a population on the other side. A military may be defeated but it is rarely possible to defeat a population. Recent events prove that war is foolish without clear, *achievable* goals, a supportive population, and a military up to that specific task. One of the prime causes of War are previous wars. War whether won or lost is a bell that can't be unrung, a 12 month war can bring 12 generations of enmity. As General Colin Powell said *"**If you break it: you own it**."*

Mid-Term

Wars go very wrong through failure to appreciate the full cultural, political and military picture. It is even more crucial to understand this if today's wars are grinding cultural antipathy with little to shoot at – an eternal urban insurgency. Effective and flexible military prowess will be as important as ever but more important will be broad-based **global monitoring**, political and cultural analysis, and scenario development – all of a quality not yet seen. But this quality Peace-keeping will still be cheaper than war.

Long-Term

As Clausewitz says, **war is <u>not</u> an independent phenomenon**. In war-time the generals take control of all the khaki bits, but a society that is not mobilized for peace will need to fight unnecessary wars. All nations will need to marshal their best resources (largely knowledge-based) for success in both peace and war. In comprehending and managing the threats to peace – *Poverty, Civil War, Water Wars*, ... -- all military and civil intelligence must be harnessed toward the national and global good.

THREAT #5: CIVIL WAR

And I will give unto thee, and to thy seed after thee, the land wherein thou art a stranger, all the land of Canaan, for an everlasting possession; and I will be their God. (Genesis 17:8)

Civil war is defined by what it is not – *not* war between fielded forces of nation states. Because there is often no "army" to be defeated, internecine inconclusive lethality can continue for decades, even centuries. Similarly, **insurgency** is defined as *not* civil war but it is just a matter of degree.

Insurgencies can be victorious; the Long March of the Communist forces in China, or the uprising by American merchants against good King George. The longest running civil war today is said to be the struggle since 1948 by the **Karen** in **Myanmar** (Burma) but the **Philippines** (1960s), **Thailand** (1960s), **Somalia** (1977), **Sri Lanka** (1983) are just some of the other conflicts that extend over decades.

But this Guinness book of records approach misses a crucial point. The southern Thailand conflict actually arises in Siamese annexation of an Islamic Sultanate in the 16th century; the **Moro** ("Moor") insurgency in the southern Philippines originates in the Spanish conquest of 1571. The *Troubles* in **Northern Ireland** date to victory by William over James II at the Boyne in 1690. Deep rifts in the **Balkans** date to when and where the Ottomans were halted in the 15th century. What may be civil war in all but name may be called an *insurgency* or *terrorism* for rhetorical reasons as with present-day **Iraq**, invented in 1932 when Whitehall sought to unite three Ottoman provinces (*Mosul, Baghdad* and *Basra*) into a new impossible entity.

Foreign intervention in civil wars is a gamble and the US had a run of bad luck – backing the **Taliban** in **Afghanistan**, the **Shah** in **Iran**, **Iraq** against **Iran** -- a geopolitical three-in-a-row loss. This points to intrinsic dangers of taking sides in "local" conflicts, or systematic short-sightedness in US foreign policy.

Intervention such as this often escalates into a **proxy war**. As the roots of civil wars and insurgencies are often very deep -- like a village feud in Calabria -- the origins are so distant that which party is clearly "right" or "wrong" is meaningless. The cycle of violence can only be solved with adult supervision and the only legitimate "adult supervision" at present – apart from some land-giving God – is the **United Nations** and **International Courts**.

69

Near-Term

A jury of the world will find few civil wars or insurgencies to have a *clear good guy* or *bad guy*. Any genuine interest in solving a conflict requires a juristically neutral appreciation of the harms, the claims and the logically possible judgments.   As with civil society, conflict that disrupts the public order – "world peace" -- can only be effectively resolved in the context of rule-of-law. Nation states unable to solve conflict must – in the broader interest -- surrender to international **juristic** solutions.

Mid-Term

There is an array of conflict-resolution methods starting from the proposition that most conflicts – with wisdom and effort – can be transformed from a **zero-sum game** into rational new arrangements that maximize each side's needs. Failure to understand that arises from the primitive reptilian brain; curable in most cases. The "jury of the world" will readily see what is just in the case of most disputes if the logical alternatives – often a complex of rights and duties – is derived from the true origins of the conflict.

Long-Term

The UN is the worst form of conflict resolution except all the others that have been tried.[40] The **veto**-based Security Council ensures that any civil war soon becomes a proxy war, in principle if not in reality – a race for "our side" to win rather than the conflict be justly resolved. Any use of the UN's palpable powers is thwarted or perverted. Any effective system for global intervention and solution of civil wars necessarily depends on retirement of the veto power.

THREAT #6: GENOCIDE

> **Of the cities of these people thou shalt save alive nothing that breatheth: But thou shalt utterly destroy them; namely, the *Hittites*, and the *Amorites*, the *Canaanites*, and the *Perizzites*, the *Hivites*, and the *Jebusites*. -- Deuteronomy 20:16-17**

---

[40] *Pace* Winston Churchill on democracy. He was also fond of saying that Americans always did the right thing, they just tried everything else first.

70

The distinction between war and genocide is a modern one. Throughout history, a lost battle often meant genocide for an entire population. In more modern times, most conflicts -- certainly not all -- have been about political suzerainty and control of resources. That said, the finger has never been far from the trigger of leaving alive *nothing that breatheth* – the **Japanese** in Nanking, **Germany** in Russia, **Russia** in Germany, and some isolated cases in every war by all armies since. Since 1945, over seventy million people have been killed in at least 55 genocides and systematic political killings. Most of these people have been killed by their own governments.

The *Convention on the Prevention and Punishment of the Crime of Genocide* was adopted by the UN General Assembly on 9 December 1948 (*entry into force* 12 January 1951) following the systematic slaughter by the German *Third Reich*. The Convention defines genocide as any act – whether during war or not –committed with intent to destroy, in whole or in part, a ***national*, *ethnical*, *racial*** or ***religious*** group, as such: Since some States refuse extradition for political crimes, the Convention specifically states that acts of genocide may *not* be classed as ***political crimes*** for the purpose of extradition. The full scope of acts constituting genocide is not widely known – (Article 2) **killing**, serious bodily or mental **harm**, inflicting **conditions of life** calculated to bring about physical destruction, imposing measures intended to **prevent births**; **transferring children** of the group to another group. In short, genocide is not just mass murder with racial motivation. It starts not with the act of killing but with the act of **differentiation** and then any acts that disadvantage that differentiated group.

This clearer understanding of genocide (as defined in the Convention) shows where the term is often misused. It explains why the UN has seemed to vacillate over **Darfur**. If the circumstances show that a group is being massacred not because of *who* they are but because of *where* they are living (consuming precious water resources perhaps) the label of genocide may not apply. Media may be vociferously critical of this but that is to miss the point and the true strength of the Convention. ***Mass murder*** is unlawful in all circumstance, in time of war or not and such acts are no less actionable for not falling within the Convention. The true power of the convention is to make unlawful acts which were policy of even Western governments in recent generations. The *conditions of life* provisions (as well as killing) would apply to in numerous cases to the treatment of Amerindians in North and South America; the *transferring children* provision would apply in many colonized places with indigenous populations (the *"Lost Generation"* cases in Australia). Similarly, the Convention probably applies to **China**'s "cultural genocide" in **Tibet**.

Differentiation (discrimination) is the key; not killing. Article 3 describes punishable acts, apart from acts of genocide, to include *conspiracy*, *incitement*, *attempt*, and *complicity* to commit genocide. Because the Convention requires signatories to promulgate local legislation against applicable acts, several developed nations have instituted *racial vilification* legislation. In some places this has led to absurd extremes of political correctness.

Genocide-Watch has done much work in this area and its lobbying contributed to creation of an office of *Special Advisor on the Prevention of Genocide* in the UN in July 2004. The first occupant, Juan E. Méndez of Argentina, has a staff of two. Though this initiative is laudable, lobbyist say little will be achieved without an arms-and-legs component, a *Genocide Prevention Center*, which would collect and analyze. Genocide-Watch has produced a ***predictive model*** based on *The Eight Stages of Genocide* characterized as *classification*, *symbolization*, *dehumanization*, *organization*, *polarization*, *preparation*, *extermination*, *denial*. A collection and analysis center would use models such as this to feed a threats and warnings system. But member states – for reasons best known to them and suspected by others -- continue to deny UN agencies the independent ***intelligence*** function such a Center would need.

Ethnic cleansing, forced relocation, systematic privation all have roots in identification (*classification*) of a group as somehow inferior or hostile. Examples abound -- the **Turkish** massacre and deportation of *Armenians*, the **German** deportation and massacre of *Jews*, *Slavs*, *Gypsies*, and others, **Japan** in China, **Italy** in Ethiopia, *Hutu / Tutsi* in **Burundi** and **Rwanda**, various massacres in former **Yugoslavia**. Possibly the list also includes **Indonesia** in East Timor and **Sudan** in Darfur but it would probably *not* include the killing fields of **Cambodia** which claimed two million lives, 30% of the population, because victims were of no particular group but each and every person an apocalyptic regime saw as a threat. This is one of the capricious consequences of the concept of genocide – the trivializing of *non-genocidal* mass slaughter, ***politicide*** as it is sometimes called. The *disappeared* of Latin America should bring as much outrage and retribution as any genocide.

The only authority the UN has is ceded to it by member states. Many see little reason to be optimistic that member states, and the even more problematic Security Council, will overcome their "idolatry of national sovereignty" sufficiently to authorize and implement the necessary mechanisms for fast, authoritative, and forceful intervention in genocide events. The UN is routinely blamed for being slow, indecisive, or incompetent but that, failing proof to the contrary, is a function of member states. *Chapter VII* of the UN Charter sets out the UN Security Council's powers to maintain international peace and security. The Council can declare Chapter VII to be applicable to an issue such as a process of genocide and (under Article 42) *may take such action by air, sea, or land forces as may be necessary to maintain or restore international peace and security.* The Security Council has not yet used these *peace-making* powers to prevent or stop genocide.[41]

Near-Term
Populations need to be taught that there are more sins in the world than genocide. In the modern connected world, genocide in fact is the most easy of high crimes to identify and, more importantly, to foresee and prevent. By contrast arbitrary serial killing by the State – *politicide*, *democide*, *extra-judicial killing* – is far more difficult to foresee and track and thus a more deadly threat. Charges and rumors of these acts should be taken just as seriously as genocide. Similarly *race crimes* appearing in Germany, UK and other parts of Europe are obvious warnings of a deep, perhaps intractable political problem.

Mid-Term

The underpinning immorality behind genocide is **collective punishment** – persecution of a group for perceived shortcomings of a few. Some would claim that Israel's recent action in **Lebanon** and wide allied netting in **Afghanistan** are examples of collective punishment and that perception does nothing to uphold global moral standards. The **US** has resisted profiling in its Homeland Security efforts but this almost certainly will be to its cost which may bring a

---

[41] Some factual material is from http://www.genocidewatch.org. OSS.Net, Inc. has been privilged in the past to retain two of the foremost genocide scholars in the world, Dr. Greg Stanton, and Mr. John Heidenrich, MA.

popular racial backlash that will undo any laudable motives. Classification – associated with respectful treatment --for clear and present national security reasons would be specifically permitted under the *Covenant on Human Rights*.

Long-Term

Globalization is bringing a time of the greatest immigration and ethnic mixing ever experienced. Although Man is a great trader he also seems to wired for distrusting strangers. Even if States are convinced that genocide (any arbitrary murder) is a perfidy, their populations may take longer to convince. It will be increasingly necessary to educate populations -- from *Sesame Street* to the Senate – that global admixture is here to stay and that discrimination, collective punishment, race-based vilification or violence will come to no good. Genocide is just the tip of that iceberg.

THREAT #7: OTHER ATROCITIES

Atrocity is an *informal* term for a range of acts proscribed in the *International Covenant On Civil And Political Rights* of 1976 (**torture**, **slavery**, **child labor**, **child soldiers**,…), for acts against the laws of war (**war crimes**), for acts that are culturally determined to be particularly heinous such as **desecration of a corpse**, **child sexual exploitation**, and willful acts against cultural property (**iconoclasm**). *Any* aggravated violent act against person or property might be seen as an atrocity in a loose sense but it is the act itself and the circumstances that will determine if an offence under any applicable law has been committed. For instance to burn Muslim battle-dead is a practical health measure, or an atrocity, depending on cultural perspective. Thus, atrocity in the broadest sense is a value (*subjective*) term.

The purpose of the Covenant (and various conventions relating to War) is to codify acts that the signatories agree are reprehensible and agree to proscribe in local laws. Many states may already have ways of outlawing and punishing the acts but often only in an indirect or rarely used way – deprivation of liberty (for slavery), aggravated assault (for torture), low level immigration offences (for human trafficking). For these nations, it is a consciousness-raising, coordination and standardization exercise. For those nations who routinely practice torture (usually in police custody) or condone slavery as a traditional institution, it is a way for the world community to encourage adherence to a standard of behavior perceived to be morally superior.

Atrocities are a special case of **human rights** abuses but not all human rights abuses are atrocities. Imprisonment without trial is not an atrocity as such, unless the prisoner is subjected also to inhumane and degrading treatment. The Covenant allows the government of a State to temporarily *suspend* some of the rights in cases of civil emergency (if it notifies other signatories), but none of the provisions forbidding atrocity. In other words, under this international instrument there is *never* a lawful excuse for commission of an atrocity.

Just as the real value of the Convention on Genocide is proscription of those acts that invariably *precede* genocide, hence providing a form of early warning, the value of the Human Rights Covenant is that it sets a high standard which can not prevent isolated atrocities but can offer pressure against institutionalized and/or State sanctioned atrocities.

Killing is objective; mistreatment is not -- cultural variations and sensitivities abound. There is anecdotal evidence that Filipino and Indonesian maids are, by Western standards, routinely treated "atrociously" in **Saudi Arabia**, as low paid slaves subjected to cruel and inhumane treatment. Whether the treatment of "guest workers" of this type is contrary to the Covenant would be open to investigation. Several Islamic nations, including "moderate" ones such as **Malaysia**, order public whipping as a punishment for some offences. To Western sensitivities, whipping is often thought to be "barbaric" and an "atrocity". In contrast, other cultures see imprisonment in a small room for many years as cruel, unnatural, and an atrocity.[42]

International Covenant On Civil And Political Rights was adopted in December 1966 and entered into force 23 March 1976.
Near-Term

The UN Human Rights mechanism has sometimes received bad press in the West because it has brought shortcomings in developed nations such as treatment of ***illegal immigrants***, or of ***indigenous populations*** to public attention. From its position on the non-barbaric moral high ground, it is difficult for a developed nation to see that an outsider could have any useful criticism or be motivated by any decent purpose. That common reaction is counter-

---

[42] Some factual material is from http://www.hrweb.org

productive to the global purpose of Human Rights protection and undermines the patently good purpose of UNHCHR.

Mid-Term

There are reports of severe Human Rights violations every day – from systematic torture of prisoners in **Algeria** to organ harvesting in **China**. Often UNHCHR does not have the resources nor the diplomatic backing to investigate or act on accusations such as this. The work against atrocities needs daily support; not lip service every decade or so.

Long-Term

If political dissidents are summarily executed and their organs harvested for profit, or if prisoners are routinely tortured and mutilated, it ultimately makes little difference in a distant country. Politics is the art of the possible – and the necessary – and States will avoid diplomatic incidents if they can and if their own self-interest is not affected. This is why the activities of UNHCHR as an honest broker established under international Covenant should be supported in every particular. Only when UNHCHR reports are taken as seriously as a crime wave next door will one of the main goals of the UN be accomplished.

THREAT #8: PROLIFERATION

Proliferation once referred to the *Treaty on the Non-Proliferation of Nuclear Weapons* (**NPT**) of 1970, an agreement of the nuclear *haves* and most *have-nots* that things should stay just like that. However, there were two other important aspects to NPT – the Treaty overtly agreed that this was an interim arrangement directed towards eventual total nuclear *disarmament*, and that technologies for peaceful use of *nuclear energy* were not only permitted but were to be cooperatively shared. The *haves* were the five *nuclear-weapon states* defined in the NPT, **China**, **France**, **Russia**, **UK**, **USA**, who happened to be also the *Big-Five* of the Security Council. But disarmament 30 years later is just as distant; the nuclear-weapon states continue to refurbish and maintain nuclear arsenals and the principle of proliferating nuclear technology without the chapters on weaponizing that technology has proven a noble and naïve ideal. During NPT and contrary to it, **South Africa** built, tested and later disassembled nuclear weapons and several countries, including **Brazil** and

Libya, toyed with the capability and abandoned it. Today, it is an open secret that **Israel** has nuclear weapons from an unknown source and in an unknown state of readiness, and **India** and **Pakistan** have proven their nuclear capability – all contrary to NPT. Several other countries are regarded as *nuclear-capable states* – **Netherlands, Germany, Canada, Japan** -- they have everything needed to produce nuclear weapons except the political will. Of headline current interest is the controversy over whether **Iran** and **DPR Korea** have weapons capability.

This situation coincides with the view that "clean, green" nuclear energy is an obvious fix for the environmental disaster-in-waiting caused by the burning of fossil fuels. Wider use of nuclear technologies for energy raises the spectre of proliferation in a broader sense – proliferation of spent and part-spent radioactive byproducts from the *nuclear fuel cycle*. Although the 30-year old Australian *synroc* technology now seems to be a secure and irreversible means for the safe sequestration of spent fuels, a thousand more nuclear flowers blooming throughout the world offers an obvious challenge for non-proliferation efforts. Highly accurate auditing of materials in and materials out is one measure but in recent years some audits have found a useful quantity of weapons-grade material missing ... or a ***rounding error*** in the audit; no-one knows for sure. A thousand rounding errors world-wide magnify the chance of usable quantities of weaponisable materials changing hands without trace.

For these several reasons, the NPT principles have obvious practical shortcomings and *UN Security Council Resolution 1540* was promulgated in 2004 to address these. The core articles ...

> *Affirming* that prevention of proliferation of nuclear, chemical and biological weapons should not hamper international cooperation in materials, equipment and technology for peaceful purposes while goals of **peaceful utilization should not be used as a cover for proliferation**;

> *Decides that* all States shall refrain from providing any form of support to **non-State actors** that attempt to develop, acquire, manufacture, possess, transport, transfer or use nuclear, chemical or biological weapons and their means of delivery;

... are in very plain language and clearly more street-wise than NPT. Importantly, this is an instrument under **Chapter VII** of the *UN Charter* hence enforceable under the UN's ultimate powers of coercion and enforcement. Also, the subject suddenly includes **chemical** and **biological** materials, and it importantly forbids proliferation into the hands of ***non-State actors***. Although the only *peaceful* uses for these substances is research into antidotes to their non-peaceful uses, the letter of the resolution would allow any state to share or develop manufacturing technologies for these "peaceful purposes". Also, any country could build manufacturing capability (for "peaceful purposes") because the varying shelf-life of CB substances and pathogens requires periodic replenishment. So *Resolution 1540* is unfortunately, like the NPT, little more than a pious wish and, in the absence of an outright universal ban on possession of these substances, it does little to curtail *de facto* proliferation.

As the world approaches a cycle where *non-State* actors are an equal or greater threat to industrialized nations than conventional enemies, proliferation assumes new nuances. The *fear* of CBR(N) WMD is a ***force multiplier*** in ***asymmetric*** tactics and immense costs are brought upon any nation protecting itself against the threat of a CBR incident. For the present, a multi-megaton air-burst bomb is unlikely, but a taxi loaded with 10 kilos of highly radioactive waste blown up in Time Square (or Trafalgar Square) would have a cumulative cost almost as great.

Near-Term

Pious hopes are little protection against bad actors State or non-State of any ethnicity, politics or religion. The technologies and materials that were the subject of proliferation measures are already proliferated widely enough to now get anywhere else with the right theft, bribe, or accident. Although a CB attack by non-State bad actors is *possible* rather than *probable*, the consequences are such that it is an *acute hazard* and should be treated as such. It is unlikely that civil and military authorities in the US have sufficient planning in place to meet this hazard.

Mid-Term

Pandora's box is open. Getting the woes and pestilence back in the box will be very difficult – but that simply translates as very expensive. It is do-able and expensive. Security intelligence agencies throughout the world will believe they have some grasp on where hazardous technology, know-how and materials are and where they are moving, but the slight embarrassment on the **Iraq** assessment blunts confidence in this somewhat. Nothing short of a world effort, underpinned by instruments in the tradition of NPT and Resolution 1540, is urgently needed to start an exhaustive Inventory of CBRN materials throughout the world to last microgram. Obviously an agency similar to IAEA with expertise and powers across the range of CBRN would be key to that project.

Long-Term

Nuclear-generated power does seem to have long-term possibilities. If current experimental work in *fusion* by the **ITER** (International Thermonuclear Experimental Reactor) project is successful this may prove to be spectacularly so – also, there will be none of the waste products produced in *fission* technologies and the technology will not lend itself to use by non-State actors. That may bring a time when *chemical* and *biological* agents are the only possible agents of WMD threat. But the nature of the world will be much determined by political wisdom displayed in the next five years and how successful any inventory and roundup of CBR material has been. A new concern may come from substantial work in recent years on *non-lethal weapons*. This may produce a new era of proliferation of simple, easily deployed debilitating economically crippling weaponry -- *Weapons of Mass Discomfort*.

THREAT #9: TERRORISM

The "war on terror" must fail because it is a self-defeating slogan. To make war on a tactic -- a raid, a breakout, an asymmetric attack on civilians, the use of chemical weapons -- makes no sense. These tactics have worked well throughout history and will continue to. 'Terrorist" tactics were used by Americans against the British in the 1770's, by the Israelis against the British, by Algerians against the French. Progress is only possible if the problem is clearly defined … as **global militant Islam**. It may be political correctness that prevents that definition, or it may be that there is a genuine misunderstanding of the problem. Once confronted, the origins of **global militant Islam** are largely well-defined and, with sufficient cooperation by a range of nations, is a relatively simple problem to treat.

Near-Term

In the near-term, the US may find it necessary to consolidate a broader support base in its global campaign against "terrorism" and will find it necessary to reach détente *en-bloc* with entities such as the **European Union** and the **Organization of the Islamic Conference**. But much depends on how the situations in **Iraq** and **Afghanistan** develop. How each is *perceived* within one or two years -- as a job well done, a quagmire, or a strategic withdrawal – will affect US credibility for several administrations.

Mid-Term

Nations such as **Saudi Arabia**, **Indonesia**, and **Turkey** are best placed to depict violent Islamic militantism in clear contrast with global Islam but they can not join the "war on terror" to the extent the US expects while it remains a US war rather than a universal hazard because that would sacrifice their credibility at home. It seems unavoidable that the only way to build a general resilient consensus against **global militant Islam** is at the **United Nations** level and with the consent of concerned nations.

Long-Term

In the mid to longer term, the **United Nations** will either grow in stature and its ability to respond to crises or, for practical purposes, cease to exist. In this time scale there will be increasing pressure on the voting rules of the **Security Council** so that global interests are expressed as a consensus or some majority rather than the often sordid interests of one of the veto Powers. Through such reforms the UN would have a new legitimacy to tackle global challenges such as the "terrorism" of that day, or worse challenges such as epidemics and climate change.

THREAT #10: TRANSNATIONAL CRIME

Estimates vary widely on the value of transnational organized crime (**TOC**) -- the FBI uses an estimate of $1 trillion per year. A key instrument in addressing TOC world-wide is the *United Nations Convention against Transnational Organized Crime* of September 2003 which commits signatories to introduce a range of measures such as the creation of domestic criminal offences, frameworks for multilateral juristic and police cooperation, and extradition.*

The UN Office on Drugs and Crime (**UNODC**) finds that TOC groups commonly comprise 20-50 persons involved in 5 or more countries. UNODC has defined five TOC *typologies – standard hierarchy, regional hierarchy, clustered hierarchy, core group, criminal network –* that move beyond the *mob boss* model to the reality of actual groups. This is useful for tactical purposes and helps agencies achieve a common vocabulary.[43]

TOC has diversified from traditional domains of local mob crime -- "numbers racket", protection, prostitution, and **illicit drugs** – to take full commercial advantage of globalized markets and the internet. The same network that moves drugs across the world can be adapted to transfer arms, explosives, cash, or untaxed tobacco. Organised Immigration Crimes – **people smuggling**, **human trafficking** – can move illegal immigrants, sex slaves, criminals or terrorists across the world. TOC moves into areas of *petty* crime when the rewards are sufficient, displacing local petty criminals or recruiting them (stolen motor vehicle). In this way TOC underpins much local crime. Similarly, TOC moves into new profitable areas such as **identity theft**, **phishing**, **intellectual property crime** (fake/unlicensed brands), **cultural property crime** (smuggling of artifacts), and **environmental crime (illegal dumping, wildlife smuggling, illegal logging** and, soon, **water theft**). TOC also *enables* other illegal activities by supply of **false documents**, protection, assassinations, and (in the UK) hire of weapons for criminal activity by other parties. TOC activities lend themselves to high degrees of product integration and vertical and/or horizontal integration – enslaved sex-workers or foot-soldiers are often addicted to the drugs traded by the same criminal enterprise.

But any mutation of TOC uses the traditional tools – **suborning of officials**, violence and coercion, secrecy, and willingness to break laws. Common to all activities is **cash** which is paramount in unlawful transactions. This creates a continual need for *money-laundering* for conversion into real assets such as property, legitimate businesses or laundered (seemingly lawful) cash.

TOC activity comprises a multitude of criminal acts, but agencies must focus on the enabling organization. To make a conviction for a single crime will often

---

[43] Facts are drawn from sources including …
http://www.soca.gov.uk —
http://news.bbc.co.uk/hi/english/static/in_depth/uk/2001/life_of_crime/crime.stm —
http://www.fbi.gov/hq/cid/orgcrime/ocshome.htm —
http://www.unodc.org/pdf/crime/publications/Pilot_survey.pdf

be counter-productive. TOC groups have such organizational and financial depth that they generally survive the neutralization of individual members. Also any minor agency success may merely teach the TOC how to improve its operations. Hence **intelligence** and **counter-intelligence** are crucially important, as is *proactive* policing rather than reactive policing instinctive to compliance officers. Compliance agencies must adapt to the changing methods and interests of TOC sometimes by reinventing themselves. In the UK the **Serious Organised Crime Agency (SOCA)** was launched in April 2006, bringing together the *National Crime Squad*, the *National Criminal Intelligence Service*, and elements of *Customs* and *Immigration* that dealt with TOC. In the US, the **FBI Organized Crime Program** addresses TOC in geographic units such as *La Cosa Nostra and Italian Organized Crime, Asian Criminal Enterprises*. Some in the UK envy the US **RICO** (*Racketeer Influenced and Corrupt Organizations*) Act, purpose-built anti-racketeering legislation introduced in 1964, but others fear the slippery slope of legislation based on a *guilty until proven innocent* principle. One successful example of new structures for new challenges is **Europol**, established in 1999 with intelligence and proactive policing functions (not to be confused with **Interpol**, which has served as a documentation exchange since establishment in 1923).

Philosophically it is *legality* itself that is one enabler of TOC which can only operate in illegal ("**black market**") environment. Alcohol prohibition created the *speak-easy* which became a revenue stream for organized crime. States such as **Netherlands** that *license* rather than outlaw prostitution and some drugs have eradicated criminal revenue, <u>and the cost of law enforcement</u>, in those commodities.

UNODC and others have emphasized the global *nexus* between **corruption**, **terrorism** and **crime**; for instance, "terrorists" may buy illicit weapons or materials from transnational syndicates with global reach and know-how. This nexus is crucial but must include aspects of **aid** and **foreign affairs**. Officials who are found corrupt in diversion of foreign aid are more easily suborned by TOC. **North Korea**'s strategic **counterfeiting** of $100 *super-notes* finds obvious synergies with money laundering and other TOC activity. In the **Philippines** it is now difficult to distinguish between separatist raising funds and simple crime in actions such as **kidnapping for ransom**. Also in the Philippines a numbers racket (*jueteng*) is so wide spread as to have implicated the husband of President Arroyo.

The reality is that Transnational Organized Crime is a ***fifth estate*** (and ***fifth column***) just as dangerous as to save live terror from Islamic fundamentalism.

Near Term

Governments that are themselves not directly involved in TOC are easily impressed of the need for enforcement by the loss of revenue. In fighting for elusive budgets this is effective enough but it misses that point that TOC suborns and perverts the Rule of Law itself. Just as some argue that "terrorism" is a political and policing issue rather than military, key politicians and officials need to recognise that TOC is not just a police or revenue matter but subversion just as dangerous as any bombing to the health of a society.

Mid-Term

Much good work has been done by UNODC and others on the metrics and topology of TOC but largely within the silo of compliance agencies. A better, more revealing picture may come from coordination between these agencies and **diplomatic** and **security intelligence** agencies. Demarcation between many insurgencies and mere criminal activity may become clearer. Also, the direct role of states such as **North Korea** in TOC may be better understood through an exchange of information from political as well as policing silos.

Long Term

As robber barons (***core nominals***) amass greater wealth across generations and become firmly entrenched behind legitimate businesses or in distant countries, TOC will be seen as truly a world-wide fifth estate. The laws and practices of first the tiniest and then larger nations will be suborned as mere tools and fronts for a sinister force ultimately more deadly than the minority views of Osama bin Laden. In one dimension, a policy of ***zero- tolerance*** is needed; in another **legalization** of those things that make TOC possible.

Readers are encouraged to keep abreast of these ten threats through the free Public Daily Brief that provides scrolling headlines and RSS feeds on each, and then each week provides a summary with color-coded alert levels for each of the ten threats, twelve policies, and eight challengers. For each threat there is also a persistent Uniform Resource Locator (URL) that consists of the threat forecast (done once a year) along with the cumulative weekly summaries for each threat in reverse chronological order.

It is easy to lose sight of these realities, but whether we are interested in reality or not, reality is surely interested in us, and it is time we started taking life on this planet seriously.[44]

---

[44] As the author learned from one of the books by Alvin and Heidi Toffler, Trotsky was fond of saying "you may not be interested in war, but war is interested in you." The next fifteen years will give us an opportunity to directly integrate open source intelligence in all languages through serious games, to real-world budgets of all nations and organizations. It will soon be possible to clearly and quickly identify, in compelling terms, those decisions that are not in the public interest. Public intelligence in the public interest could well be the single most important factor in how well we enter the future as a species.

Chapter 6:
The Open Source Intelligence
(OSINT) Story, 1988 to date

MEMO (DOI: 25 June 2004)

Public Intelligence Must Supersede Secret Intelligence

Imagine an America in which public intelligence supersedes secret intelligence, and elitist corruption is displaced by an informed democracy in which consensus conferences at every level assure that "We the People" all serve the public interest.

Trade-Off Decisions: What $100M Will Buy & Why Secrecy Hurts the Taxpayer

Let us begin by defining what $100M will buy. $100M will buy a Navy warship, or an Army brigade, or 1000 diplomats, or 10,000 Peace Corps volunteers, or a water desalination plant doing 100M cubic meters of water a year, or a day of war over water in the Middle East.

Today these trade-off decisions are made by a policy process that is neither public, nor in the public interest. We need to create an atmosphere where secret intelligence processes and products—which cost the US taxpayers between $35 billion and $50 billion a year—cannot easily be manipulated or ignored in what amounts to a betrayal of the public trust.

The issues of how and what we can know as a Nation about the real world also need to be protected and distinguished from illegal secret agreements among politicians and private sector campaign contributors. In my view, public intelligence in support of public policy is half the solution—the other half, as championed by Senators John McCain and Joe Lieberman, among others, is complete campaign finance reform.

Copyright & Patent Reform Needed to Fully Exploit New Knowledge

One area where openness could contribute directly to national security and prosperity is in copyright and patent reform. These processes are used today to protect inefficient and socially-costly products and processes, keeping useful knowledge out of the public domain solely to protect profits that impose a heavy external diseconomy on the public—the technologies of portable, environmentally-friendly power alternatives are one example. In essence, as things now stand, wars are fought, secret military bases established, subsidies given, deficits encroaching on the future amassed, all without adequate public review.

Thomas Jefferson Had It Right: Educated Citizenry = Public Intelligence

There is a simple democratic solution. It is called public intelligence. My vision is rooted in what our Founding Father, Thomas Jefferson, articulated: "A Nation's best defense is an educated citizenry." I am the evangelist for something called Open Source Intelligence or OSINT. Like open source software, and open spectrum, OSINT is, I believe, a foundation for our future... .our *bright* future.

Open Source Intelligence (OSINT) Is the Wedge in Three Different Revolutions

OSINT is the wedge in the door for three different revolutions:

1) Intelligence reform—If we get OSINT right, at very low cost, just 5% of what we spend now on secret intelligence, we can increase by a factor of 100, perhaps 1000, perhaps even 10,000, what America can know about itself, about the world, and about the possibilities for peace and prosperity.

2) Acquisition reform—Iif we get OSINT right, we will realize that we still need $500B a year for national security, but we must invest these taxpayer dollars in different ways—we can cut the heavy metal military to half this amount; substantially increase our special operations and gendarme "white hat" capabilities for delivering humanitarian assistance under combat conditions; substantially increase our homeland security through an emphasis on intelligence and prevention; and redirect $100B a year toward faith-based diplomacy, a dramatic increase in our foreign assistance including a digital Marshall Plan, and a focus on eliminating dictatorships that spawn terrorism, poverty, and genocide.

3) Governance reform—OSINT restores the morality of capitalism, including the proper calculation of the negative economic costs including ignored social costs, creates an informed citizenry, and makes true democracy possible around the world—the only way of actually containing and then eliminating terrorism.

Learning Matters I: What the Marines Could Not Get From the Spies

Now, given that the Director of Central Intelligence (DCI) has said that intelligence returns to America the greatest "bang for the buck", something I happen to agree with, how is it that we are failing, at great expense, to get it right? Let me tell you two short stories.

The first story deals with my epiphany, a very expensive Republican word for the more Democratic "aha." It was my great privilege to be the senior civilian responsible for designing and opening the Marine Corps Intelligence Command, our Nation's newest all-source intelligence production facility. Being a former spy, and having no reason to question my faith in secrets, I spent $20 million of the US taxpayers' money on ensuring that we had all the special equipment needed to get direct access to all of the secrets—the human spy secrets, the signals secrets, the imagery secrets, and the other secrets so secret that, like Pogo, I have had to forget them.

Imagine my shock, when I actually had to produce intelligence for the Marine Corps generals responsible for policy, for acquisition, and for operations, in discovering that 80% of what I needed in the way of raw information was not secret, not online, not in English, and not available from anyone in the national or defense intelligence communities.

It turns out there is a simple explanation. The Marine Corps must concern itself with the Third World, the under-developed countries where most genocide, poverty, terrorism, crime, and other natural and man-made disasters occur. The Center that I helped create was funded precisely because our Marine Corps leaders understood that we had spent over 50 years obsessing on the Soviet Union and the nuclear threat, and all of this other stuff—what is known as

87

"Global Coverage", had been neglected. Despite the fact that the Commandant of the Marine Corps called for a major shift in U.S, intelligence in 1988, the national intelligence bureaucracy and the national politicians that this bureaucracy supports, have refused to change their focus. As recently as July of 1997,[45] the DCI himself made a decision that he was in the business of doing secrets about hard targets, not "all-source" intelligence about global issues and lower tier countries in Africa, Asia, and Latin America, where most global problems are spawned.

Learning Matters II:
What the Public Cannot Get From Its Own Embassies

Now a second story, to put this in the context of your typical American collection environment overseas, i.e. the U.S. Embassy and the loose collection of U.S. government organizations that are represented overseas in that environment.

There are four things you need to know about the U.S. Embassies and other U.S. Government capabilities overseas that you pay for:

First, they are generally not yet "wired", which is to say that most Embassy employees do not have access to the Internet and cannot use the Internet as a basic tool for obtaining and sharing unclassified knowledge essential to our national security and national prosperity.

Second, within any given Embassy, the Foreign Service Officers or FSOs, the elite from the Department of State, labor under numerous burdens. They are in the minority in their own Embassies, outnumbered by the mélange of officers from other departments and agencies, none of whom really care what the Ambassador wants from them. They have lost their secretaries to budget cuts, resulting in the junior officers becoming very expensive clerks. They are without any realistic budget for buying local knowledge legally and ethically. Finally, they are limited by the physics of the 24-hour day and the politics of who is willing to meet with them in the national capital area—their lack of funds precludes routine travel in to the provinces.

---

[45] See "The Challenge of Global Coverage," by Boyd Sutton, as posted to the OSS.Net web site. A quick link is available via http://www.oss.net/BASIC.

Third, within any given Embassy, there are two ways for information to be sent back to Washington: electronically, or via the diplomatic pouch in hard-copy. Electronic transmissions require staff coordination across all Embassy section, pouch hard-copy dispatches do not. The result: less than 10% of what we capture goes electronically, with the result that 90%, send via the diplomatic pouch, is not visible to the rest of the government, and more often than not is filed or discarded and thus not exploited as it should be.

Washington Is Operating on 2% of the Relevant Available Unclassified Information

This is why I came to the conclusion, in my second graduate thesis studying three Embassies with which I was familiar, that Washington is operating on 2% of the relevant unclassified multi-lingual information that can and should be known in support of our foreign relations decisions.

Spies Have Too Much Money, Diplomats Do Not Have Enough

Fourth, and carefully separated from our Embassies, contrast this with the unlimited funding available to your clandestine officers that operate throughout the country, but have one rather interesting condition for listening to a local person: that person must be a traitor. They must agree to betray their country or their tribe or their organization or their family, either for money or because of a mutual interest that generally is not consistent with the interests of the host country's leadership.

In summary, it is my view that we are wasting at least 10 billion dollars a year going after secrets out of context, and we are failing to spend a modest 1 or 2 billion going after open sources of information that are much more valuable to our national security and prosperity when taken in the aggregate, in near-real-time, and in the original languages where nuances are clear.

What is Open Source Intelligence or OSINT?

Now, what is OSINT, you may ask. Let me begin with the quasi-official definition that I have put forward over the past 15 years, and then explain that with two relatively short stories.

89

Definition of OSINT

Open Source Intelligence (OSINT) combines the proven process of intelligence (requirements definition, collection management, source discovery and validation, multi-source fusion, and compelling actionable presentation) with a deep and broad understanding of what open sources of information (OSIF) are available in 29+ languages. While legally and ethically available, roughly 80% of those sources are not known to and not exploited by standard bureaucratic elements of the U.S. Government such as the Foreign Broadcast Information Service (FBIS) of the Central Intelligence Agency. The Department of State, which has the statutory responsibility for collecting, translating, and interpreting open sources of information relevant to U.S. foreign policy and national security, gave up its responsibility and its competency in this arena during the Cold War. Internationally, a number of nations, notably Australia, Norway, South Africa, and Sweden, have created specialist units to focus on OSIF/OSINT, with considerable success.

Proving the Point I:
Testimony to the Aspin-Brown Commission on Future of Intelligence

First, the Burundi Exercise. In August 1995, it was my privilege to testify the Aspin-Brown Commission on the future of intelligence, and more specifically, focused on what reforms were needed to make American intelligence effective. Had their recommendations been implemented, I do not believe 9-11 would have occurred. At the end of my testimony, as I was about to leave for the airport to speak to hackers in Las Vegas, General Les Aspin asked me if I would be willing to do a *pro bono* benchmark exercise—me and my Rolodex against the entire US Intelligence Community. I readily agreed. He turned to Britt Snider, the dynamic and very knowledgeable Staff Director and said, as I recall: "Burundi. By 1030 on Monday." This was a Thursday, at the end of the day. I called my assistant from the car, told her who to alert, and had her send an additional fax to my hotel in Las Vegas, where I spent the day persuading my counterpart CEOs to donate roughly $100,000 in free services to make my point.

By 1030 Monday—the early delivery time for Federal Express—the Commission received the following:

90

- From LEXIS-NEXIS in Dayton (OH), one of the finest commercial online subscription services—there are others, such as Factiva and DIALOG, but they were the best for this specific task—a list of the top ten journalists reporting on the genocide happening in Burundi and Rwanda, all immediately available for debriefing.

- From the Institute of Scientific Information in Philadelphia (PA), publisher of the science and the social science citation directories—this is a very clever way of identifying the most influential authorities based on who else has quoted them or cited their work in other work published later—a list of the top 100 experts in the world, cutting across all cultures and countries, on the Burundi situation—all available for immediate debriefing, and also helpful in identifying the unpublished experts within governments and non-governmental organizations.

- From Oxford Analytica in Oxford (GB), which published superb Presidential and CEO-level strategic reports, a series of 22 two-page executive summaries of the situation in Burundi in relation to risk, UN operations there, and US foreign policy objectives or lack thereof.

- From Jane's Information Group outside London (GB), two separate products were received. The first was a complete summary of all stories published in the various Jane's publications, such as Jane's Intelligence Review, on Burundi. This collection of one-paragraph summaries provided a superb overview of the historical and current situation unique to Jane's. A second product, created overnight for this purpose, was a series of one-page tribal "orders of battle", essentially describing tribal leadership, tribal manpower, and tribal capabilities including what are called "technicals" or normal small trucks with mounted machine-guns.

- From East View Cartographic in Minneapolis (MN), a list of all immediately-available Russian military combat charts

91

(charts are geospatially accurate about contour lines and cultural features, where maps are simply generic guides to roads and other features) for the entire country, all at the 1:50,000 tactical level, essential for carrying out military and humanitarian assistance operations. This is very important because the United States of America does not have such maps for 90% of the world, having focused on the Soviet Union and aviation charts instead of ground truth in the Third World.

- Finally, from SPOT Image of Toulouse (FR), through its US affiliate in Reston (VA), and belatedly as I recall, since I met them a couple of weeks after the exercise, confirmation that all of Burundi was available in the form of commercial imagery, less than three years old, cloud-free, and inexpensive for being already in an archive.

This is the power of open sources of information. We did not produce intelligence for this test case—tailored answers to specific questions—but you can see how impressive the private sector can be when properly engaged. The US Intelligence Community had almost nothing—they are not structured to do overnight open source collection and their secret collection is focused on hard targets and also difficult to redirect. The provided a regional map of the area, the chapter from the World Fact Book, and a regional economic study that was very inaccurate because it applied American assumptions to African economics. There may have been one or two other small things also provided, but you get the idea.

Proving the Point II: The Problem with Spies

As I have learned over the years, first as a spy—a clandestine case officer—then as a specialist seeking to help CIA exploit emerging Internet and other advanced information technologies—and finally as the senior civilian responsible for creating our Nation's newest national intelligence facility, the Marine Corps Intelligence Command—our national intelligence service is neither truly national, nor all-knowing. We have two problems.

First, **the biggest problem with spies is that they only know secrets**. Think about that. They have access to—at best—less than 10% of what can and should be known in order to make informed decisions. This problem stems from a combination of excessive focus on secret technical collection, excessive use of official cover and acceptance of secret information from other governments, most of which cannot be trusted, and two deliberate decisions that will haunt us forever after 9-11: a refusal to invest in processing what we collect, and a refusal to take open sources of information seriously. This culture of secrecy, which extends to other governments, also imposed what is called the "third party rule," meaning that even when information is known to be of value to multiple other countries, it cannot be shared directly—the originator must be asked to provide it directly and bilaterally—a very inefficient way of sharing, and a major contributor to the failure of Europe, Asia, and America to prevent the 9-11 debacle.

Second, however, **the spies also have a mind-set that prevents sharing**. For a spy, a secret shared is a secret lost forever. Both the FBI and the CIA as well as NSA—the National Security Agency that eavesdrops on everyone but processes fewer than a million out of every billion or so messages it collects—a processing rate of 1%, at best—have a culture of secrecy that is so deep as to have become an obstacle to achieving our goals. Even now, two years after 9-11, we have not achieved proper sharing despite direct orders to do so, in part in part because we are not yet serious about intelligence reform.[46] As recently as March of 2004, I have learned that the most senior FBI leaders have not been able to get the CIA and NSA to include the names of American citizens *known to be supporting terrorism* in messages about terrorism. The FBI is forced, still, now, two years after 9-11, to go back to CIA and NSA, point out that the law permits reporting on US citizens when they are known to be supporting terrorists or are known agents of a foreign power.

Seven Tribes, Seven Standards, Seven Issues: The Way Forward

Now, for the second story, the seven tribes, seven standards, and seven issues. In the course of spending $20 million of the taxpayer's hard-earned funds on the Marine Corps, I discovered that 80-90% of what we need to know to keep America safe from terrorists and other unconventional threat, and to further our economic prosperity, public health and education, and ecological prosperity—is

---

[46] As this book goes to press on 30 August 2006, this is still the case, and we have two immortal quotes: Dick Cheney telling the heads of the FBI and CIA "you guys don't cooperate worth shit," and George Tenet, then Director of Central Intelligence, telling the assembled heads of the allied intelligence services, "We don't know shit." For more background see the author's many reviews of non-fiction works at Amazon.

not secret, not online, not in English, and not available from anyone in Washington, D.C. or other major foreign capitals. It is all open source information, most of it is not digital, and most of it is in 29 languages, and in some instances a further 10-20 important dialects, none of which are understood by US intelligence officers, with a handful of exceptions.

As I cast about for solutions to the challenge of Global Coverage, to the need for finding ways to share the burden of 24/7 monitoring of the seven major issues that we must solve if we are to survive as a species on this planet, I realized that our concept of national intelligence was neither national nor intelligent. I already knew about spies and military intelligence as well as law enforcement, and of course academics and journalists. Beginning in 1988 I went on to explore business intelligence, then found religious intelligence and by 1994 began writing about creating smart nations with truly national and even global intelligence, through the harnessing of the distributed intelligence of the Whole Earth. My 1992 article in *Whole Earth Review*, entitled "E3i: Ethics, Ecology, Evolution, and Intelligence: An Alternative Paradigm for National Intelligence" was ridiculed by some as "assuring my place on the lunatic fringe." My earlier articles in the *American Intelligence Journal*, from 1988 through 1992, and my later article in *Government Information Quarterly* as well as various chapters and speeches and additional testimony to Presidential and Congressional bodies, were simply ignored.

It was not until I attended a Dutch conference in 2002, sponsored by the Netherlands Intelligence Studies Association, that I found this final story. I call it, with help from many brilliant minds that have spoken at my annual conferences, "Seven Tribes, Seven Standards, Seven Issues."

We Have Seven Intelligence Tribes, Not Just the One Secret National Tribe

There are seven intelligence tribes in every nation—and we must have nations, for they are the only body that could and should protect the public interest instead of selfish private interests.

First, we have the **national intelligence tribe**—the spies and the signals and imagery and other technical intelligence specialists, and the all-source analysts that serve national government policy makers, usually just a handful of individuals. We still need this tribe, but we must make it smarter and connect it to the real world of open sources.

Second, we have the **military intelligence tribe**—the strategic, operational, tactical, and technical intelligence specialists that support military policy, military acquisition, and military operations.

Third, we have the **law enforcement intelligence tribe**—preventive policing, pro-active counterintelligence, a tribe very much in its infancy, but doing well in some areas such as London, where Scotland Yard has grown wisely.

Fourth, we have the **business intelligence tribe**—business intelligence is too often confused with data mining, middle managers think they know everything they need to know, and the competition rather than the customer is the focus of effort, but at least the tribe exists.

Fifth, we have the **academic intelligence tribe**—many brilliant scholars and diligent students, all eager to contribute the world brain, held back mostly by a lack of connectively and structure. This tribe is actually the most important tribe with respect to helping governments detect tax avoidance and import-export pricing fraud, or crop insurance and medical claim fraud. It is also the most important in terms of historical understanding and cultural intelligence research.

Sixth, we have the **ground truth tribe**, consisting of a handful of investigative journalists that actually leave their hotel rooms to go into the jungle, or Chechnya, or the mines of Papua New Guinea, and a vast multitude of non-governmental (NGO) and international governmental (IGO) specialists, among whom the World Bank and the European Centre for Conflict Prevention (ECCP) stand out. This tribe lacks processing power, and needs to be fully integrated into the world brain that is emerging.

Seventh, and finally, we have the **citizen intelligence tribe**, where I group religions, civil societies, and neighborhood associations as well as labor unions and individual "lone scouts." Faith-based diplomacy, empowered labor unions, energized "cultural creative" associations, and citizens who share values and information for the common good comprise the foundation as well as the glue for bring all the tribes together, across national and cultural boundaries.

The Seven Tribes Need Seven Standards To Enable Sharing

There are also seven standards and seven issues that I will name but not discuss today. The seven standards areas where we must develop generic "good enough" means of sharing the burden of global intelligence are:

- Collection (Data Capture)
- Processing (Data Mining)
- Analytic Tool-Kits
- Analytic Trade-Craft
- Defensive Security & Counterintelligence
- Overt Action
- Mind-Sets—Leadership, Training, & Organizational Culture

We Can Begin Building the World Brain By Focusing on Seven Issues

The seven issue areas where we can begin organizing the world brain functions of weekly reports, expert forums, distance learning, virtual libraries, shared calendars, shared directories, virtual budgets (don't move money, just deconflict spending), and a global "plot" that anyone can use to navigate the vastness of our newly-shared global digital intelligence community are:

- Co-Intelligence—Creating the World Brain
- Democracy through Faith-Based Diplomacy and Consensus Conferencing
- Digital Divide, Digital Marshall Plan
- Ecological Economics—Pricing to the Value of Life
- Faith-Based Education for Humanitas
- Public Health—Mental, Physical, Cultural, & Economic
- Rules of the Road—Moral Capitalism & the Public Interest

Putting It All Together

Now let us conclude by taking this story to its logical conclusion, ten years into the future.

96

In ten years' time, it will be fashionable for each of you to see yourself as a member of one of the seven tribes, and to wear a pin such as I am wearing, that instantly connects you to strangers who share your vision, your values, your commitment to saving the future by husbanding the commonwealth through public intelligence applied to public policy.

In ten years' time, with the Internet as the backbone for global connectivity, including the necessary tools for protecting privacy as well as confidences, these tribes will be well-established at the local, state or province, national, and regional levels. Governments will be important partners, but citizens and civil societies will do the leading.

In ten years' time, every issue and every location of common concern to our "intelligence minutemen" will have an Internet "hub" that is well-structured and replete with validated information. Such a hub will have eight functional offerings, and be maintained by volunteers around the world who are proven and trusted must as the developers of LINUX are proven and trusted.

Eight Points of the World Brain Node on Anything of Public Interest

These eight offerings will be, in increasing order of importance:

- Weekly Report—change, early warning, cost implications Virtual Library—all that can be known, easily visualized and accessed, distributed
- Distance Learning—basic, intermediate, and advanced self-study on every aspect, in every language[47]

---

[47] There are many nuances of strategy and the practice of OSINT that are simply not understood by bureaucrats focused on day to day support to the secret agencies. The fact is, as we explore later in the book, but wish to emphasize here, that the "end game" for war and peace is squarely centered on belief systems and life-long education. The first power that can provide free online education in all languages, and free access to all substantive information relevant to the humanities and sciences, wins and wins big. The Broadcasting Board of Governors (BBG), not the Department of Education, is the right place to craft a program that is well-rooted in the principles of public diplomacy and virtual diplomacy. Diplomats, not spies, warriors, or bureaucrats, should use education to achieve global stabilization and reconstruction objectives that could never be realized with simple aid, trade, or military might.

- Calendar—of conferences and events, all monitored for the group by local minds
- Directory—of interested and qualified parties, self-validating
- Active Map—of the time, space, costs, benefits, and imminent dangers
- Expert Forum—certified, well-behaved, public, distilling wisdom on the fly
- Virtual Budget—the reality of what is being spent, easily redirected by consensus

Citizen-Centered Intelligence, Networking, & Influence

My second book, entitled *THE NEW CRAFT OF INTELLIGENCE: Personal, Public, & Political*, begins with a preface that outlines my vision of how citizen or public intelligence will supersede secret intelligence and decision-making by the elites, for the elites. At every level, from neighborhoods to counties, to nations and regions, I see citizens being able to get the information they need, connect immediately with like-minded others regardless of race, religion, nationality, or occupation, establish consensus, and impose the will of the people on the elected officials and the hired bureaucrats.

Small Obstacles

There are several small obstacles. The first is an educational system that focuses on rote learning rather than learning how to learn and work with others. We have to change that. The second is the manner in which elected officials are compensated, where wealthy corporations have the influence to avoid taxes and violate the public interest. We have to change that. The third is the manner in which bureaucrat decisions—and especially homeland and national security decisions—are not subject to public review. We have to change that. Finally, the fourth—one you can take on if you wish—is the inattentiveness of the public. Between mediocre public education and the alternative reality portrayed by our really dumbed down media industry, we have a Nation of drones that are sleep-walking over the chasm created by elites who have betrayed our trust—some out of ignorance, others out of greed. This revolution is going to be a bottom-up revolution, and it starts right here with you. Get organized, focus on public intelligence as your tool for restoring the power of We the People, and begin the hard task of helping every waitress, every truck driver, every member of the working poor as well as the lower middle class, understand that it is their life, their brain, their attention to these details, that will determine whether or not we save this Nation and this world for our fulfillment and the fulfillment of our children.

Two Sources of Public Intelligence

I commend to you my web site, www.oss.net as a source of continuing education and networking among the seven tribes, and my 750+ reviews of national security and global issues non-fiction books at Amazon.com, where the people's intelligence is visible for all to appreciate. I am sponsoring books by others about each of the seven intelligence tribes, and I hope you will share with me—and with those that visit our web site, any stories of your own as they emerge over the next few years.

The other leading source for understanding Collective Intelligence is a the web site for the Co-Intelligence Institute created by Tom Atlee, at http://www.co-intelligence.org. I also recommending a general Google search for "Collective Intelligence" as a number of new sites are emerging each day.

Conclusion

We are all a family, a family of informed citizens of good heart, and we need to help one another into the future. The new craft of intelligence is personal, public, and political. It supports peace and prosperity. I ask for your help in communicating the vision to every citizen in every country. For myself, I dedicate the remainder of my life to telling this story. Thank you.

Signature of the Author
Robert David Steele (Vivas)

Chapter 7:
Intelligence Affairs:
Evolution, Revolution, or Reaction?

Michael A. Turner's article, "Intelligence Reform and the Politics of Entrenchment," in the Fall 2005 issue (*IJIC* 18/3), is one that I found gripping, compelling, and illuminative.[48] He clearly explains why we many published intelligence reformers, from Allen to Bauer to Berkowitz to Codevilla to Gentry to Goodman to Gerecht to Fialka to Godson to Johnson to Levine to Odom to Riebling to Steele to Treverton to Wiebes to Zegart, have failed all these years. I am reminded of Machiavelli:

> *"There is nothing more difficult to plan, more doubtful of success, nor more dangerous to manage than the creation of a new system. For the initiator has the enmity of all who would profit by the preservation of the old system and merely lukewarm defenders in those who would gain by the new one."*

An example of the status quo thinking is a recent RAND document, "Toward a Revolution in Intelligence Affairs" by Deborah G. Barger, (TR-242-CMS, 2005). Upon close examination, I have found that the document is reactionary rather than revolutionary. Indeed, the footnotes are completely focused on what has been said by those who failed to protect America from 9-11, and completely ignorant of any—literally any—of the many sources on intelligence reform available to those who are open to ideas from the outside.

I decided to look at this situation more closely, and I have identified three competing approaches to the eradication of intelligence incompetence such as the Americans have displayed so profoundly since the end of the Cold War. The reactionary approach, reflected in both the RAND study and the recent

---

[48] This is the author's draft of the the the edited version that appeared in *International Journal of Intelligence and Counterintelligence* (IJIC), Volume 19, Number 1 (Spring 2006), pages 187-189.

101

selections of deputies to the Director of National Intelligence (DNI) who cannot, by any stretch of the imagination, be considered anything other than "business as usual" choices, is one we will dismiss right now. The DNI, with the best of intentions, will fail. He will fail because he was not willing to consider external solutions or external deputies. Drawing on a very weak and shallow bench, he has fielded a group of second and third stringers who will not prevent another 9-11, and will probably embarrass the White House in multiple ways. As Michael Turner states so clearly, the DNI and the people around him are the *status quo ante*, not the reformers.

An intelligent examination of the potential for evolution or revolution within intelligence affairs must begin with an understanding of these two terms. Evolution is a gradual process in which something changes into a different and usually more complex or better form. We emphasize here both "different" and "more complex" or "better." An evolutionary approach to intelligence reform would, at a minimum, expand the concept of national intelligence to embrace what the Swedes are calling M4 IS: multinational, multiagency, multidisciplinary, multidomain information sharing at all levels of classification, and to embrace what we ourselves call the "seven tribes" of intelligence—not only national and military, but law enforcement, business, academic, ground truth (nongovernmental organizations and media), and citizen (including labor unions and religions) networks. Such an approach would retain the capability to collect and exploit secrets, but it would establish a new national Open Source Agency as the 9-11 Commission has recommended, and it would emphasize sharing over secrecy, with open source intelligence (OSINT) as the baseline for sharing, rather than a cosmetic after-thought, as is now the case.

A revolution in intelligence affairs (RIA), in contrast to an intelligent evolution, is a drastic (that is to say, sudden, and far-reaching) change in ways of thinking and behaving. Such a revolution would be characterized by a true sense of national crisis, such as occurred after Pearl Harbor, or Sputnik. The Global War on Terror (GWOT) is a political affectation today in America, not a true national endeavor, our earnest defense endeavors not-with-standing. Indeed, while the Americans play at GWOT, the Chinese, Indians, Iranians, and Russians—with active interest from the Brazilians, Indonesians, Malaysians, Pakistanis, and Venezuelans—are eating our lunch in South America and taking over Africa, at the same time that Latin America is being invited to invest in Africa and trade with Asia. Behind the scenes, the common agenda

102

among these players, with Europe sitting foolishly on the sidelines, is the displacement of America as a super-power—the relegation of America to co-equal status with that lonely island called England.

A true revolution in intelligence affairs would radicalize and internationalize American education overnight, shifting billions from guns to brains; it would democratize US politics (electoral reform, so that every American's vote counts, which is not the case today); it would eliminate US support for the 44 dictators that pretend to support GWOT while raping and pillaging the commonwealth of billions whose poverty threatens America vastly more than any terrorist gang; and it would strive for nothing less than a cultural revolution, a revolution of the American mind, a restoration of American ideals of informed democracy and collective intelligence at home first, then globally. Now *that* is a revolution.

I have set in motion certain initiatives that show promise, and I am heartened by the simultaneous emergence of other initiatives known as "collective intelligence," or "wisdom of the crowds," or "the power of us." The bottom line is that $30 Motorola cell phones, when combined with Google Enterprise, CISCO's new content-based routing systems, and IBM's DB2 with Omni Find, have changed the balance of power. The old paradigm was elites hoarding secret knowledge, making unilateral decisions for short-term gain by the few. The new paradigm is bottom-up consensus—multinational and multicultural consensus, relying on open sources in all languages, and intimately respectful of the long-term—what the Native Americans call "seventh generation thinking."

Open Source Intelligence (OSINT) is intimately connected to the restoration of the original values of the Republic—informed democracy and moral capitalism. We now have cause for celebration. *St.*

Chapter 8:
Intelligence in Denial:
The Need for Independence

Jennifer Sims's article, "Foreign Intelligence Liaison: Devils, Deals, and Details," (*IJIC* 19/2 Summer 2006) is quite wonderful in all respects save one: it deals only with secret government to government intelligence liaison, and makes no reference at all to the many non-secret, non-governmental, and non-intelligence liaison and information sharing arrangements that have been under development for the past eighteen years, and are just now about to explode into global reality.[49] Bottom-up collective public intelligence is here to stay, and the new standard, defined by the Swedish Ministry of Defence, is Multinational, Multiagency, Multidisciplinary, Multidomain Information Sharing (M4IS). As I note in on the inside flap of my latest book,[50] "Sharing, not secrecy, is the operative principle." While now obvious to the rest of the world, it is necessary for this readership to add that it is the sharing of non-secrets, among non-governmental organizations, that is the defining aspect of M4IS, and governments, while they may be the catalysts for such arrangements, are largely the beneficiaries, not the benefactors of M4IS.

---

[49] This chapter has been accepted for publication in a forthcoming issue of the *International Journal of Intelligence and Counterintelligence* (IJIC), the foremost journal in the field. It is provided here to help Congress understand the continued incapacity of even the most educated participants in the secret intelligence world—their mind-sets will never allow them to give full reign to open source exploitation, whether from inbred naivete or out and out knavery—unable to resist the urge to repress OSINT to protect the Naked Emperor SECRETUS. The national open source capabilities outside the U.S. Intelligence Community must be earnest in their support of the secret missions of that community, but completely independent of its repressive influence.

[50] *INFORMATION OPERATIONS: All Information, All Languages, All the Time—The New Semantics of War & Peace, Wealth & Democracy* (OSS International Press, 2006, with a Foreword by Congressman Rob Simmons (R-CT-02) and a Technical Preface by Dr. LCdr Robert Garigue, RN Canada (Resigned)). A 50-slide briefing on the book, with words in Notes format, is at www.oss.net/IO.

In as much as my own article on "Peacekeeping Intelligence," based on a presentation in Sweden in December 2004, subsequently appeared in the next issue (*IJIC* 19/3 Winter 2006-2007), I will say no more about the seven tribes, or the *other* rather obvious fact that open source information in 185 languages, including 12 still-relevant variations of Arabic, now comprises 80% or more of what we as a *government* need to collect, process, and analyze. Despite this, we not only spend less than one-tenth of one percent of our total secret intelligence budget on open sources *but also* the Assistant Director of National Intelligence for Open Source (ADDNI/OS)—to whom we have pledged our complete support contingent on his honoring his promises—is not a Program Manager, has no real authority, and lacks any staff other than (the last we knew) two people on rotation. This is simply not serious, one reason why the Department of Defense is completely justified in going its own way.

I agree whole-heartedly with my friend Jennifer on the matter of information and intelligence metrics,[51] one reason why Team OSS includes Thomas J. Buckholtz, author of *Information Proficiency, Your Key to the Information Age*. Tom has led the knowledge-management, computing, and telecommunications practice for the 4,000,000-person Executive Branch of the United States federal government. He also led a program that catalyzed $100,000,000 in recurring annual benefits for a $6 billion corporation—in other words, metrics can help enhance one's Return on Investment (RoI).[52] However, and I say this as one who supported Marty Hurwitz, then Director of the General Defense Intelligence Program (GDIP) when Marty tried to do this in 1990-1992, there are two major flaws in all prior and current approaches to metrics for intelligence: flaw #1 is that they are not tied to policy outcomes (more on that below), and flaw #2 is that no one—and especially the high-end defense technical collection agencies—is held accountable for failing to show a reasonable return on investment in the larger context of our total intelligence analysis needs.

---

[51] This somewhat important insight by the author is relegated to endnote 9 in the cited article.

[52] Our data mining partner, the Texas Data Mining Research Institute, has documented 20:1 returns on investment, with $4M a year in data mining identifying and eradicating $80M a year in fraud within a specifically targeted industry. Within the Silicon Valley Hackers Conference, there is a slightly different but still important metric that has been long agreed to: publishing one useful bit of information to the Internet leads to 100 new bits being sent to the author without solicitation, with ten of them being useful—hence a 10:1 relative noise ratio, but also a 10:1 return on investment for sharing.

My observation on connecting intelligence to budgets and inter-agency behavior, that is to say, rational unified national security programs in touch with reality, will no doubt inspire sighs of exacerbation from all those who remain in denial and continue to believe there should be a wall between intelligence and policy. These are the same people who—with the exception of Joe Markowitz and Gordon Oehler—have refused to take open sources of information and lower-tier instability threats seriously from 1988—when Commandant of the Marine Corps Al Gray made this an issue in his seminal article, "Intelligence Challenges of the 1990's" as published in the *American Intelligence Journal* (Winter 1988-1989)[53]—to this very moment.

History is the context for intelligence and policy metrics. This is about ends, ways, and means—about sustainable outcomes that must be guided by intelligence, but can only be achieved through wise policy.[54] Our failure to break with a policy intent on invading Iraq without regard to reality or intelligence or a coherent grand strategy—and our compounding failure to resign our commissions and go directly to the American public (here I include the Joint Chiefs of Staff, not only the leadership of the U.S. Intelligence Community (IC)—will stand in history as a much greater failure than that associated with 9-11. I plan two metrics-related initiatives in the next few years.

1. Over the next few years we will begin cross-walking the entire U.S. Federal budget against reality, with a focus on diplomatic, information, military, and economic (DIME) investments. Henceforth, the public will see very clearly the relationship between how we do or do not spend the taxpayer dollar wisely, and the growing threat to our future security and prosperity, both of which must be defined globally. This will be done for each of the Combatant Commanders (COCOM) as their understanding of the art of the possible matures, for it is the COCOMs that are ultimately the hubs for inter-agency campaign planning in the real world. Over a year ago we warned on our web site of Al Qaeda's planned "death of a thousand cuts" against oil and related above-ground water

---

[53] General Gray's article is easily found by using the link offered in the Open Page Open Source Intelligence Familiarization Guide, at http://www.oss.net/BASIC.

[54] Wisdom in my view is a combination of consistent morality (the Golden Rule applied both internally and externally), a proven policy process that allows all legitimate stake-holders to air their views and concerns in a timely and deliberate fashion; and adequate Intelligence and Information Operations (I2O).

and electrical conduits. Today we have Exxon on the one hand saying there is no threat to the continuing supply of oil,[55] and on the other hand an excellent summary of Al Qaeda material from the Center for Islamic Studies and Research,[56] which confirms our earlier diagnosis: Bin Laden understands two things that our Administration does not: 1) the most vulnerable attack points for impacting on U.S. energy costs are in Saudi Arabia, Nigeria, and Venezuela; and 2) raising the cost of oil is vastly more harmful to America than killing troops, and has the rather lovely (from an Al Qaeda perspective) outcome of transferring vast amounts of additional wealth from the West to the Muslim countries exporting oil, as well as populist Latin American leaders who share their disdain for this Administration. Now that is a metric: if Al Qaeda can take oil prices to triple their existing costs; and our combined collective national intelligence fails to devise an energy independence plan as well as make the case for withdrawing U.S. troops from Muslim countries, then shame on us, we deserve whatever fate the Gods have in store for us.

2. As a longer term objective, we want to see clients committed to M4IS sponsor a detailed data-mining of history, beginning with the digitization of Chinese and Iranian history, as these are the two lynch-pin countries for their respective regions. Metrics can be over-lain on a historical issue-matrix that shows public statements by the other party; American posturing and ignorance of the meaning of those statements; consequent behaviors by the other party, and the resulting long-term cost to America for having failed to pay attention to the lessons of history or the open source statements in proper context.

On that note, please allow me to expand with two observations on the two excellent articles on intelligence reform. The one by Arthur S. Hulnick, on "U.S. Intelligence Reform: Problems and Prospects," and the other by Robert

---

[55] As published on their web sites and numerous advertisements in the media, with one in particular, appearing on the Federal Page of the *Washington Post* on 2 March 2006, to which we responded with a press release and a letter to Exxon's leadership. On the next day, to its credit, *Energy Bulletin* featured the OSS press release, with a supporting online Comments from *Scientific American*. The various links are at www.oss.net within the Collective Intelligence portal page, Comments and links for 2 and 3 March 2006 respectively. Our original Comments on the "death of a thousand cuts" Al Qaeda strategy is in our review of Robert Pape's *Dying to Win: The Strategic Logic of Suicidal Terrorism*, at http://www.oss.net/extra/news/?id=2693.

[56] The Op-Ed "An Energy Pearl Harbor" by Gal Luft of the Institute for the Analysis of Global Security was carried by the Post on 5 March 2006 but is more easily reviewed at http://www.evworld.com/view.cfm?section=communique&newsid=11223.

108

D. Vickers Jr., on "The Intelligence Reform Quandary. I take no issue with either except in the following two respects:

1.   The U.S. Intelligence Community (IC) appears oblivious to the fact that Information Operations (IO) is the new boss in town. I confess to having had to learn this myself, but I am fortunate in being close to some very special people in defense, and they have taught me not only that secret intelligence is a minute fraction of all the information that must be collected and made sense of, but that both secret and open source intelligence (OSINT) are themselves—even with the very considerable contributions OSINT has been making since General Peter Schoomaker directed its integration in 1997 across all Special Operations Forces commands and practices[57]—less than 20% of the total that must be integrated, made sense of, and acted upon in a timely fashion. While select elements of the IC understand the importance of both secret and open geospatial information, of the urgent need to integrate all U.S. Government (USG) operational, logistics, acquisition, and administration information in near-real-time, with all state, local, and tribal law enforcement and select related civilian transportation and other infrastructure data, including financial data, the IC as a whole appears nearly catatonic when it comes to dealing with this larger inter-agency IO reality, and never mind the implications of doing so on an M4IS basis!

2. Large Scale Internet Exploitation (LSIE) and internal data mining are not the full solution. I do completely support the LSIE initiative, and hope that an appropriate mix of capabilities are selected from the private sector to migrate the Foreign Broadcast Information Service (FBIS) toward being able to do LSIE in 185 languages and 12 Arabic variations—certainly I would not consider for even a moment the same people that screwed up Trailblazer at the National Security Agency (NSA) or so many other programs for the Federal Bureau of Investigation (FBIS) and across varied elements of defense. The days of proprietary special programming is over! The days of sweetheart deals and incremental increases in massive omni-bus contracts and a complete lack of accountability for failing to be effective in massive data-mining efforts that are only text-based (and generally only demonstrated in English) and that fail to scale or meet their speed and relevance targets, are over. It is medium and

---

[57]   Today, for under $1M, the OSINT Branch at SOCOM answers 40% of all Global War on Terror (GWOT) requirements using only open sources. CIA has had similar results documented in the 1990's.

small businesses that have been the pioneers, with select larger enterprises like International Business Machines (IBM) also re-inventing themselves and doing a better job of also integrating medium and small providers of "best in class" capabilities. The current trend in government contracting toward mandated 33% and more enforceable earmarked small business sub-contracting is a good one. The questions that FBIS has devised for LSIE are truly impressive, and in combination with the Solicitation from the National Ground Intelligence Center (NGIC), offer some hope for the future. There are, however, two elements from the Open Source Center (OSC)/FBIS approach to OSINT that are Missing in Action (MIA):

> a. Off-line information and direct observation remain vastly more important to the security of our Nation and specifically of our Armed Forces and Foreign Service personnel overseas. As the Chief of Staff of the Army recently noted in his Posture Statement to Congress, "The greatest source of our intelligence are the Iraqi people in these towns."[58] To that we would add a variety of localized monitoring needs specific to IO that FBIS has failed to prepare for and must now abdicate to others: the mapping of key communicators across all dimensions of society, and their relationships to competing views of key concepts such as the Caliphate, or the incidental killing of Muslim bystanders by suicide bombers; the in-depth monitoring of school papers and texts that can help us map major directions in teaching and learning by an entire emergent generation that are harmful to our future prospects; the deep exploration of history and particularly official statements on any given issue going back 200 years (e.g. China on the Spratley Islands, or Iran on its alternative to the Caliphate). I could go on. The Internet remains less than 20% of the open source environment that must be monitored, and is not to be confused with electronic mail patterns, instant texting, shared images, the deep web, or the growing migration of voice communications into free but difficult to track Internet offerings.

---

[58] A detailed extract, Comments, and links are at the 1 March 2006 section of the Strategic Peacekeeping Portal Page at www.oss.net.

b. All that we must accomplish to survive, stabilize, and prosper cannot be done in isolation from our coalition partners. This is why the Coalition Coordination Center (CCC) at the U.S. Central Command (USCENTCOM)[59] may be, together with the IO global monitoring initiatives of the U.S. Strategic Command (USSTRATCOM) and the direct observation initiatives of the U.S. Special Operations Command (USSOCOM), one of the single most important resources available to us as we strive to actually understand the "lower tier" world that Boyd Sutton and Keith Hall told George Tenet in July 1997—after a comprehensive year-long review at the Assistant Secretary level across the entire USG—would require no less than $1.5 billion a year as an "insurance policy" for early warning on issues not adequately covered by classified means. They were told "fu-ged-ab-oud-it" by George Tenet, the same individual who chose to ignore the Aspin-Brown recommendations on OSINT.[60]   Multinational Information Operations Centers (MIOC) are the logical adjunct to the well-conceived Joint Intelligence Operations Commands or Centers (JIOC), as is a National Inter-Agency Collaboration Center (NIOC) at the U.S. Northern Command (USNORTHCOM). They will both provide, and benefit from, the commercially-based Open Source Information System – External (OSIS-X) that is being implemented for varied international clients and

---

[59] Our briefing on the possibilities for multinational information operations centers, one for each COCOM, as presented to representatives of the 90 nations on 27 January 2006 at CENTCOM, can be seen at www.oss.net/MIOC.

[60] Both the original unclassified text report on "The Challenge of Global Coverage" as written by Boyd Sutton, and his powerpoint presentation to an international audience on 18 January 2006, can be seen at the general conferences portal page beginning I2O '07 at www.oss.net. The Aspin-Brown recommendations, based in part on my winning the Burundi exercise against the entire IC with six telephone calls, found our access to open sources to be "severely deficient" and recommended that funding for open source access be a top priority and that open sources also be a top priority for DCI attention.

relies heavily on SILOBREAKER[61] as the common delivery, sense-making, and information-sharing platform.

I will end with two observations:

1. The IC (and the larger USG) are inside-out and upside-down, and denial remains the order of the day. I very much admire a cartoon that recently appeared in *The Intelligencer*, and have inserted it below certain that the Association of Former Intelligence Officers (AFIO) will permit its reproduction. As this issue of *IJIC* so richly communicates, most of those associated with or commenting on the IC remain fixated on the chaotic kludge of secret bi-lateral, mostly technical stovepipes that have developed over the past 50 years, and largely oblivious of the urgent need for starting with OSINT (right-side-up) instead of secret technical collection (upside down), and for starting with our coalition partners (outside in) rather than unilaterally (inside out).

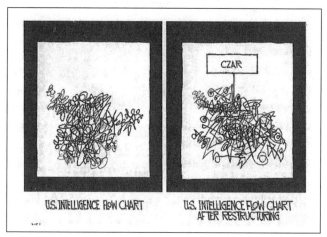

---

[61] SILOBREAKER, at www.silobreaker.com, is available to the public (both sources and the over-arching analytic-toolkit) for $398 a year. It is superior, and cheaper, as well as full of more relevant information, than any of the traditional commercial aggregators of information for sale by the document, who continue to offer raw text in isolation from sense-making tools, or the "free" search engines that take your time instead of your money and offer no sense-making tools whatsoever. It has replaced a tailored capability we have been using for 10 years at a cost of $150,000 a year.

2. Public collective intelligence is emergent, from the bottom-up. It was citizens armed with cell phones that prevented the third airplane from hitting its intended target on 9-11, and it is citizens armed with OSINT that will from this day forward begin confronting the Enrons, Exxons, and Executive leaders (as well as legislators) who choose to ignore reality and mis-serve the public interest through the abuse and manipulation and side-lining of secret or proprietary intelligence. Intelligence has become personal, public, and political, and I for one plan to keep it that way. The line is drawn: use open sources and serve the public interest. Or not. *St.*

Chapter 9:
Open Source Intelligence:
The Strategic Value to the Nation

Executive Summary

Open Source Intelligence (OSINT) is the only discipline that is both a necessary foundation for effective classified intelligence collection and analysis, and a full multi-media discipline in its own right, combining overt human intelligence from open sources, commercial imagery, foreign broadcast monitoring, and numerous other direct and localized information sources and methods not now properly exploited by the secret intelligence community. OSINT is uniquely important to the development of strategic intelligence, not only for the government, but for the military, law enforcement, business, academia, non-governmental organizations, the media, and civil societies including citizen advocacy groups, labor unions, and religions for the simple reason that its reliance on strictly legal and open sources and methods allows OSINT to be shared with anyone anywhere, and helps create broader communities of interest through structured information sharing.

It can be said that at the strategic level in particular, but at all four levels of analysis (strategic, operational, tactical, and technical) generally, the secret intelligence communities of the world are inside-out and upside-down. They are inside-out because they persist in trying to answer important questions with unilaterally collected secrets, rather than beginning with what they can learn from the outside-in: from the seven tribes[62] and the 90+ nations that form the Coalition. They are upside down, at least in the case of the United States of America (USA) and selected other major powers, because they rely too much

---

[62] The "seven tribes" are a concept developed by the author and include government, military, law enforcement, business, academia, the ground truth tribe (non-governmental organizations and the media), and the civil sector tribe (citizen advocacy groups and societies, labor unions, and religions).

on expensive overhead satellite systems, instead of bottom-up ground truth networks of humans with deep historical, cultural, and localized knowledge.

In the long-run, I anticipate that OSINT will displace 80% of the current manpower and dollars devoted to secret sources & methods, and that this will offer the taxpayers of the respective nations a Return on Investment (RoI) at least one thousand times better than what is obtained now through secret sources and methods. A proper focus on OSINT will alter the definition of "national" intelligence to embrace all that can be known from the seven tribes across both the home nation and the coalition nations, and will dramatically reform intelligence, electoral processes, governance, and the application of the national, state, and local budgets in support of the public interest.

Strategically, OSINT will restore informed engaged democracy and moral capitalism, a new form of communal capitalism, in America and around the world. OSINT is, at root, the foundation for the emergence of the World Brain, and the empowerment of the public.

The bulk of this chapter will focus on OSINT and intelligence reform at the strategic level, but it is essential that the reader appreciate the implications of OSINT for electoral, governance, and budgetary reform so as to better realize the enormous implications of the revolution in intelligence affairs[63] for which OSINT is the catalyst.

---

[63] This term, "Revolution in Intelligence Affairs," is abused by loosely-educated individuals who know nothing of revolution and little of all-source intelligence. For a critique of the abuse of the term, and a discussion of the three options for intelligence reform, see the author's "Intelligence Affairs: Evolution, Revolution, or Reactionary Collapse," *International Journal of Intelligence and Counterintelligence* 19/1 (Spring 2006). In a forthcoming issue the author comments on "Intelligence in Denial." Both are provided in this book as chapters 7 and 8 respectively.

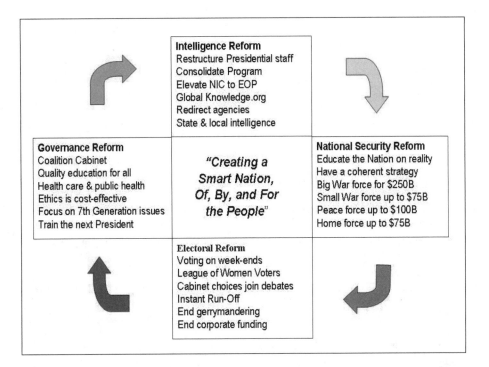

Figure 3: Four Strategic Domains for Reform Catalyzed by OSINT[64]

The impetus for reform across all four strategic domains could emerge from within any one of the four. If the economy collapses and the war on Iraq combined with an attack on Iran cause a clear and present danger to emerge in the form of global Islamic counter-attacks that are asymmetric and indiscriminate as well as widespread, we can anticipate not just the ejection of the extremist Republicans, but also of the complacent and equally corrupt and ignorant Democrats.[65]

---

[64] NIC: National Intelligence Council. EOP: Executive Office of the President. It is important to observe that the Global Knowledge organization, now called an Open Source Agency, is intended to be completely independent of both Presidential and Congressional manipulation. This chart is discussed in more detail in the final section on Governance Reform. This illustration is drawn from "Citizen in Search of a Leader" as prepared 8 January 2003 and posted to www.oss.net. Additional detail on each reform domain can be found in that document.

There is a growing awareness within the public, described by some as "smart mobs," or "wisdom of the crowds," or—our preferred term—Collective Intelligence, that it is now possible for individuals to have better intelligence based on open sources and methods, that is being made available to—or acknowledged by—the President.[66] We will see, within the next four years, a dramatic increase in both historical accountability,[67] and current accountability for actions impacting on future generations and other communities.

---

[65] This is a practical professional discourse on OSINT, not a political diatribe, but it is essential for those who have the most to gain from OSINT, citizens, to understand that the extremist Republicans have driven out the moderate Republicans (including the author) while the inept Democrats have alienated both the conservative Democrats and the New Progressives. For an excellent and erudite discussion of why the prevailing mood of the country may well be "a pox on both parties," see Peter Peterson, *RUNNING ON EMPTY: How The Democratic and Republican Parties Are Bankrupting Our Future and What Americans Can Do About It* (Farrar, Straus and Giroux , 2004). Peterson was a Cabinet Secretary under Nixon and Chairman of the Council on Foreign Relations. He joins numerous other moderate Republicans who have published books dismissive of the Republican Party as it has been hijacked by the religious extremists, the neo-conservatives, and corporate war-profiteers. The Democratic leadership is equally corrupt, but so inept as to be incapable of either governing or holding the Republicans accountable.

[66] Howard Rheingold, *SMART MOBS: The Next Social Revolution* (Basic Books, 2003); James Surowieki, *The Wisdom of the Crowds* (Anchor, 2005); and Pierre Levy, *Collective Intelligence: Mankind's Emerging World in Cyberspace* (Perseus, 2000). Three other essential references are H. G. Wells, *World Brain* (Ayer, 1938), Howard Bloom, *GLOBAL BRAIN: The Evolution of Mass Mind from the Big Bang to the 21st Century* (Wiley, 2001), and Tom Atlee, *The Tao of Democracy: Using Co-Intelligence to Create a World That Works for All* (Writer's Collective, 2003). Robert Steele addresses the concepts and doctrine for actually "doing" collective public intelligence in *THE NEW CRAFT OF INTELLIGENCE: Personal, Public, and Political* (OSS, 2002).

[67] It is now clearly documented that both the White House and the Senate knew that Peak Oil was upon us during varied hearings conducted from 1974-1979, and deliberately concealed this fact from the public, and failed to alter energy policy, in order to avoid alarming citizens or angering them over prices, while continuing to reap the rich dividends of bribery from the oil companies. This is a single specific example of where retrospective impeachments would be appropriate as a means of telling all elected officials that they will be held accountable not just today, but into the future as their treasonous betrayal of the public trust becomes known.

Electoral reform will be inspired by citizens realizing that both the Republican and Democratic parties have been come corrupt as well as inept at representing the public interest.[68]

Governance reform will be inspired by citizens realizing that in today's world, we need a networked model of governance that elevates intelligence to the forefront—decisions must be made in the public interest and be sustainable by consensus and conformance to reality, not purchased by bribery from special interests who seek to loot the commonwealth and/or abuse their public power to pursue the ideological fantasies of an extremist minority.

Budgetary reform will be inspired by citizens who understand that we still need to be able to defend ourselves, but that waging peace worldwide is a much more cost effective means of both deterring attacks and of stimulating sustainable indigenous wealth that is inherently stabilizing.

OSINT and Intelligence Reform

Open Source Intelligence (OSINT) should be, but is not, the foundation for all of the secret collection disciplines, and it could be, but is not, the foundation for a total reformation of both the governmental function of intelligence, and the larger concept of national and global intelligence, what some call Collective Intelligence or the World Brain.[69]

---

[68] With the utmost respect for all those now serving in the Senate and the House of Representatives, it is a hard fact that cannot be denied that Congress and the Executive today appear to represent corporations rather than their constituencies. Policy and legislation is drafted on Wall Street and mandated down to Washington. The literature is also quite clear in documenting that Congress now suffers from three major flaws: 1) a propensity of long-standing incumbents to shake down lobbyists for contributions rather than "succumbing" to bribery; 2) an unconstitutional mandate by party leaders that their members toe the party line instead of vote for their constituents' best interests; and 3) an unconstitutional and quite shocking abdication by Congress of its role as the FIRST branch of government (Article 1), instead forcing party members to serve as "footsoldiers" for the White House. Nothing could be further from the intent of the Foundation Father, and any Member that fails to feel the mood of the country is at risk.

[69] There are 20,000 pages on OSINT at www.oss.net, and a one-page list of key familiarization links covering history, context, practice, policy, and reference are at www.oss.net/BASIC. To this day, the secret intelligence world refers with disdain to OSINT as "Open Sores."

119

War. In failing to meet the mandate to inform policy, acquisition, operations, and logistics, secret intelligence has contributed to the "50 Year Wound"[70] and failed to stimulate a redirection of national investments from military capabilities to what General Al Gray, then Commandant of the Marine Corps, called "peaceful preventive measures."[71]

Secret intelligence became synonymous with clandestine and secret technical collection, with very little funding applied to either sense-making information technologies, or to deep and distributed human expertise. The end result at the strategic level can be described by the following two observations, the first a quote and the second a recollected paraphrase:

Daniel Ellsberg speaking to Henry Kissinger:

> *The danger is, you'll become like a moron. You'll become incapable of learning from most people in the world, no matter how much experience they have in their particular areas that may be much greater than yours" [because of your blind faith in the value of your narrow and often incorrect secret information].* [72]

---

[70] The single best book on the cost of the Cold War is Derek Leebaert's *The Fifty-Year Wound: How America's Cold War Victory Has Shaped Our World* (Back Bay Books, 2003). Chalmers Johnson has written two books in this genre, the more recent, listed here first, is more methodical than the other: *The Sorrows of Empire : Militarism, Secrecy, and the End of the Republic* (Metropolitan Books, 2004), and *Blowback : The Costs and Consequences of American Empire* (Owl, 2004 re-issue). See my partial list of books on blowback at http://tinyurl.com/qrcdu. An entire literature on "why people hate America" has been developing, along with US-based critiques of immoral capitalism and virtual colonialism.

[71] General Alfred M. Gray, Commandant of the Marine Corps, "Global Intelligence Challenges in the 1990's," in *American Intelligence Journal* (Winter 1988-1989). Despite four years of effort by the Marine Corps, the National Foreign Intelligence Board (NFIB) and the Military Intelligence Board (MIB) refused to address General Gray's recommendations that we change our priorities from worst-case least probably to most probable emerging threats, and that we invest in open sources. Had we done so from 1988-2000, in those twelve years we would probably have collected enough open sources in Arabic and other languages to understand the threat represented by Bin Laden in terms compelling enough—because they were *public*—to mandate sustained effective action by all relevant national capabilities.

General Tony Zinni, speaking to a senior national security manager:

> *"80% of what I needed to know as CINCENT I got from open sources rather than classified reporting. And within the remaining 20%, if I knew what to look for, I found another 16%. At the end of it all, classified intelligence provided me, at best, with 4% of my command knowledge."*[73]

Secret intelligence may legitimately claim some extraordinary successes, and we do not disagree with Richard Helms when he says that some of those successes more than justified the entire secret intelligence budget, for example, in relation to Soviet military capabilities and our counter-measures.[74] However, in the larger scheme of things, secret intelligence failed to render a strategic value to the nation, in part because it failed to establish a domestic constituency, and could be so easily ignored by Democratic presidents and both ignored and manipulated by Republican presidents.[75]

In this first section, we will briefly review both the failings of each aspect of the secret intelligence world, and summarize how OSINT can improve that specific aspect.

---

[72] Daniel Ellsberg, *SECRETS: A Memoir of Vietnam and the Pentagon Papers* (Viking, 2002). This is his recollection of his words to Henry Kissinger, then National Security Advisor to President Richard Nixon. The three pages on the pathological effects of falling prey to the cult of secrecy, on pages 237-239, should be forced rote memorization for all who receive clearances.

[73] General Tony Zinni, USMC (Ret.), former Commander-in-Chief, U.S. Central Command (CINCCENT), as recounted to the author on 4 April 2006 by a very prominent individual close to varied National Security Council and defense personalities, who desires to remain anonymous.

[74] As recounted in Richard Helms, *A Look over My Shoulder : A Life in the Central Intelligence Agency* (Random House, 2003)

[75] Cf. Robert Steele, *ON INTELLIGENCE: Spies and Secrecy in an Open World* (AFCEA, 2000, OSS, 2003) with a Foreword by Senator David Boren (D-OK), whose efforts to reform national intelligence in 1992 were undone by a combination of Senator John Warner (R-VA) and then Secretary of Defense Dick Cheney. The book remains the single most comprehensive public critique of the shortfalls of the secret world. For a list of other books critical of the past and offering a vision for the future, see my varied lists at Amazon.com. ***Reform can be revenue and job neutral district by district and state by state.***

History

The history of secret intelligence may be concisely summarized in relation to three periods:

- Secret War. For centuries intelligence, like war, was seen to be the prerogative of kings and states, and it was used as a form of "war by other means," with spies and counter-spies, covert actions and plausible deniability.[76]

- Strategic Analysis. During and following World War II, Sherman Kent led a movement to emphasize strategic analysis. Despite his appreciation for open sources of information, and academic as well as other experts, the clandestine and covert action elements of the Office of Strategic Services (OSS) and the follow-on Central Intelligence Group (CIG) and then Central Intelligence Agency (CIA), grew out of control, well beyond what President Harry Truman had envisioned when he sponsored the National Security Act of 1947.[77]

- Smart Nation. Since 1988 there has been an emergent movement, not yet successful, but increasingly taking on a life of its own in the private sector outside of government. Originally conceptualized as an adjunct to secret intelligence, a corrective focus on open sources long neglected, it was soon joined by the Collective Intelligence movement that has also been referred to as "smart mobs" or "wisdom of the crowds," or "world

---

[76] Cf. Walter Laqueur, *A World of Secrets: The Uses and Limits of Intelligence* (Basic Books, 1985). Many other books give accounts of secret warfare going back into time, but culminating in the behind the lines operations in World War II, and then the "dirty tricks" of the 20th Century.

[77] Sherman Kent, *Strategic intelligence for American world policy* (Princeton, 1951). This is a classic. In reality, Kent did not achieve his vision for two reasons: because the clandestine service took over the Central Intelligence Agency and subordinated the analysts, and because in so doing, they cut the analysts off from the world of open sources that were the mainstay of Kent's vision in the first place.

122

brain." H. G. Wells conceptualized a world brain in the 1930's. Qunicy Wright conceptualized a world intelligence center in the 1950's. Others have written about smart nations, collective intelligence, global brain, and the seven tribes of intelligence.[78]

Although the U.S. Intelligence Community has individuals that respect the value of open sources of information, and every major commission since the 1940's has in some form or another called for improved access to foreign language information that is openly available, the reality is that today, in 2006, the United States of America (USA) continues to spend between $50 billion and $70 billion a year on secret collection, almost nothing on all-source sense-making or world-class analysis, and just over $250 million a year on OSINT. This is nothing less than institutionalized lunacy.

The future history of secret intelligence is likely to feature its demise, but only after a citizen's intelligence network is able to apply OSINT to achieve electoral, governance, and budgetary reform, with the result that secret intelligence waste and defense acquisition waste will be converted into "waging peace" with peaceful preventive measures and a massive focus on eliminating poverty, disease, and corruption, while enabling clean water, alternative energy, and collaborative behavior across all cultural boundaries.[79]

Requirements

---

[78] Robert Steele is the primary author on the concept of "smart nation." Among the early works were "Creating a Smart Nation: Information Strategy, Virtual Intelligence, and Information Warfare," in Alan D. Campen, Douglas H. Dearth, and R. Thomas Goodden (contributing editors), *CYBERWAR: Security, Strategy, and Conflict in the Information Age* (AFCEA, 1996); "Creating a Smart Nation: Strategy, Policy, Intelligence, and Information," *Government Information Quarterly* (Summer 1996); "Reinventing Intelligence: The Vision and the Strategy," *International Defense & Technologies* (December 1995), bilingual in French and English; and "Private Enterprise Intelligence: Its Potential Contribution to National Security," paper presented to the Canadian Intelligence Community Conference on "Intelligence Analysis and Assessment," 29 October 1994, reprinted in *Intelligence and National Security* (Special Issue, October 1995), and also in a book by the same name, 1996.

[79] The sections that follow deliberately relate OSINT to reform of the secret elements of the intelligence cycle. Complete multi-media lectures, a total of eight, are easily accessed via www.oss.net/BASIC.

Requirements, or Requirements Definition, is the single most important aspect of the all-source intelligence cycle, and the most neglected. Today, and going back into history, policymakers and commanders tend to ignore intelligence, ask the wrong questions, or ask questions in such a way as to prejudice the answers. There are three major problems that must be addressed if we are to improve all-source decision support to all relevant clients for intelligence:

1. <u>Scope</u>. We must acknowledge that all levels of all organizations need intelligence. We cannot limit ourselves to "secrets for the President." If we fail to acknowledge the needs of lower-level policy makers, including all Cabinet members and their Assistant Secretaries; all acquisition managers, all operational commanders down to civil affairs and military police units; all logisticians; and all allied coalition elements including non-governmental organizations, then we are not being professional about applying the proven process of intelligence to the decision-support needs of key individuals responsible for national security and national prosperity.

2. <u>Competition</u>. We must acknowledge that open sources of information are vastly more influential in the domestic politics of all nations, and that it is not possible to be effective at defining requirements for secret intelligence decision-support in the absence of a complete grasp of what is impacting on the policy makers, managers, and commanders from the open sources world.

Consider the figure below.[80]

---

[80] A variation of this chart appears on page 53 of the author's *ON INTELLIGENCE*. It is based on differing renditions as used by Greg Treverton in teaching the Intelligence Policy Course at Harvard University in the 1980's, and Jack Davis teaching at CIA on challenges to intelligence analysis effectiveness.

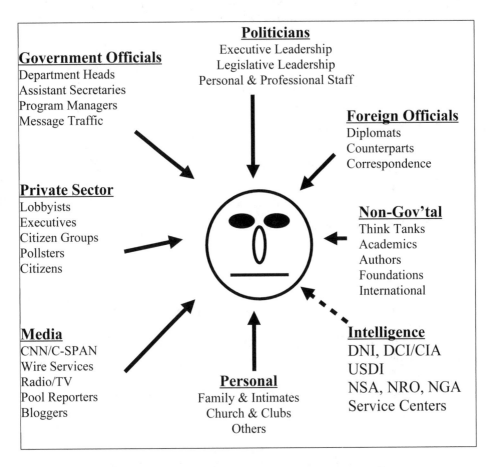

Figure 4: Competing Influences on the Intelligence Consumer

3. <u>Focus</u>. Third, and finally, we must acknowledge that at the strategic level, our focus must of necessity be on long-term threats and opportunities that are global, complex, inter-related, and desperately in need of public education, public recognition, and public policy that is sustainable, which is to say, non-partisan or bi-partisan. Consider, for example, the following findings from the

Report of the High-level Panel on Threats, Challenges and Change, *A more secure world: Our shared responsibility*[81]

• Economic and social threats including	95%
○ poverty,	99%
○ infectious disease and	95%
○ environmental degradation	90%
• Inter-State conflict	75%
• Internal conflict, including	90%
○ civil war,	80%
○ genocide and	95%
○ other large-scale atrocities	95%
• Nuclear, radiological, chemical, and biological weapons	75%
• Terrorism	80%
• Transnational organized crime	80%

Figure 5: OSINT Relevance to Global Security Threats

The average utility and relevant of OSINT to these global threats is—on the basis of my informed estimate—82.5%, which comes very close to the generic "80-20" rule. We must conclude that any nation that persists in spending 99.9 percent of its intelligence funds on collecting secrets,[82] and less than one half of

---

[81] (United Nations, 2004), The endeavor benefited from the participation of The Honorable LtGen Dr. Brent Scowcroft, USAF (Ret), former national security advisor to President George Bush. Terrorism is either fifth on this list or seventh if the first is counted as three. The report, 262 pages in length, can be seen at http://www.un.org/secureworld/report2.pdf. Both the report, and our collected works on intelligence, and completely consistent with the findings of the erudite scholar-practitioner Michael Herman's *Intelligence Power in Peace and War* (Cambridge, 1996), where he concludes that at the strategic level, non-intrusive open sources of information and advanced analytics are vastly more important than secret sources and methods, which tend to shine in tactical situations where force on force remote surveillance can make a difference. That tactical advantage, however, is rapidly being overtaken by commercial and networked capabilities (including human surveillance networks with cell phone videocamaras, to the point that the cost and secrecy of the U.S. Intelligence Community can no longer be justified.

126

one percent of its intelligence funds on OSINT, is quite literally, clinically insane (or insanely corrupt) at the highest levels.

In all three of the above cases, only OSINT can deliver a solution that is affordable, practical, and infinitely shareable with all stake-holders both in and out of government.

Collection

Secret collection has made three fundamental mistakes across several generations of management:[83]

1.   Denigrated OSINT.   It chose to ignore open sources of information, assuming that the consumers of intelligence were responsible for their own OSINT, and that OSINT would not impact on secret collection. In fact, OSINT can dramatically reduce the cost and the risk, and increase the return on investment in secret sources & methods, simply by helping with targeting, spotting, assessment, validation, and the over-all strategic context of what needs to be collected "by other means." It merits very strong emphasis that this failure to respect open sources of information falls into three distinct forms:

> •   Complete disrespect for history in all languages. There is no place within the U.S. Government where one can "see" all Chinese statements on the Spratley Islands, or all Iranian statements on the competing Caliphate concept, or all Brazilian statements on alternative energy sources. We simply do not compute history, and consequently what little we know about current events and threats is known is isolated ignorance of history.

---

[82]   It merits comment that according to the Commission on the National Imagery and Mapping Agency, as published in December 1999, most of the intelligence money is spent on esoteric collection systems, and almost none at all is spent on actually making sense out of the collected information.

[83]   The author has served in the clandestine service (six tours, three overseas), supported strategic signals intelligence acquisition operations, and been a member of the Advanced Program and Evaluation Staff (APEG) with responsibilities for national level validation of current and future secret imagery collection programs.

- Complete abdication of any responsibility for monitoring, understanding, and engaging sub-state or transnational entities as major factors in both international affairs, and as threats or potential allies in domestic security and prosperity.

- Finally, almost complete abdication for more nuanced topics other than standard political-military calculations, with very important sustained failures to collect information on socio-economic, ideo-cultural, techno-demographic, or natural-geographic matters. This has been compounded by an extraordinary laziness or ignorance is relying almost exclusively on what can be stolen or obtained readily in English—the USA simply does not "do" the key 31 languages,[84] much less the totality of 185 languages necessary to understand the sub-state threat and the global network of cause and effect.

2. <u>Official Cover</u>. We have relied almost exclusively, at least in the USA, on "official cover" for our spies, and known trajectories for our satellites. Non-Official Cover (NOC), which does not offer any form of diplomatic or other official immunity from incarceration or eviction, has been treated as too expensive, too complicated, and not worthy of full development. The result has been the almost total compromise of all U.S. secret agents and case officers overseas, as well as their varied not-so-secret thefts of the codebooks of other

---

[84] The languages that OSS and its partners use to follow terrorism and other topics properly are as follows: Arabic, Aramaic, Berber, Catelan, Chinese, Danish, Dari, Dutch, English, Farsi, Finnish, French, German, Indonesian, Irish, Italian, Japanese, Korean, Kurdish, Kurmanji, Norwegian, Pashto, Polish, Portuguese, Russian, Serbian, Spanish, Swedish, Tamil, Turkish, and Urdu. Arabic variations include Andalusi Arabic (extinct, but important role in literary history); <u>Egyptian Arabic</u> (Egypt) Considered the most widely understood and used "second dialect"; Gulf Arabic (Gulf coast from Kuwait to Oman, and minorities on the other side); <u>Hassaniiya</u> (in Mauritania); Hijazi Arabic; Iraqi Arabic; Levantine Arabic (Syrian, Lebanese, Palestinian, and western Jordanian); Maghreb Arabic (Tunisian, Algerian, Moroccan, and western Libyan); Maltese; Najdi Arabic; Sudanese Arabic (with a dialect continuum into Chad); and Yemeni Arabic.

128

nations. We not only don't know what we don't know, we are in denial about the basic fact that what we do know has been compromised.

3. <u>Failure to Process</u>. Finally, and this applies to both clandestine human collection and secret technical collection, we have failed, with deliberate ignorance at the management level, to devote any resources of significance to processing—to sense-making. Today, eighteen years after the needed functionalities for an all-source analytic desktop toolkit were published, we still do not have a desktop analytic toolkit. Today, despite major advances in the private sector with respect to machine-speed translation, and machine-speed statistical, pattern, and predictive analysis, the large majority of our classified intelligence analysis is still done the old-fashioned way: reading at human speed, cutting and pasting, attempting to make sense of vast volumes of secret information while lacking equivalent access to vast volumes of open source information (and especially open source information in any language other than English), limited by the physics of the 24-hour day.

OSINT combines the proven process of intelligence with the ability to collect, process, and analyze all information in all languages all the time. We collect, at best, 20% of what we need to collect, at 99% of the cost, and we spill most of that for lack of processing capabilities. It can be said, as an informed judgment, that Washington is operating on 2% of the relevant strategic information necessary to devise, implement, and adjust national strategy.[85] We should not be sending spies where schoolboys can go, nor should we be ignoring scholarship in all languages.

There will still be a need for selected clandestine human operations, especially against organized crime and translation terrorist groups, but they will need to shift toward non-official cover, and multinational task forces. Secret technical collection will need to emphasize commercial collection first, dramatically refocus secret collection, and shift the bulk of the future resources toward processing—making sense of what we do collect—and toward close-in technical collection inclusive of beacons for tracking bad guys and bad things.

---

[85] This is a very serious indictment of both the policy community and the intelligence community. It is based on direct observation in three Embassies overseas (three tours), on a second graduate thesis on strategic and tactical information management for national security, and on eighteen years of advocacy during which over 40 governments have been helped to enhance their access to and exploitation of open sources of information.

Collection Management will require draconian reform. Instead of defaulting to the tasking of secret collection capabilities, an enlightened collection manager will first determine if they can FIND the information for free in their existing stores of knowledge; then determine if they can GET the information for free from allied government or any of the seven tribes; and then determine if they can BUY the information from a commercial provider, ideally a localized provider with direct indigenous access, in the time and with the operational security (e.g. cover support plans) appropriate to the need. Only if the first three options are unsuited to the need should the collection manager be tasking secret sources and methods, and even that will have to change to accommodate new possibilities from multinational secret task forces able to leverage the collection capabilities of varied countries, many of them vastly superior to the USA when it comes to both deep cover clandestine human penetrations, and the related ability to place close-in secret technical collection devises.[86]

OSINT is, without question, the catalyst for a revolution in how we collect intelligence and how we go about using public intelligence in the public interest.

Processing

Apart from our failure to actually invest in processing (known within the US Intelligence Community as Tasking, Processing, Exploitation, and Dissemination, or TPED), we have made three consistent mistakes over time that have made it virtually impossible, and now unaffordable, to actually do automated all-source analysis:

1. No Standards. We failed to establish data standards that could be used at the point of entry for both secret and open sources of information. This applies to both information sources, and information software. Not only was the intelligence community much too slow to adopt commons standards such as

---

[86] The author spent a tour in the Collection Requirements and Evaluations Staff (CRES) at the CIA, and also consulting in the 2000-2001 timeframe to ICMAP, the attempt by the Deputy Director of Central Intelligence for Administration (DDCI/A) to reduce duplicative tasking of the varied classified collection disciplines. Neither CIA nor the new Open Source Center have a full grasp of how to access all information in all languages all the time, and ICMAP continues to focus on triage among the classified systems, without regard for what can be found, gotten, or bought.

eXtended Markup Language (XML) Resource Description Framework (RDF), Web Ontology Language (OWL), Simple Object Access Protocol (SOAP), today it is either ignorant of or reluctant to move ahead aggressively with Open Hypertextdocument System (OHS)[87] and eXtended Markup Language Geospatial (XML Geo), or the more recent Information Economy Meta Language (IEML).[88] The obsession with security, and the pathology of limiting contracts to the established firms in the military-industrial complex who profit from proprietary softwares and human "butts in seats" rather than real-world low-cost answers, can be blamed for the chasm between the secret intelligence world and the real world of open sources and standards.

2. <u>No Geospatial Attributes</u>. In the fall of 1988 it was made known to the U.S. Intelligence Community and clearly articulated by the author at a meeting of the General Defense Intelligence Program (GDIP), that in the absence of geospatial attributes for every datum entering the all-source processing system (actually an archipelago of private databases), that machine-speed all-source analysis and fusion would be an impossibility. Despite this, the individual secret collection disciplines of clandestine human intelligence (HUMINT), signals intelligence (SIGINT), and imagery intelligence (IMINT) refuse to do anything other than persist with their human analytic reporting that provides date-time-group (DTG), and geographic place names where known, but no standard geospatial attributes for relating information to a map. Today Google Earth is being used in extraordinary ways to visualize relationship databases of real estate, shipping, and other important topics, and the individual citizen is

---

[87] This is the only standard that may not be readily apparent when this chapter is published. Invented by Doug Englebart, also the inventor of the mouse and hypertext, this standard enables linkage of related content to take place at the paragraph level, which also allows copyright compliance to be executed at the paragraph level, for pennies instead of dollars.

[88] XML Geo has been developed by the talented people at the National Space and Aeronautics Administration (NASA) but there is no evidence that they and the National Geospatial Agency are in close communication over this critical matter. IEML has been developed by Professor Pierre Levy, who is also the author of the extraordinary book, *Collective Intelligence: Mankind's Emerging World in Cyberspace* (Persues, 2000) Professor Levy will be presenting his globally-important capability at our annual conference on 18 January 2007, following Howard Bloom, who will speak about his book, *Global Brain.: The Evolution of Mass Mind from the Big Bang to the 21st Century* Conference information is at http://www.oss.net/IOP. Held each year from 1992 to date, this is a permanent event that will go on for the next decade, at least.

light years ahead of the average "cut and paste" analyst at the federal, state, and local levels.

3. No Integration. There is no one single place where all known information comes together. Despite critical concerns raised by every Congressional and Presidential commission since the 1940's, the U.S. Intelligence Community has continued to be "flawed by design,"[89] and persisted in the turf wars between the Central Intelligence Agency (CIA) and the Federal Bureau of Investigation (FBI), between the FBI and the Drug Enforcement Administration (DEA), between FBI and the Department of Justice (DoJ), and between the Departments of State and Defense. Within the Department of Defense (DoD), the services have not only competed with one another, but actively conspired to fabricate and manipulate intelligence to exaggerate the threats relevant to their budget share. A corollary of this abysmal situation is that processing within the stovepipes has been focused on the delivery of documents rather than on making sense of all of the information in the aggregate. With the exception of selected efforts at the National Security Agency, the Army's Intelligence and Security Command, and the U.S. Special Operations Command, virtually all civilian and military analysts are still in cut and paste mode, and do not have the tools for pattern or trend analysis or anomaly detection, much less predictive analysis.

In processing, it is machine speed translation and statistical analysis, based on standards and global distributed information integration, that permits early warning, anomaly detection, and structured analysis that can be completed in a timely—that is to say, relevant—manner. OSINT is where the real innovation is occurring, and I anticipate that within ten years, the secret world will be sharply restricted to no more than 20% of its present cost and size, while the balance of the funding is re-directed to a mix of OSINT that can be shared with anyone, and a massive re-direction of two-thirds of the secret intelligence budget toward global online education in all languages.[90].

Among the corrective measures required in secret processing, which OSINT will facilitate, are a shift toward the Internet as the common operating environment; the adoption of open source software to provide a generic access

---

[89] Amy Zegart, *Flawed by Design: The Evolution of the CIA, JCS, and NSC* (Stanford, 2000).

[90] Members and others may rest assured that our planned reforms are job and revenue neutral from constituency to constituency. This can be done rationally and gradually.

and collaborative sharing environment for all seven tribes;[91] the development of 24/7 "plots" at every level of governance in which all information can be seen in time and geospatial context;[92] and the creation of a national skunkworks with an anti-trust waiver for the public testing and certification of all open sources, softwares, and services. Rapid promulgation of free wireless within urban areas and in the Third World will help accelerate both sharing in the North and West, and uploading of useful information from the East and South.

Analysis

In evaluating the failure of analysis, it is important to understand that most U.S. analysts are too young, too inexperienced in the real world, and too isolated from foreign or even U.S. private sector experts, to realize that the secret information they are receiving is out of context, often wrong, and largely irrelevant to strategic analysis. Their managers are too busy trying to be promoted or to win bonuses or please the White House (or the representative of the White House, the Director of Central Intelligence (DCI)). As a result, the strategic analysis vision of Sherman Kent has been dishonored and largely set aside. There have been three major failures in analysis over time.

1. <u>Hire Young</u>. The intelligence management philosophy in both the national civilian hires and at the military theater and service center levels has combined

---

[91] It is a fact that 90% of the information that we need to gain access to is controlled or obtainable by non-governmental, academic, civil, and generally foreign organizations that cannot afford the gold-plated and generally pathologically dysfunctional information technology systems that the beltway bandits have been selling to the secret world for decades. In order to create a global information sharing environment where we can get much more than we give in the way of content (what we can provide is processing power), it is essential that we establish generic open source software suites of tools, such as the Defense Advanced Research Projects Agency (DARPA) has done with STRONG ANGEL, so that all relevant contributors can join the Open Source Information System (OSIS) via inexpensive collaborative toolkits and access ports.

[92] Information technology has not been an obstacle to the creation of 24/7 "plots" but rather mind-sets and bureaucratic inertia. For a stimulating and truly enlightening account of both the early mistakes and later successes of the British in World War II in using "plots" to track and anticipate the movements of submarines (a skill applicable to today's terrorists), see Patrick Beesley, *Very Special Intelligence: The Story of the Admiralty's Operational Intelligence Centre, 1939-1945* (Greenhill, 2000). As with all books cited, a summative review by Robert Steele, with key points itemized, can be read at Amazon.

"hire to payroll" with obsessive lazy security parameters that have resulted in an analytic population that is largely young, white, and mostly bereft of overseas experience and especially long-term residency in foreign countries. On the one hand, budgets have been used to hire low and promote over time, treating analysis as an entry-level hiring challenge rather than a mid-career sabbatical challenge; this has been deeply and pathologically influenced by a low-rent security philosophy that has combined paranoia over foreign contacts (and relatives), with an unwillingness to spend the time and thoughtfulness necessary to clear complicated individuals that have led complicated lives. This personnel management failure stems from the larger philosophical management failure, which confuses secrets with intelligence, and thus demeans expertise from the open source world while assuming that young analysts will succeed because they have access to secrets, rather than because of any application of analytic tradecraft such as might take twenty years to refine.

2. <u>Hard Target Focus</u>. In keeping with the military-industrial complex and its desire to profit from the Cold War, the national and military intelligence communities devoted virtually their entire budgets and most of their manpower to the "hard targets" (generally, Russia, China, Iran, India, Pakistan, Libya, and —hard to believe but true—Cuba). They ignored all of the "lower tier" issues and Third World countries,[93] and also focused only on very big threats, not on very big opportunities for peaceful preventive measures where a few dollars invested in the 1970's might have eradicated Anti-Immune Deficiency Systems (AIDS) or dependency on Middle Eastern oil. This was of course in keeping with policy preferences, and even when the CIA did excellent work (for example, accurately forecasting the global AIDS epidemic), it could safely be ignored because its work was not available to the public or even to most Members of Congress. A very important consequence of this narrow focus was

---

[93]   Despite General Gray's concern in 1988, and years of effort by the author that culminated in testimony to the Aspin-Brown Commission resulting in a finding that our access to open sources was "severely deficient" and should be a "top priority" for funding; and despite a report commissioned by DCI George Tenet and delivered by Boyd Sutton in July 1997 on "The Challenge of Global Coverage"—a report recommending that $1.5 billion a year be spent on open sources as an insurance policy, consisting of $10 million a year on each of 150 topics of lower tier countries spawning terrorism, crime, disease, and other ills, Tenet, his predecessors, and his successors have consistently refused to focus on anything other than secrets for the President. The Global Coverage report is easily accessible via www.oss.net/BASIC.

134

the complete failure to ensure that all of the sources of national power—diplomatic, informational, military, economic (DIME)—were funded, acquired, fielded, and applied in a coherent and timely manner. The entire military-industrial-intelligence complex has been skewed toward a heavy metal military —a few big platforms or big organizations—that are only relevant 10% of the time. We are completely unprepared for, we are not trained, equipped, or organized, for small wars, waging peace, or homeland defense. This is still true —truer that ever—in the aftermath of 9-11 and the invasions and occupations of Afghanistan and Iraq.

3. Local Now. Finally, U.S. Intelligence (and many foreign intelligence communities) focused on the local now instead of the global future. "Current Intelligence" dominated the President's Daily Briefing (PDB), and over time longer-term research fell by the wayside. This problem was aggravated by a draconian editing process in both the national civilian and theater or service level military, where a twelve month research project could be subject to eighteen month editing cycles, such that the work was out of date or thoroughly corrupted by the time it was finally released to a relatively limited number of policymakers. With most of the intelligence products being released in hard-copy, or messages that were printed out and not saved electronically, the overall impact of U.S. intelligence production, and especially Codeword production, must be judged as marginal.[94]

---

[94] There are a handful of books that really emphasis the importance of history and the continuing strategy relevance of historical factors including morality and birth control (or not). Among them: Will and Ariel Durant, *The Lessons of History* (Simon & Schuster, 1968), Richard Neustradt and Ernest May, *Thinking In Time : The Uses Of History For Decision Makers* (Free Press, 1988), and Stewart Brand, *The Clock of the Long Now: Time and Responsibility: The Ideas Behind the World's Slowest Computer* (Basic, 2000), John Lewis Gaddis, *The Landscape of History : How Historians Map the Past* (Oxford, 2004). Included here are two books on the strategic implications of losing history, and failing to notice fact: Robert Perry, *Lost History: Contras, Cocaine, the Press & 'Project Truth* (Media Consortium, 1999), and Larry Beinhart, *Fog Facts : Searching for Truth in the Land of Spin* (Nation Books, 2005).

OSINT is "the rival store."[95] Whereas I spent the first eighteen years of my campaign to foster an appreciation on OSINT and focusing on the urgency of integrating OSINT into secret sources toward improved all-source analysis, I plan to spend the next eighteen years burying 80% of the classified world. They are too expensive, too irrelevant, and pathologically anti-thetical to the new and correct Swedish concept of Multinational, Multiagency, Multidisciplinary, Multidomain Information Sharing (M4IS).[96] OSINT analysis will in the future be the benchmark by which classified sources and methods are judged to be relevant and cost-effective, or not. The Director of National Intelligence (DNI) has chosen to remain focused on secrets for the President. So be it. OSINT, from a private sector and non-governmental foundation, will capture all the other consumers of intelligence. The day will come when "clearances" are severely devalued and open source access—international open source access in all languages all the time—is ascendant. The DCI must serve all levels of the government, all seven tribes, and must balance between open and closed sources so as to inform decision-makers—and their publics—in order to preserve and enhance the long-term national security and prosperity of the USA. Secret sources and methods—and the existing military—have demonstrably failed in both regards.

Analytic tradecraft notes are available online and should be consulted.[97] All-source analysts should not be hired until they have first proven themselves as masters of all open sources in all languages relevant to their domain and not be considered for mid-career hire unless they are one of the top 25 cited authorities in the field. They must know how to leverage their historian, their librarian, and the Internet. They must know how to identify and interact with the top 100 people in the world on their topic, regardless of citizenship or clearances. Finally, they must understand that they are—and must be trained to be—

---

[95] This term was first used by Alvin Toffler to describe the author, his company, and OSINT. See the chapter on "The Future of the Spy" in which 5 of the 12 pages are focused on OSINT, in *War and Anti-War: Making Sense of Today's Global Chaos* (Warner, 1995). All of the books by the Tofflers, who now write as a team, are relevant to the information era, but *Powershift: Knowledge, Wealth, and Power at the Edge of the 21st Century* (Bantam, 1991) is rather special.

[96] This term (M4IS) was first introduced by the Swedes at the Third Peacekeeping Intelligence Conference held in Stockholm in December 2004. The Swedes have replaced the Canadians as the neutral third party of choice.

[97] Goggling for "analytic tradecraft" is always useful. The actual notes from Jack Davis can be accessed via www.oss.net/BASIC.

managers of customer relations and requirements definition; of open sources; of external experts; and of classified collection management. Analysts must know and practice the "new rules" for the new craft of intelligence, with specific reference to being able to actually do forecasting, establish strategic generalizations, and drill down to the neighborhood and tribal levels, not simply hover at the nation-state level.[98]

Covert Action

Covert action consists of agents of influence, media placement, and paramilitary operations. Covert action assumes two things that may once have been true but are no longer true: that an operation can be carried out without its being traced back to the USA as the sponsor; and that the fruits of the operation will be beneficial to the USA. In each of these three areas, the USA has acted with great disdain for the normal conventions of legitimacy, accountability, morality, and practicality, and today the USA is suffering from what is known as "blow-back"—it is reaping the dividends from decades of unethical behavior justified in the name of national security, but unfounded upon any substantive grasp of long-term reality.

1. Agents of influence are individuals bribed covertly who are charged with getting their governments or organizations to pursue a course of action that the USA deems to be necessary, but which may not be in the best interests of the indigenous public or its government. Regardless of what one may think of the local country and its government and public, what this really means is that agents of influence are responsible for disconnecting local policies from local realities, and imposing instead a reality or choice selected by the US Government. This is inherently pathological. There are certainly some success stories—support to Solidarity in Poland, for example, but this was a capitalization on the fall of communism, not the cause.

2. Media placement uses individuals, generally foreign journalists, who are bribed covertly to create and publish stories that communicate an alternative view of reality, one sanctioned by the US Government but generally at odds with the actual facts of the matter. There is a constructive side to media

---

[98]   As with all observations in this chapter, the specifics are easily accessible via www.oss.net/BASIC, in this case as "New Rules for the New Craft of Intelligence," under Practice, where other guides to analytic tradecraft may also be found.

placement, for example the promulgation of information about atrocities committed by dictators or Soviet forces, but generally the US Government supports most of the dictators it deals with, and reserves this tool for deposing individuals that dare to oppose predatory immoral capitalism or virtual colonialism.   Consequently, most media placement activities consist of propaganda seeking to manipulate rather than deliver the truth.   Media placement by spies should not be confused with Public Diplomacy by diplomats or Strategic Communication by the military—the latter two are overt truth-telling missions, although mis-guided practitioners may occasionally stray into propaganda and the manipulation of the truth.[99]

3. <u>Paramilitary operations</u> are not only direct assaults on the sovereignty of other nations, but they tend to bring with them black markets, drug running, money laundering, corruption, and the proliferation of a culture of violence and the small arms with which to do indiscriminate violence. The Phoenix program of assassinations in Viet-Nam, the support to the contras and the mining of the Nicaraguan harbors (an act condemned by the World Court), the arming of the Islamic fundamentalists for jihad in Afghanistan, join the planned overthrows of the governments of Chile, Guatemala, Iran, as causes of long-term and costly "blow-back." Of all of these, Iran is the most interesting. Had we allowed the nationalization of the oil in Iran and the fall of the Shah, we might today have both a non-fundamentalist Iran as a bulwark against the radicals from Saudi Arabia, but we might also be less dependent on oil, and less subject to the whims of the extraordinarily corrupt Saudi regime and its US energy company allies.

OSINT is the anti-thesis of all three forms of covert action. As David Ignatius noted so wisely in the 1980's, overt action rather than covert action delivers the best value in both the short and the long run. Promulgating the tools for truth—cell phones, wireless access, access to the Internet—is a means of fostering informed democracy and responsible opposition. It is also a means of creating stabilizing indigenous wealth.   OSINT provides a historical and cultural foundation for achieving multi-cultural consensus that is sustainable precisely because it is consensual.   As Jonathan Schell documents so well in *The Unconquerable World: Power, Nonviolence, and the Will of the People*, there

---

[99] Cf. Robert Steele, *INFORMATION OPERATIONS: All Information, All Languages, All the Time* (OSS, 2006) and—more focused on the military as well as free, *INFORMATION OPERATIONS: Putting the I Back Into DIME* (Strategic Studies Institute, February 2006). The latter is easily found by Googling for the title.

are not enough guns in the world to force our way or protect our borders.[100] Only by fostering legitimacy, morality, charity, and full participation of all, can we stabilize the world to the mutual benefit of the USA and the rest of the world.

OSINT, in addition to being vastly superior to covert action as a means for establishing reasonable goals that are sustainable over time, is also very well suited to documenting the extraordinary costs of historical covert actions. Only now is the public beginning to understand the lasting damage caused by the US sponsorship of assassination attempts against Fidel Castro, capabilities that were ultimately turned against the unwitting President, John F. Kennedy, and his brother Robert. We have sacrificed our national values, and our international credibility at the alter of covert action, and we are long overdue for a deep "truth and reconciliation" commission that evaluates the true costs of covert action, and that then defines much more narrowly the conditions and protocols for engaging in covert action in the future.

Counterintelligence

Strategic counterintelligence is completely distinct from tactical counterintelligence.[101] In strategic counterintelligence, one is looking for emerging threats at the strategic level, not individual penetrations of specific organizations. This is an area where OSINT should, but does not, shine. The US Intelligence Community—and consequently the US policy community—have completely missed the end of cheap oil, the end of free water, the rise of Bin Laden and the rise of pandemic disease, even global warming, precisely because national counterintelligence was focused obsessively on penetrating foreign security services, and not on the strategic environment where natural and other threats of omission and commission were to be found. There are three areas where strategic counterintelligence can benefit considerably from comprehensive OSINT, inclusive of the digitization and statistical analysis of all available historical information.

---

[100] Jonathan Schell, *The Unconquerable World : Power, Nonviolence, and the Will of the People* (Owl, 2004).

[101] The author spent a tour at the national level responsible for offensive counterintelligence against a denied area county, and was also responsible for global oversight of recruitment efforts against all representatives of the same government.

1. National education. Thomas Jefferson said that "A Nation's best defense is an informed citizenry." This is absolutely correct, and even more so today, when central bureaucracies are no match for agile networked transnational groups. The USA has failed to understand the strategic implications of its lack of border control, its mediocre educational system designed to create docile factory workers, and the trends toward obesity, insularity, and indifference that characterize the bulk of the population today. We have gone hollow for lack of focus.

2. Environment. The Singapore military was stunned by the emergence of Severe Acute Respiratory Syndrome (SARS), but unlike the U.S. military—they got it. They realized they were responsible for defending Singapore against all threats, not just man-made or man-guided threats, and added national health and border security against airborne, waterborne, and human or animal borne diseases, to their charter. Similarly, the Singapore police have an extraordinarily nuanced and enlightened understanding of their global and regional information needs and responsibilities in relation to deterring and resolving all forms of crime impacting on Singapore. In the USA, and globally with dire consequences for the USA, there are threats associated with the environment and how it changes (including water, energy, and raw material resources) that are simply not understood, not acknowledged, and not being acted upon responsibly by any US Administration, be it Democratic or Republican.[102]

3. Ideology. There are two ideological threats to US security today, one external, the other internal. The two together are very troubling. Externally, the radical and violent fundamentalist stream of Islam has been armed and energized by jihad in Afghanistan, in Chechnya, and in Iraq. Other small jihads in Indonesia, the Philippines, and southern Thailand, as well as selected locations in Muslim Africa, add to this threat. Internally, US Christian fundamentalists—these are the people that graduated from rote reading of the Bible to the Left Behind fiction series—have assumed a terribly excessive importance in extremist Republican circles, in part because the Texas corporate energy interests chose to make common cause with them. The Middle East, oil,

---

[102] In general the reader is referred to the 678+ books reviewed by the author at Amazon over the past five years. Dr. Col Max Manwaring, USA (Ret) has edited *Environmental Security and Global Stability: Problems and Responses* (Lexington, 2002) and there is an entire literature on ecological economics as well as on the health of nations, relating disease, poverty, and the environment.

and the almost cult-like extreme religious right, have hijacked American democracy. The American left, nominally but not intelligently led by the Democratic party (which is as corrupt as the Republican party, but more inept), meanwhile, abandoned faith and God and the sensible calming effect of religion as a foundation for community and ethics.[103] The American ideology of capitalism has also been corrupted. Immoral predatory capitalism, and pathologically inept formulas for "developmental economics" as imposed on failed states by the International Monetary Fund (IMF) and the World Bank, have given rise to populism and other forms of indigenous resistance now witting of the collusion between their corrupt elite and immoral foreign capitalism that are in combination looting the commonwealth of many peoples.[104]

In all three of these cases, OSINT has an extraordinary role to play. Under the leadership of Congressman Rob Simmons (R-CT-02), a moderate Republican with an extraordinarily deep background in both intelligence and on the Hill, the campaign continues for a national Open Source Agency funded at $3 billion per year, under the auspices of the Department of State (as a sister agency to the Board of Governors that controls the Voice of America and other public diplomacy outlets). However, fully half the budget is intended to fund fifty Community Intelligence Centers and networks across the country (each receiving $30 million at Full Operating Capability or FOC). These centers are

---

[103] On this vital topic, see on the internal threat, two books: Kevin Philips, *American Theocracy : The Peril and Politics of Radical Religion, Oil, and Borrowed Money in the 21stCentury* (Viking, 2006), and Michael Lerner, *The Left Hand of God: Taking Back Our Country from the Religious Right* (Harpers, 2006). On the external threat, while there are numerous books on radical Islam, the best overall discussion of ideology as a means of changing the pecking order among social groups, and grabbing real estate and resources, is offered by Howard Bloom, *The Lucifer Principle: A Scientific Expedition into the Forces of History* (Atlantic Monthly, 1997). The book includes a prescient discussion of Sunni versus Shiite, as well as of religion as an ideology used to capture resources.

[104] Among the most obvious and hard-hitting current references on immoral capitalism are Clyde Prestowitz, *Rogue Nation: American Unilateralism and the Failure of Good Intentions* (Basic, 2004), John Perkins, *Confessions of an Economic Hit Man* (Plume, 2005), William Greider, *The Soul of Capitalism : Opening Paths to a Moral Economy* Simon & Schuster, 2004), and, most recently, Jeffrey Sachs, *The End of Poverty : Economic Possibilities for Our Time* (Penguin, 2006). There is a separate literature on "virtual colonialism" and the inner anger that a U.S. military presence inspires, particularly in Muslim countries.

needed for two reasons: first, to provide 119 and 114 numbers for citizen mobilization (119 alerts all cell phones within a 5 kilometer radius) and citizen neighborhood watch inputs (114 receives cell phone photos, text messages, any form of information, all with geospatial and time tags); and second, to serve as dissemination nodes for transmitting to all schools, chambers of commerce, churches and synagogues and mosques, labor unions, civil advocacy groups, and so on, the wealth of "real world" information to be collected, processed, and shared, free via the Internet, by the Open Source Agency. This will impact very favorably on the environment, as these centers will help citizens at the county, state, and regional levels understand, with precision, where each of them stands with respect to access to clean water, alternative energies and related lifestyle choices, and global threats to their children and grandchildren based on easy access to the actual U.S. federal budget in relation to real world threats and needs.   Militarism will be reduced, poverty and disease will be eliminated, and the USA can rejoin the community of nations as a force for good.   Finally, all competing ideologies can be subject to scrutiny and understanding, and the majority of Americans who are not part of the nutty right can come together consensually to limit the damage these people can do to the Republic, while also holding their political and corporate allies accountable for serving America as a whole rather than a lunatic fringe element.

Dramatically redirecting national intelligence toward OSINT will substantially reduce the cost of secrecy, estimated by the Moynihan Commission as being on the order of $6 billion a year (probably closer to $15 billion a year today),[105] and will also eliminate perhaps 70% of the costs associated with establishing the trustworthiness of individuals being considered for clearances. The security and clearance system of the U.S. Government is broken beyond repair. Not only does it take over two years from most investigations to be completed, but they are generally sub-standard investigations that go through the motions and generally do not detect basic aberrations, such as a fascination with child pornography and online molestation of children, as was the case recently with a senior manager in the Department of Homeland Security. The fact is that most sheriffs and other state, local, and tribal officials are not "clearable" for a variety of reasons, and we may as well recognize that not only is OSINT better suited for most national intelligence information sharing, but we really do not need most of the grotesquely expensive and dysfunctional Top Secret"

---

[105] *Report Of The Commission On Protecting And Reducing Government Secrecy* (GAO, 1997), available at http://www.fas.org/sgp/library/moynihan/.

compartments" (over 400 of them, half in the civilian world and half in the military world) and all the attendant costs, including the costs of ignorance stemming from compartmented information not being shared. At least at the strategic level, we need a national intelligence system where we are less concerned about betrayal from within, and more focused on emerging strategic threats to our long-term security and prosperity, threats that must not be limited to man-made capabilities, but include animal borne diseases and other environmental conditions that tend to be shut out from national security decision processes.

Accountability, Civil Liberties, and Oversight

As all of the preceding sections should have made clear, OSINT is the essential contributing factor to dramatically improving the accountability and oversight of the U.S. Intelligence Community and the policymakers, acquisition managers, and operational commanders that respond to White House direction. OSINT is also a means of dramatically enhancing not just civil liberties, but civic engagement in the practice of democracy. By providing citizens at every level with structured OSINT on any issue for any zip code or other geographic grouping, and by making it possible for citizens to immediately connect with other like-minded citizens and with accountable officials, OSINT in practice is an enabler of a new form of constant engaged informed democracy. Civil liberty infractions will be broadcast or podcast, rapidly aggregated, and civil pressure brought to bear. By harnessing citizens as part of the "home guard" and empowering them with immediate and understandable access to indications and warning information, we will dramatically improve the reporting of relevant information, and—through the Community Intelligence Centers—be able to process, make sense of, and act on—or discount—the "bottom up" dots that I am convinced will comprise at least 50% of the relevant dots needed to prevent the next 9-11.

It is also important to emphasize that at the strategic level, we need to be concerned not just with accountability and oversight of secret intelligence, but with the much larger issue of whether Congress and the Executive are being responsible in representing the public interest. For this reason we include very brief but vital sections at the end of this chapter on OSINT and electoral reform, governance reform, and budgetary reform. OSINT is the ultimate means by which citizens may hold their government accountable, protect their civil liberties over time, and contribute to the pursuit of happiness by one for all and all for each. It's called a commonwealth!

Strategic Warning

Although CIA has done some fine work on global threats, and I particular like the work done under John Gannon as Assistant Director of Central Intelligence for Analysis & Production (*Global Trends 2015*, which led to *Global Trends 2020*),[106] on balance the U.S. Intelligence Community has failed abysmally at strategic warning because of some fundamental operational and philosophical failures.[107]

Operationally, despite fifty years of extraordinarily generous funding for multi-billion dollar satellite systems, the U.S. Intelligence Community still cannot do wide area surveillance, real-time change detection, or "the last mile" inclusive of seeing into urban area, under jungle canopy, and into the deep ravines of mountainous terrain.

Philosophically U.S. Intelligence has been a disaster in strategic terms. The cult of secrecy limited "intelligence" to "secrets for the President" and left everyone else, from Cabinet-level leaders to military acquisition manager and operational commanders, to Governors and Mayors, completely without "decision-support." Perhaps worse, the U.S. Intelligence Community has refused to recognize the seven tribes of intelligence, shutting out, for the most part, state, local, and tribal officials with overseas knowledge, business travelers, academics, non-governmental observers, journalists, labor union leaders, religious travelers, and so on. The obsession with government secrecy over public sharing has cost this Nation fifty years of time—the one strategic factor that can not be bought nor replaced[108]—and at least 3 billion souls of good will. U.S. Intelligence is a small part of the overall federal government,

---

[106] Both are available online.

[107] No disrespect is intended in neglecting to address the standard works on strategic warning. The author's concept of strategic warning is much broader than now exists within both the secret intelligence world, and the academic world that writes about the secret intelligence world.

[108] Colin Gray, *Modern Strategy* (Oxford, 1999). An eight point summary is at Amazon. A superb monograph on strategy (83 pages) by Dr. Col (Ret) Harry (Rich) Yarger, "Strategic Theory for the 21st Century," is easily found online by Googling the author and title.

and it merits comment that most of our problems today cannot be blamed on U.S. Intelligence as much as on a Congress and Executive all too eager to ignore, for example, the Peak Oil warnings of 1974-1979 in order to keep the bribes going and the public docile. This is not, however, to excuse the U.S. Intelligence Community, in as much a focus on OSINT from 1988 onwards would have done much to illuminate and correct the policy errors that benefited from secrecy, obscurity, and public inattentiveness.

Strategic Sharing

The U.S. Intelligence Community is incapable today, five years after 9-11, of creating a single consolidated watch list of suspected terrorists. The U.S. Government as a whole is incapable of sharing everything that it knows for lack of collaborative mindsets, willing management, interoperable systems, and coherent data sets.   There are three primary impediments to the U.S. Intelligence Community ever being able to share readily:

1. High Side Security. The obsession with security is occasioned in part by the fact that the secret intelligence world, even though it has "compartments," has never learned to disaggregate secret from non-secret information. Everything is stored at the "high side," at the highest possible level of security, meaning that nothing can be shared with anyone who is not cleared for the highest level of security, however unclassified the information might be.

2. Third Party Rule. The secret world has for decades operated under a "third party rule" that prohibits the sharing of any information received from one party, with another party. This rule is extremely detrimental to multi-lateral sharing, and imposes enormous time, manpower, and dollar costs when something needs to be shared and the sharing must be coordinated. The default condition of the secret world is "do not share."

3. Legacy Systems. As John Perry Barlow noted in an article in *Forbes*,[109] if you want to see the last remnants of the Soviet Empire, go visit the CIA and look at their computer systems. The U.S. Intelligence Community as a whole is still mired in 1970's technology managed by 1950's mind-sets, totally out of touch with 21st Century information networks, both machine and human.

---

[109] John Perry Barlow, co-founder of the Electronic Frontier Foundation, "Why Spy?" in *Forbes*, 10/07 2002, at http://www.forbes.com/asap/2002/1007/042.html.

OSINT is going to be the catalyst for M4IS and strategic sharing. OSINT is the only discipline that can easily distribute the collection, processing, and analysis burden across all coalition nations (e.g. the ninety nations comprising the U.S. Central Command coalition), and also the only discipline whose products can easily be shared with non-governmental organizations as well as state, local, and tribal authorities all over the world who will never qualify for "clearances." It will be our challenge in the next eighteen years to develop an alternative global intelligence community that relies almost exclusively on "good enough" open sources, and that consequently forces the secret world into proving its "added value" in relation to cost, risk, and time, on every topic, every day.

Emerging Prospects

Apart from increased public access to the Internet, inclusive of electronic mail, the deep web, and the dramatically increased availability of free multi-media communications and information sharing capabilities, several factors are supportive of a displacement of secret sources and methods by open sources and methods:

1. Digitization. It is a mistake to believe that all relevant information is being digitized today. Tribal histories (e.g. those from Iraq) and vast quantities of important information are still being produced in Industrial Era mediums, and Friday sermons by Islamic imams as well as the sermons by all the other faiths, are not part of the digital revolution. In strategic terms, however, digitization is extremely important for three reasons:

- Most current information from mainstream and niche media as well as individual publishers and bloggers, in all languages, is now available digitally.
- Historical information, including policy and financial statements of great importance to specific nations, industries, organizations, and tribes, can now be affordably and effectively digitized.

- Hand-held devices are rapidly becoming a primary means of collecting and sharing information, with imminent prospects of being able to harness, selectively, all that any group of individuals can see and hear and think, and is willing to upload as needed.

2. <u>Visualization</u>. Digital information, including historical information, can now be visualized, not only in relation to content analysis and links between paragraphs and among individuals, but in relation to a geospatial foundation such as Google Earth provides in rudimentary but quite compelling terms. This is moving OSINT well beyond secret sources and methods because it can draw on a much greater body of information and expertise in real time, and apply all modern machine analytic tools with fewer security, legal, and policy constraints. The centralized unilateral secret bureaucracies are losing ground—rapidly—to distributed open multinational networks.

3. <u>Peer-to-Peer (P2P)</u>. "Ground truth" is taking on a whole new meaning as individuals exercise the power to share complex information directly with one another, eliminating the intermediary journals, web sites, and government or media offices that in the past have played the role of editor, judge, and broker of meaning and value.

The power of OSINT at the strategic level can simply not be exaggerated nor underestimated for the simply reason that it harnesses the distributed intelligence of the Whole Earth, in real time as well as in historical memory time, across all languages and cultures. There isn't a bureaucracy in the world that can match its networked power. To drive that point home, consider the game of baseball. In today's secret environment, government bureaucrats accustomed to unlimited budgets and secret methods continue to try to win the game by bribing a player (Clandestine Intelligence), putting a "bug" in the dug-out (Signals Intelligence), trying to "sniff" the direction and speed of the ball (Measurements & Signatures Intelligence), or taking a satellite picture of the field every three days (Imagery Intelligence). The new craft of intelligence simply integrates the audience. It uses the collective wisdom of all the participants. It encourages the crowd to participate. Any catch by the audience is an out! Open source intelligence harnesses what *everyone* sees and knows. It changes the rules of the game. Any catch in the stands is an out. *That* is how we win against asymmetric opponents who know our Achilles' heels all too well.

OSINT and Electoral Reform

The USA is a Republic. An extraordinary characteristic of Republics is that voters have the power to dissolve the government should it become so ineffective or destructive as to warrant its termination. The Constitution, and the voters, are the foundation of the American democracy, not the three branches of government. If the Executive is mendacious, the Congress corrupt, the Judiciary unrepresentative of the values of the people, then the public has the power to change the rules of the game for elections. It is OSINT that can be used by citizens to break away from the grid-locked mainstream parties, and develop new networked means of demanding minimalist changes such as suggested by Ralph Nader and enhanced by the author: voting on week-ends so the poor don't lose work; restoring the League of Women Voters as the arbiters of multi-party debates; demanding that Presidential candidates announce their Cabinets in advance of the election, and including at least the Secretaries of Defense and State, and the Attorney General, in Cabinet-level debates; applying the instant run-off concept to ensure a true majority election; and of course ending gerrymandering and corporate funding for any elected official.

OSINT and Governance Reform

Government at the Federal level has become incompetent, not for lack of good intentions but because of the very issues to scale (too big, too slow) that were anticipated by Kirkpatrick Sale in 1980,[110] and it is also wasteful of the taxpayer dollar for two reasons: special interest corruption both in Congress (bribery) and in the Executive (revolving-door favoritism); and an industrial era structure that is largely disconnected from reality to the point that ideological fantasy can supplant a reasoned policy process.

At a minimum, the Republic needs a Coalition Cabinet and some means of assuring the citizenry that Presidents will not be able to simply appoint cronies from their own party; the Executive needs to be restructured to provide for integrated policy development, not just national security policy development; strategic planning focused out seven generations (over 200 years) must be demanded and be publicly transparent and accountable; and the fundamentals of national power must be mandated: quality education for all, health care for all, and an end to poverty at home. Presidents and their teams must be elected for their ability to govern rather than campaign.

---

[110] Kirkpatrick Sale, *HUMAN SCALE* (New York: Prager, 1980).

148

Congress, in my personal opinion, must move toward proportional representation in each house, with leadership positions and office assignments based on a more parliamentary form of dividing responsibilities and authorities, rather than the current "winner take all" system that is now seen by the American people as a major destabilizing influence in legislative politics.

OSINT will make all of this possible, sooner than later if a national Open Source Agency is created as a new fourth branch of government, independent of Congress and the Executive, with a lifetime appointment for its Director, and a Board of Directors comprised of former Presidents, Leaders of the Senate and House, and retired Supreme Court Justices.

OSINT and Strategic Budgetary Reform

Finally, we come to budgetary reform. OSINT has already made it clear that we have a Department of Defense costing $500 billion a year (not counting the cost of the war in Iraq) that is relevant to only 10% of the threat (state on state warfare), that is largely incompetent at small wars and homeland defense, and that we are, as a Republic, not investing properly in peaceful preventive measures inclusive of the spread of participatory democracy and moral capitalism. The Return on Investment of our "Big War" military is not only not there, the existence of that Big War force leads ignorant Presidents and their mendacious Vice Presidents to seek out wars as an option for capturing "cheap" oil (never mind the cost in blood, spirit, and treasure).

The American Republic specifically, and all other countries, are long over-due for what I call "reality-based budgeting." OSINT will restore sanity and sensibility to the public treasury and how it is applied, in the present with a grasp of the lessons of history such that we might embrace the future wisely.

There is, in the immortal words of Arnie Donahue[111] in 1992, "plenty of money for OSINT." There is also plenty of money for participatory democracy and moral capitalism. Our problem has been that we have allowed the mandarins of secrecy to pretend to be informing the President, rather narrowly and very expensively, while failing to demand that the Republic develop a public intelligence capability suitable for directing public policy and public spending in an intelligent sustainable manner.

9-11, the Iraq War, and the varied accomplishments—or mistakes—of the Bush Administration may stand in history as a bright turning point in the history of the Republic. One doubts that anything less might have awakened the somnolent public.

---

[111] At the time, Donahue was the ranking director with the Office of Management and Budget (OMB) for all Command and Control, Communications, Computing, and Intelligence (C4I), and one of a handful of individuals with all of the codeword clearances. His boss, Don Gessaman, the ranking civil servant at OMB for National Security inclusive of Programs 50 (International Relations) and 150 (Defense), guided the establishment of Code M320 for defense expenditures on OSINT in 2000. OSINT is seen by the IC as a threat that should not be out-sourced, and by OMB as a function that can be accomplished in the private sector and therefore should be out-sourced to the fullest extent possible.

Part III:
OSINT Honors & References

The illustration below is a depiction of the Lifetime Award for professionalism in the discipline of Open Source Intelligence (OSINT). Twelve were awarded in 2006, the eighteenth year of struggle to communicate common sense across forty governments, but especially into the U.S. Government.

Figure 6: Lifetime Award for OSINT Achievement

This portion of the book is intended to help busy Members of Congress and citizens who do not have time to visit the electronic web sites.

Chapter 10: OSINT Honors

While those in the U.S. Government nominally responsible for OSINT have been incapacitated, a robust international community has formed, led largely by military officers and their librarians.   140 Golden Candle Awards and 12 Lifetime Awards, provide a very fast summary of who has actually be active in the OSINT world. The U.S. Army has been especially noteworthy.

Chapter 11: OSINT References

This document, while available electronically with hot links to each document, in included to make the point to Congress and to the public that there are 30,000 pages from over 600 contributing speakers and authors spanning over 40 countries with successful OSINT programs that are operationally oriented, technically nuanced, and able to keep pace with their customers most urgent needs. No element of the U.S. Government can claim such a collection, nor such sustained interest in breaking new ground that helps America make the most of all information in all languages all the time.

Chapter 12: The Failure of U.S. Intelligence

This briefing is available both electronically and on DVD to any Member or Congressional staff. The U.S. Intelligence Community is not able—even with $60 billion a year—to achieve full competency with secrets. It would be ludicrous to entrust them with creating the very "rival store" they have fought bitterly to defeat all these years. Congress and the public need an Open Source Agency to serve as an honest broker for what can be know using legal sources.

Chapter 13: How NOT to Spend The Taxpayer's Treasure

Congress needs a Congressional Public Intelligence Office to help it understand the ten threats, twelve policies, and eight challengers as a system of systems. The Executive is not going to do that for Congress, but the Smart Nation Act could dramatically improve all oversight missions, by providing for both open source and secret intelligence support to each Congressional jurisdiction.

Chapter 10:
OSINT Honors

Lifetime Awards (First 12 in 2006)[112]

Alvin & Heidi Toffler

Alvin and Heidi Toffler are the original researchers, visionaries, cartographers, path-finders, and mentors for a legion of pioneers who have created the future. The writing is but the tip of the their influential iceberg--their personal relationships worldwide, and the manner in which they inspire and introduce special people to one another, is without equal in this world.

Mrs. Kathy Steele, Saint

Mrs. Kathy L. Steele has been, since 1988, "home base" for her husband Robert, and mother to three children conceived and raised amidst the turmoil, sweat, tears, and consequences of one man's fight to restore common sense to the U.S. Intelligence Community and other intelligence communities. Her loyalty, tolerance, good humor, and enormous capacity for dealing with uncertainty mark her as a saint. Nothing accomplished by her husband would have been possible without her unwavering support.

Mr. Arno "The Curious" Reuser

Mr. Arno Reuser, Arno the Curious, is a Master Librarian who has done more for the practice of Open Source Intelligence (OSINT) in support of national security than anyone else in Europe. He has been a pioneer in the exploitation of badly-delivered OSINT from private sector vendors, writing original PERL programs to make sense of their feeds; he has known how to make the most of the Internet; and above all, he has known how to find and engage human intellects around the world, each capable of producing unique tailored knowledge not available online or in print. He is the Master Librarian of the OSINT world and all seven intelligence tribes.

---

[112] All awards, including photographs or seals for recent years, and links where provided, can be seen online at www.oss.net by clicking on OSINT Honors in the lower left column of the Home Page.

Robert Young Pelton

Mr. Robert Young Pelton is perhaps the greatest journalist-adventurer on the planet. This is a man that gets kidnapped by accident, is recognized by the leader of the kidnappers, and is promptly released with apologies and an honor guard. His book *World's Most Dangerous Places* and his TV series *Come Back Alive* are among the most extraordinary "ground truth" offerings available to the public and admired by the spies. In his every waking moment, in his every action, in his every report, he embodies the true spirit of Open Source Intelligence (OSINT).

Dr. Joseph Markowitz

Dr. Joseph Markowitz is without question the most qualified Open Source Intelligence (OSINT) pioneer in the ranks of those presently in or retired from U.S. government service. As the only real chief of the Community Open Source Program Office (COSPO) he tried valiantly to nurture a program being systematically undermined by both the leadership and the traditional broadcast monitoring service. When he moved on to advise the Defense Science Board, he served America well by helping them fully integrate the need for both defense open source information collection and exploitation, and defense information sharing with non-governmental organizations. His persistent but diplomatic efforts merit our greatest regard.

Dr. Ran Hock

Dr. Ran Hock has done more than any single individual to educate both government and private sector parties with respect to the value of the deep web. He has single-handedly trained hundreds of individuals in the nuances of this major new intelligence resource base. Emphasizing individual analytic skills and common sense rather than arcane expensive and generally unproductive technologies, he represents the intersection of integrity, intelligence, and intuition in the service of all legitimate governments and organizations.

Professor Robert Heibel

Professor Robert Heibel, a veteran of the Federal Bureau of Investigation, is unique for having established both an undergraduate and a graduate program in intelligence and research analysis. His pioneering efforts have provided varied intelligence communities with very high-quality individuals, properly trained, at a time when their respective countries need them badly. His development of

154

training materials that did not exist, of a training program that did not exist, of a philosophy of education in the national service that did not exist anywhere else at the time, is worthy of the highest regard.

Mr. Ben Harrison, OSINT Pioneer

Mr. Ben Harrison is a master of both the military bureaucracy, and the global open source intelligence (OSINT) world. He has been a pioneer in all respects--helping the larger Department of Defense Community understand OSINT; creating innovative solutions for his own Command, the U.S. Special Operations Command; and helping teach others about the basics of OSINT. Within the U.S. Department of Defense, he is the tip of the spear for DoD OSINT.

Detective Steve Edwards, MBE, UK

Detective Steve Edwards, Member of the British Empire, has been the foremost law enforcement pioneer in the field of Open Source Intelligence (OSINT), and it is with heartfelt admiration that we applaud his recent recognition by the Queen of England. His gentle, self-effacing, sober appreciation of the nuances of crime, private sector offerings, and government needs for innovation have enabled him to bring disparate personalities and capabilities together in a most effective manner.

LCdr Andrew Chester, RN, Canada

LCdr Andrew Chester, RN, Canada, has distinguished himself, first, as a pioneer for the exploitation of Open Source Intelligence (OSINT) within and throughout the North Atlantic Treaty Organization (NATO) and the Partners for Peace (PfP), and subsequently as a trainer and practitioner with an especially constructive influence upon the international military environment.

Dr. Vint Cerf, Parent of the Internet and Mentor to Google

Dr. Vinton Cerf, one of several founding parents of the Internet, inspiration to the global Internet Society, and today a mentor to Google, which seeks to place all information at the disposal of the people of the world, is without question one of a handful of individual who have impacted on every person's life, whose life's work could be said to prove the point that information can deter conflict and create stabilizing indigenous wealth.

Mr. Mats Bjore, Sweden

There is no other person who has created a national open source intelligence capability, with recognition from the Royal War Academy for doing so; then gone on to rationalize McKinsey knowledge management in the Nordic region, then created the foremost international commercial intelligence practice in InfoSphere AB, and concluded with the creation of Silobreaker, a combination of sources and tools that takes the information industry to a new level. Mats Bjore is the ultimate Long Range Reconnaissance Philosopher-Warrior.

Mr. Steve Arnold
For his constant demonstration of the utility of Open Source Intelligence (OSINT) in the understanding of social networks, emerging technologies, and cultural realities. As a world-renowned authority on information and communications, with a deep understanding of the public policy value of open source information, he has made himself available around the world, and had much more influence than most realize. His publication of the book, "The Google Legacy," is a mere milestone in one of the most distinguished information careers in the world.

Golden Candle Awards (annual distinctions)

Scotland Yard, Specialist Crime Directorate
IOP '06. For their continuing diligence and professionalism in handling the difficult tactical and strategic needs of law enforcement intelligence operations aimed at disrupting and deterring terrorists, arms merchants, and other organized criminals. With special recognition for Mr. Colin Ehren and Mr. Chris Stock, their accomplishments in using Open Source Intelligence (OSINT) to nurture public safety and order, set the standard for all others.

Prof. Michael Andregg, Chief OSINT Shrink (USA)
IOP '06. For academic excellence and support to the dual concepts of Open Source Intelligence (OSINT) across all seven tribes of intelligence, and the urgent need for intelligence reform, inclusive of a psychological re-orientation away from compartmented lunacy and toward inclusive openness. Professor Andregg embodies the concept of Information Peacekeeping--conflict deterrence and stabilizing wealth creation through the sharing of open information in all languages.

Mr. Estolano "Ben" Benavides, U.S. Army Master Trainer

IOP '06. To Mr. Estolano "Ben" Benavides, for being the original Open Source Intelligence (OSINT) ranger and pathfinder for the Long Gray Line long before OSINT became fashionable. As an original contributor to the paper on open source information exploitation for the military intelligence officer under the leadership of LtCol Rob Simmons, USAR (today Congressman Rob Simmons, R-CT-02), and as a Master Trainer who catalogs useful web sites spanning all topics where open source information can contribute to Army and defense policy, operations, acquisitions, and logistics, Ben Benavides is not only in a class by himself, he is "the class before 1."

Mr. Scott Bird, Mr. Scott Bird

IOP '06. For over ten years, as a strictly personal interest, Mr. Scott Bird has studies Open Source Intelligence (OSINT) and its potential utility to increasing state revenue by detecting fraud and waste, and in reducing state costs by identifying faster, better, cheaper alternatives. This year his work culminated in an extraordinary presentation of his personal views to an international audience of government and industry, views that were validated and appreciated by all present. He is a pioneer in state-level OSINT applications, and recognized as such by the award of this Golden Candle.

Ms. Karen George, UK Government Senior Librarian, Home Office

IOP '06. For innovation and leadership at the national government level, inclusive of vision and integrative direction in the library professional, with the direct consequence of developing and enhancing an environment of enthusiasm and appreciation for Open Source Intelligence (OSINT) by civil servants and government officers in the United Kingdom.

Dr. Edvard Jacob, Chief OSINT Shrink (Rest of World)

IOP '06. From the very early days of the emerging Open Source Intelligence (OSINT) movement, Dr. Edvard Jacob understood that it represented a psychological and sociological "break-out" from the lunacy of compartmented secret intelligence. Over the years he has ministered to the many souls that have sought liberation and enlightenment by recognizing OSINT for what it is: a return to sanity and common sense, of, by, and for the people.

Mr. Kevin Scheid, Staff, 9-11 Commission

IOP '06. To Mr. Kevin Scheid, Senior Intelligence Service, for his sustained professionalism in studying shortfalls related to national access to open sources of information of potential intelligence value, and in working very hard to

157

introduce constructive recommendations at the national level. While serving as senior staff to the Commission on the Roles and Capabilities of the United States Intelligence Community, he contributed to their finding: "severely deficient" and their recommendation, "top priority for funding." It was not until the 9-11 Commission, however, that his diligence finally prevailed, with the inclusion on page 413 of the Report of an independent Open Source Agency. Mr. Scheid is one of a handful of individuals who have truly served America with distinction in this vital arena where all nations and organizations are able to share intelligence.

Congressman Rob Simmons, (R-CT-02)
IOP '06. To Congressman Rob Simmons (R-CT-02), who, as a pioneer in the 1990's, won his first Golden Candle as a Lieutenant Colonel commanding an open source unit, later officially recognized as the "Best Small Unit in the US Army Reserve. As a Congressman, elected in 2000, he has been diligent and faithful to the Republic in pressing for open source intelligence (OSINT) reform across both the defense and the homeland security communities. There is no more influential champion for public intelligence and open source information exploitation serving the U.S. Government today.

United Nations, Institute for Disarmament Research (UNIDIR)
IOP '06. Under the leadership of Dr. Patricia Lewis, and in pursuit of the basic mission of the United Nations Institute for Disarmament Research (UNIDIR), the development of "ideas for peace and security," this organization has demonstrated sustained excellence in the exploitation of open sources of information, and in the development of new forms of internal information management and external information sharing, that suggest it is a potential catalyst for a surge in United Nations capabilities to leverage information to deter and resolve conflict, to reduce weapons of mass destruction as well as small arms and other contributing capabilities to genocide and instability, and to increase the prospects for peace across the many regions beset by complex emergencies that reduce human security.

Sweden, Swedish Military Academy & Swedish National Defence College
IOP '06. With the strong support of General Håkan Syrén, Supreme Commander of the Swedish Armed Forces, and under the operational direction of Col Jan-Inge Svensson, Sweden has become the global leader and trusted third party of choice for peacekeeping intelligence conferences and training. Their conference in December 2004 set the stage for publication of the book,

second in the series, "PEACEKEEPING INTELLIGENCE: The Way Ahead," and their planned two-month course in peacekeeping intelligence, to be offered in March-April of each year to both uniformed personnel and non-governmental organization (NGO) specialists, assure their continued leadership in this vital endeavor that seeks to ensure Force Commanders have adequate strategic, operational, tactical, and technical intelligence from all sources, but especially open sources of information.

Croatia, Mr. Mario Profaca

IOP '06. To Mr. Mario Profaca, Croatian independent journalist, investigative reporter and war correspondent as well as a globally-recognized WWW pioneer, *for* "Mario's Cyberspace Station" web site, a OSIF goldmine and OSINT tool featured in Encyclopedia Britannica, MSN Encarta Encyclopedia, mainstream media, net guides and university digital libraries world wide. Working as a sort of "One Man Agency", Mr. Profaca is also owner and editor of Spy News OSIF/OSINT Newsletter with 1600+ subscribers and searchable archive of more than 60,000 items related to intelligence. Investigative journalist and OSINT minded, he is very fast in searching the internet and picking up underreported news and sources related to intelligence and terrorism. He represents the future of public intelligence.

The Netherlands, MajGen Patrick Cammaert, Royal Marines

IOP '06. MajGen Cammaert is recognized for his extraordinarily diplomatic and diligent furtherance of common sense and understanding at the highest levels of United Nations leadership, with respect to both the generic value of the process of intelligence to peacekeeping and conflict avoidance, and the specific value of open sources of information, including geospatial information, useful to the strategic mandate, the operational force composition, and the tactical campaign. As Military Advisor to the Secretary General from 2003-2005, and then as Force Commander of UN Forces in the Congo, he devised and began implementation of the regional United Nations Joint Military Analysis Centre (UN JMAC) program. His leadership with respect to a common standard of intelligence training for all UN civilian and uniformed personnel are likely to have a considerable impact on the future effectiveness of peacekeeping operations.

South Africa, Military and Civilian Intelligence Community

IOP '06 Under the general leadership of Minister of Intelligence Services Ronnie Kasrils, in partnership with an extraordinary collection of individuals across all elements of the South African intelligence community, and across all countries in the continent of Africa, successfully implemented both an open source software strategy, and an early warning and open source information sharing strategy. Their continental initiative, in its openness, low cost, and mutually beneficial architecture, sets the standard for multinational, multiagency, multidisciplinary, multidomain information sharing (M4 IS).

STRONG ANGEL, Defense Advanced Research Projects Agency
IOP '06. To the STRONG ANGEL team of the Defense Advanced Research Projects Agency (DARPA, for its extraordinary early grasp of the importance of both open source software and open source information as a means of enabling close collaboration and information-sharing in near-real-time between overt elements of the U.S. Government and all non-governmental organizations and their personnel who are the most important and skilled contributors to stabilization & reconstruction operations.

Open Source Exploitation Branch, U.S. Special Operations Command
IOP '06. To the Open Source Exploitation Branch of the U.S. Special Operations Command, and especially contract employees David Dillow, Angela Neale, and Matt Puls, who have excelled at devising open sources and methods supportive of national, theater, and tactical missions.

USDI, Office of the Undersecretary of Defense for Intelligence
IOP '06. To the Office of the Undersecretary of Defense for Intelligence (USDI) for the extraordinary strategic vision and transformative impact of Dr. Stephen A. Cambone's integrated approach to Strategic Communication, Open Source Intelligence (OSINT), and Joint Inter-Agency Collaboration Centers (JICC). Under his leadership and that of LtGen William "Jerry" Boykin, USA, the extraordinary professionalism of Col Vincent Stewart, USMC has produced a "tipping point" initiative that will harness the distributed unclassified intelligence of the non-governmental organizations, other governments, and private sector partiers such that we will achieve the objective of universal coverage, 24/7, in all languages, at sub-state levels of granularity (tribes and villages).

Dr. Douglas M. Johnston

OSS '04: To Dr. Douglas M. Johnston, president and founder of the International Center for Religion and Diplomacy, for his path-finding efforts with regard to Preventive Diplomacy as well as Religion and Conflict Resolution. Among his many works, two stand out for defining a critical missing element in modern diplomacy: *Religion, the Missing Dimension of Statecraft* (Oxford University Press, 1994), and *Faith-based Diplomacy*: Trumping Realpolitik (Oxford University Press, 2003). He has restored the proper meaning of faith qua earnestness instead of faith qua zealotry, and this is a contribution of great importance.

Dr. Bert Little
OSS '04: To Dr. Bert Little, Medical and Scientific Researcher and Administrator, in recognition of applied research (data warehousing and mining, and other scientific investigation methods) in financial fraud and evidence based medicine. His research has saved hundreds of millions of dollars in both arenas, both beneficial to the citizen-taxpayer. He is the author of over one hundred medical and scientific journal articles, over a dozen book chapters, and of four books, with two additional books in press. Currently he is Associate Vice President for Research and Professor of Computer Science and Mathematics, Tarleton State University, Texas A&M University System.

Johns Hopkins University Applied Physics Laboratory
OSS '04: To the JHU-APL, and especially to Capt Joseph Mazzafro, USN (Ret) and Dr. Michael Vlahos, for sustained excellence in the integration of Open Source Intelligence (OSINT) into their complex all-source analytic efforts in support of the Department of Defense. Aided by the Gibson Library, they have set a new standard.

Mr. Paul van Tongeren
OSS '04: To Mr. Paul van Tongeren, leader, educator, advocate, and pioneer in the prevention and resolution of conflict. As Executive Director of the European Centre for Conflict Prevention, his is a critical voice in facilitating peace through hinter-disciplinary study, cross-cultural communication, and the creation of Open Source Intelligence (OSINT).

Dr. Paul Ray
OSS '04: To Dr. Paul Ray, anthropologist, sociologist, political scientist, economist, and moralist, for his integrative and sustained efforts to understand and connect the power of the people to the problems of the Earth. He has

161

identified and studied 50 million Americans interested in changing the world, now known as the New Progressives.

Mr. William Greider
OSS '04: To Mr. William Greider, perhaps America's most effective voice in favor of moral behavior. His investigative journalism, national correspondence, and authorship, including *Who Will Tell the People, One World, Ready or Not*, and most recently, *The Soul of Capitalism: Opening Paths to a Moral Economy*, all empower the public.

Mr. David Kaplan
OSS '04: To Mr. David Kaplan, for his extraordinary exploitation of legal and ethical sources of information in the pursuit of investigative journalism on behalf of *U.S. News & World Report*. His studies of North Korean government corruption and of Saudi Arabian government sponsorship of terrorism, represent the best practices in his field.

Mr. Steve Denning
OSS '04: To Mr. Steve Denning, organizational storyteller extraordinaire, whose book, *The Springboard: How Storytelling Ignites Action in Knowledge-Era Organizations*, represents a new level of innovation and action in the field of Knowledge Management, one operationalized by himself within the World Bank, offering ideas instead of money.

Dr. Herman E. Daly
OSS '04: To Dr. Herman E. Daly for his early role as a founder of the field of Ecological Economics, including his leadership role in the creation of the journal for this area of ethical study, and his body of work including *Steady-State Economics* (1977) and the most recent *Ecological Economics and the Ecology of Economics* (1999).

Dr. Tore Bjorgo
OSS '04: To Dr. Tore Bjorgo, Senior Research Fellow of the Norwegian Institute of International Affairs (NUPI), for his leadership of research on terrorism and international crime. His authorship/editorship of ten books in the field represents the best combination of open sources, scholarship, and operationally-useful intelligence.

Mr. Tom Atlee

OSS '04: To Tom Atlee, founder of the Co-Intelligence Institute, for his sustained leadership in the vanguard of an informed democracy. His book, *The Tao of Democracy: Using Co-Intelligence to Create a World that Worlds for All* is in the best traditions of Thomas Jefferson, who said "A Nation's best defense is an educated citizenry."

Canadian Association for Security and Intelligence Studies (CASIS)
OSS '03: For its role as the premier professional intelligence association in the world, bringing together both scholars and practitioners for the purpose of understanding and improving the professionalization of intelligence. Open to all nations, and reflecting the extraordinary role that Canada can play as a neutral friend to all, CASIS embodies the principle, (in the words of its current President, Tony Cambell) that "the truth is so important, it must be protected by a bodyguard of professionals."

Republic of South Africa, National Intelligence Unit
OSS '03: For its renewed national commitment to the creation of both an inter-agency open source intelligence architecture, and a regional early warning network heavily reliance on multi-lingual and multi-media open sources of information. As Africa is now so clearly a test of global responsibility, the South African intelligence initiatives represent both a model for others to follow, and a portal through which other nations might make contributions while gaining access to localized intelligence about Africa's many complex emergencies.

Mr. Jack Davis, Central Intelligence Agency (Retired)
OSS '03: For a lifetime of leadership and innovation in the craft of all-source intelligence analysis, beginning with the creation of the "Friends of Analysis" online forum in the 1980's, the definition of new forms of analytic tradecraft in the 1990's, and--in the opening years of the 21st Century--the identification of new forms of value-added open source intelligence supportive of the all-source intelligence process.

Mr. James Hardee & Mr. Ben Harrison, U.S. SOCOM
OSS '03: For persistence and innovation in devising low-cost and responsive open source intelligence solutions in support of both all-source intelligence and sensitive global operations. In documenting that open sources can meet forty percent of the intelligence needs of a global command, they have established a

163

compelling justification for the funding of independent open source intelligence capabilities at every level of government.

Mr. Mats Bjore, InfoSphere A.B. (Sweden)

OSS '03: For his personal leadership, over the course of a decade, in establishing the Swedish military open source intelligence unit; in revitalizing knowledge management practices in the Nordic business intelligence world; and in creating new means of meeting global intelligence partnership needs through shared multi-lingual data capture and online secure information sharing protocols.

MajGen Patrick Cammaert, Royal Netherlands Marine Corps

OSS '03: For his sustained service at all levels of command to United Nations forces, culminating in his appointment as Military Advisor to the Secretary General of the United Nations, where he has established a "best practices" unit and strives to implement the recommendations of the Brahimi Report as they pertain to the establishment of the new craft of peacekeeping intelligence.

Mr. Peter Modafferi, Chief of Detectives, Rockland County, New York

OSS '03: For his continuing efforts, within the International Association of Chiefs of Police (IACP), to gain recognition for the value of intelligence to state, local, and tribal law enforcement.

Dr. Simon J. Pak and Dr. John S. Zdanowicz, Penn State University and Florida International University

OSS '03: For their extraordinary demonstration, with a tangible value to the public of $50 billion a year in tax fraud savings, of new methods of academic investigation into public trade records, and the consequent discovery of specific instances of import-export money laundering and financial fraud, as well as weight variances associated with the smuggling of contraband and the mis-representation of cargo.

Mr. Yossef Bodansky, Author & Researcher

OSS '03: For his global multi-lingual open source investigations into terrorism, and his extraordinary professional achievement in writing and publishing *BIN LADEN: The Man Who Declared War on America,* years before the 9-11 World Trade Center demonstration of what well-funded suicidal terrorism can achieve when intelligence and policy both fail to focus on the threat.

Mr. Tom Copeland, LEXIS-NEXIS
OSS '03: For his sustained assistance to law enforcement
government clients seeking to make better use of open sources c
and his emerging contributions to the study of the new craft of int
specific reference to terrorism.

Mr. Johan Truyens, Belgium
OSS '03: For his earnest and insightful contributions to the
intelligence, and specifically for his investigation for and writin
Ph.D. dissertation to focus on defining and enhancing the role of
intelligence in the affairs of the state, and of the United Nations.

Mr. Arno Reuser, Military Intelligence, The Netherlands
OSS '03: For his inspired leadership in migrating
military intelligence library from an archival to a discovery c
include value-added programming of incoming streams of raw d
virtual organization of distributed open source expertise.

Mr. David Jimenez, Texas Association of Crime & Intelligence A
El Paso, Texas, 17 September 2002: 21st Century Emerging Leaders
Mr. David Jimenez, Texas Association of Crime & Intelligence Ar
his deep personal commitment and inspired professionalism ii
together over 400 individuals from the six major intelligence tribes
military, law enforcement, state & local, business, & academic--to di
open and unrestricted manner the new challenges and directions of in

Global Futures Partnership, Central Intelligence Agency
OSS '02: 21st Century Emerging Leadership Award. Global
Partnership, Central Intelligence Agency. Under the leadership
Dumaine with her extraordinary vision, the Global Futures Partne
created strategic learning forums bringing the rich perspectives of th
world into the classified environment in a manner never before attemp
official but revolutionary endeavor nurtures an outside-in cha
integrating a diversity of perspectives. It is a vanguard toward a future
the lines between national and global intelligence, and between gove
and nongovernmental intelligence, are blurred into extinction.

165

. David Moore and Ms. Lisa Kirzan, National Security Agency, USA
S '02: Mr. David Moore and Ms. Lisa Kirzan. For their personal
mmitment to nurturing intelligence education and the craft of intelligence
lysis, in part by studying, defining, and then promulgating "best practices"
m both within the government and from the external private sector.

r. Leonard Paul, Community Open Source Program Office
S '02: Mr. Leonard Paul, Chief of Operations, Community Open Source
gram. For his personal commitment to upholding the Director of Central
elligence Directive (DCID) mandating a Community Open Source Program
OSP); and for nurturing the Open Source Information System (OSIS),
cing the interests of the larger Community above any lesser considerations.

r. William Hann, BSc (Hons), Free Pint
r. William Hann, BSc (Hons), Founder and Managing Editor, Free Pint. For
s extraordinary personal effort in creating a community of over 48,000
lunteers who share information about information at www.freepint.com. He
a true open source cyber-citizen and intelligence minuteman, at the forefront
peer-to-peer computing, a model for us all.

Ir. Joseph V. Latella Sr., Land Information Warfare Activity (LIWA), .S. Army
Ir. Joseph V. Latella Sr., Land Information Warfare Activity. OSS '02: For his
reless effort as Chief, Open Source Division, in creating the first
perationally-focused open source cell to provide timely, relevant, and unique
upport to globally-deployed members of the Intelligence and Security
ommand (INSCOM) of the U.S. Army. His new initiatives in media and trend
nalysis as well as Internet data harvesting have contributed directly to both
Iomeland Security and the Global War on Terrorism.

Ir. Richard Klavans, Center for Research Planning
SS '02: Dr. Richard Klavans, President, Center for Research Planning. For his
ubstantial contributions to the field of Industrial Technical Intelligence, where
e has defined "best practices" and advanced the state of the art; and for his
eadership in nurturing the discipline of business intelligence and the Society of
Competitive Intelligence Professionals.

166

Mr. William Crislip, National Ground Intelligence Center, U.S. Army
OSS '02: Mr. William Crislip, National Ground Intelligence Center. For his persistent and effective leadership, management of scarce resources, integration of open source into all-source analysis and establishment of one of the very few stable open source programs in the U.S. Department of Defense.

Foreign Military Studies Office (FSMO), Joint Reserve Intelligence Center, Fort Leavenworth
OSS '02: Foreign Military Studies Office, Joint Reserve Intelligence Center, Fort Leavenworth. For establishment of the Emerging Threat centers of excellence with emphasis on open source information, to include the establishment of a flexible World Basic Information Library and the direct support of operations by the Joint Forces Command Headquarters Homeland Security Open Source Intelligence Team based in the Ft. Leavenworth Joint Reserve Intelligence Center.

Strategic Studies Institute, U.S. Army War College
OSS '02: U.S. Army War College Strategic Studies Institute. For consistent excellence in providing the leadership of the U.S. Army and the Department of Defense with provocative, thoughtful, open source information at the strategic level, and for building bridges between the U.S. military and the global strategic community. The efforts of Dr. Steve Metz, with his work on future war and strategic asymmetry, and Dr. Max Manwaring, with groundbreaking analysis of global instability and internal war, are especially noted.

Open Source Unit, Defence Command, Norway
OSS '02: Open Source Unit, Defence Command, Norway. For their innovation and discipline in establishing a uniquely effective means of monitoring open sources in over 29 languages including Dari, Farsi, and Pashto.

European Centre for Conflict Prevention, The Netherlands
OSS '02: European Centre for Conflict Prevention. For their consistent and superior efforts to make open sources of information more readily available to those who deal with conflicts and humanitarian emergencies, to include their surveys of conflict prevention and peace building activities, and their lessons learned. Their web site, www.conflict-prevention.net, is a global resource.

Mr. Guy Kolb, Society of Competitive Intelligence Professionals (SCIP)
OSS '01: Association Executive Mr. Guy Kolb. For his sustained and arduous efforts, from 1994 to 2000, as the first professional Executive Director of the Society of Competitive Intelligence Professionals (SCIP). His recruitment and management of staff and his innovative and energetic efforts led to a growth of SCIP from 2000 to 7000 members, and a growth in annual revenues from $0.5M to over $4M a year. He is the "first facilitator" of the new discipline of business intelligence, and has brought great credit to the American Society of Association Executives (ASAE).

Maj Kristan Wheaton, USA, *The Warning Solution*
OSS '01: Major Kristan Wheaton, U.S. Army. For restoring the tradition of the statesman-warrior, and bringing to bear a unique combination of intellect, legal training, faith in the military virtues, and a deep familiarity with the many sources of conflict in the Balkan and Aegean regions. In particular, Maj Wheaton is recognized for his incisive and essential documentation of the deep chasm between early warning reports from the analyst at the front, and the attention span of the preoccupied Commander-in-Chief—his book, The Warning Solution: Intelligent Analysis in the Age of Information Overload, may come to be regarded as "Ref A" for commanders and their intelligence professionals in the 21st Century.

Mr. William Shawcross, Author, United Kingdom
OSS '01: Author-Pilgrim William Shawcross. If our new Secretary of State, General Colin Powell, might be willing to listen to just one voice, his is the voice that must be heard. Few have done more to personally investigate and then accurately report the terrible suffering and instability that characterizes the vast majority of the planet's population, and few have presented so cogently the complexities and subtleties of peacekeeping and operations other than war.

Robert Young Pelton, Come Back Alive, Discovery TV
OSS '01: Adventurer Robert Young Pelton. For the finest, deepest, most useful individual effort at collecting and reporting "ground truth" in an open, usable, reliable manner. His work is an inspiration—and a very tough baseline—that no diplomatic, military, or intelligence organization has yet been able to match in terms of either relevance or cost effectiveness.

168

Researcher A.J. Jongman, Interdisciplinary Research Programme (PIOOM), Leiden University, The Netherlands
OSS '01: Researcher A. J. Jongman, Leiden University. For a brilliant combination of research, insight, and data visualization, in partnership with those associated with the Interdisciplinary Research Programme (PIOOM), resulting in the creation of the World Conflict & Human Rights Map 2000 that portrays so effectively the global conditions of instability that no great nation can ignore.

Mr. James Bamford, Author, *The Puzzle Palace, Body of Secrets*
OSS '01: Mr. James Bamford, Author. For extraordinary investigative journalism over the course of an entire career, but in particular for two signal contributions to the literature of intelligence—The Puzzle Palace (1982) and Body of Secrets (2001). Each of these served both the public and the National Security Agency by bringing to light both the heroism and vital contributions of its cyberspace warriors, and the deficiencies in government requiring repair. To have penetrated this target using only legal and ethical means—open sources— is a testament to the author's skill.

Service de Renseignements, Ministere d'Etat, Luxembourg
OSS '01: Service de Renseignements, Ministere d'Etat, Luxembourg. For the wisdom of its leadership in recognizing and acting upon the opportunity to create a "Smart Nation" by openly consulting and embracing its business, academic, professional association, and foreign embassy counterparts, and in particular for the creation of a permanent open forum.

CINC Open Source Advisory Council (COSAC), U.S. DoD
OSS '01: CINC Open Source Advisory Council (COSAC). For efforts to significantly improve the acquisition and exploitation of open sources information relevant to operational planning and mission execution.

Supreme Allied Commander, Atlantic (SACLANT), North Atlantic Treaty Organization (NATO)
OSS '01: Supreme Allied Commander, Atlantic (SACLANT). For expeditious and enlightened leadership as the vanguard of the future intelligence architecture for the Atlantic alliance, with a strong vision for the future intelligence needs of the Partners for Peace as well as the Mediterranean Dialog nations, and in particular for the rapid establishment of the NATO Open Source Intelligence Working Group.

British Broadcasting Corporation (BBC), United Kingdom
OSS '01: British Broadcasting Corporation (BBC) Monitoring. For sustained excellence in multi-media monitoring and the effective use of unclassified information, and in particular for setting the very highest standards for global multi-media monitoring and the rapid effective commercial dissemination of their production.

Dr. Dominic J. Farace, GreyNet (The Netherlands)
OSS 21 ('00): Dr. Dominic Farace, founder and leader of GreyNet, and the foremost champion of Grey Literature acquisition and exploitation.

Mr. Philippe Lejeune, Interpol and Belgium
OSS 21 Mr. Philippe Lejeune, graduate of the Master's program in open source intelligence exploitation offered by Mercyhurst College, and now the open source focal point for Interpol, for his persistence in pursuing an unpopular idea. As an individual, he is now the "fourth musketeer" within the European law enforcement open source leadership.('00):

Commander, Joint Intelligence Center, U.S. Transportation Command
OSS 21 ('00): U.S. Transportation Command, presented to the Commander, Joint Intelligence Center, for his leadership and the accomplishments of his subordinates in establishing a new model for austerely integrating active duty, reserve, and commercial capabilities to produce open source intelligence in support of a global mission in lower tier countries.

Director of Intelligence and Information Operations, U.S. Special Operations Command
OSS 21 ('00): U.S. Special Operations Command, presented to the Director of Intelligence and Information Operations Center for his leadership and the accomplishments of the Joint Intelligence Center in establishing the first operationally-focused Open Source Cell to provide timely, relevant, and unique support to U.S. Special Operations Forces

Satellite Centre, Western European Union
OSS 21 ('00): Satellite Centre of the Western European Union for its role in demonstrating that regional intelligence has great value, and that commercial imagery and open sources comprise the most essential foundation for such regional intelligence.

Open Source Intelligence Centre, Ministry of Defence, United Kingdom
OSS 21 ('00): United Kingdom, presented to the Open Source Information Centre for its role in expanding the original concept beyond the Ministry of Defence to include the Home Office and Law Enforcement Agencies.

National Intelligence Service and Ministry of Defense (Joint Award), Republic of Germany
OSS 21 (00): Republic of Germany, presented jointly to the BND and the Ministry of Defense for their collaborative effort in creating an inter-agency OSINT architecture.

OSS '99: None awarded.

Office of Strategic Crime Assessments, Australia
EuroIntel '99: Office of Strategic Crime Assessments, Australia, for its establishment of an open source intelligence support programme that is a model for others to follow.

National Intelligence Service, The Netherlands
EuroIntel '99: National Intelligence Service, The Netherlands, for its definition of and advocacy of a European Open Source Intelligence Network.

EUROPOL, European Community
EuroIntel '99: EUROPOL, newly authorized as an independent regional agency, for its definition and advocacy of a regional open source intelligence network in support of European law enforcement.

LtCol Ian Wing, Chief of Defence Force Fellow, Australia
PacIntel '99: LtCol Ian Wing, Chief of Defence Force Fellow, Australia, for his leadership and intellectual accomplishments in both authorship on intelligence reform and in the creation and management of Australia's 1998 conference on open source intelligence, an event that brought together over 300 senior participants from across the entire Australian government.

LCdr Sean Connors, USN, Virtual Information Center, U.S. Pacific Command
PacIntel '99: LCdr Sean Connors, USN, for his role in the development of the Virtual Information Center, U.S. Pacific Command (J-08), a non-intelligence

activity sufficiently impressive to have been added to the Battle Staff of the Commander-in-Chief, U.S. Pacific Command.

Colonel Barbara Fast, U.S. Army, 66th Military Intelligence Brigade
OSS '98: Colonel Barbara Fast, Commanding Officer, 66th Military Intelligence Brigade, because her senior enlisted personnel insisted we recognize her leadership in exploiting open sources.

Autometric (Now Boeing Autometric), United States of America
OSS '98: Autometric, Inc. for its development of a robust process for integrating all forms of commercial imagery with national imagery to produce digital three-dimensional geospatial information and intelligence.

National Intelligence Community, Republic of South Africa
OSS '98: The National Intelligence Community of South Africa for its extraordinary renaissance including its successful integration of black revolutionaries into a previously white bastion of secrecy.

Mr. Tom Will, Defense Intelligence Agency, USA
OSS '98: Mr. Tom Will, Open Source Program Manager, Defense Intelligence Agency, for spending over $10 million dollars in interesting ways.

Dr. Mark Maybury, MITRE
OSS '98: Dr. Mark Maybury, leader of MITRE's Open Source Processing Research Initiative (OSPRI), for his efforts to develop an integrated web-based system for knowledge development and information-sharing.

Mr. Harry Collier, Infonortics Ltd., United Kingdom
OSS '98: Mr. Harry Collier, founding and Managing Director of Infonortics Ltd.; founder of the Association for Global Strategic Information, and a leading practitioner of open source intelligence in support of business and technical objectives.

Captain Patrick Tyrrell, RN OBE LLB, Ministry of Defence, United Kingdom
EuroIntel '98: Captain Patrick Tyrrell, RN OBE LLB, Commandant, Defense Intelligence and Security School, for his sponsorship of the open source intelligence movement within the Ministry of Defence, and his authorship of the seminal paper on a NATO/PfP Open Source Intelligence Programme.

i2 Ltd., United Kingdom
EuroIntel '98: i2, Ltd., and in particular to Mr. Mike Hunter, Managing Director, for developing data visualization technology contributing to improved open source exploitation processes.

Metropolitan Police of London (Scotland Yard), United Kingdom
EuroIntel '98: Metropolitan Police of London, United Kingdom, and Detective Constable Steve Edwards, for the establishment of the open source intelligence unit within the Intelligence Division, and the extraordinary savings achieved through the use of open sources instead of surveillance team to locate assorted felons and suspects.

National Center for Missing & Exploited Children, United States of America
EuroIntel '98: National Center for Missing & Exploited Children, United States of America, and Mr. Ruben Rodriguez Jr., Director of the Exploited Child Unit, for developing new methods of using the Internet to find and return missing and exploited children to their parents.8:

Ministry of the Interior, The Netherlands
EuroIntel '98: The Ministry of the Interior, The Netherlands, for its open source program under the direction of Mr. Frans de Ridder, and particularly its unique status as the only open source unit in the world that is co-equal to clandestine and technical collection units and under the same director of collection.

Open Source Intelligence Long Range Reconnaissance Unit, Swedish Military Intelligence & Security Directorate
EuroIntel '98: Swedish Military Intelligence & Security Directorate, for its establishment of the Long Range Reconnaissance Patrol unit for cyber-space, and its development of innovative methods of discovering and exploiting the 80% of the Internet that is not indexed. LtCol Mats Bjore, Founder and Leader.

Servizio Centrale di Investigazione sulla Criminalità Organizzata, Republic of Italy
EuroIntel '98: Servizio Centrale di Investigazione sulla Criminalità Organizzata (SCICO) della Guardia di Finanza, for its emerging commitment to the use of open sources in the war on organized crime.

173

SPOT IMAGE S.A., Republic of France

EuroIntel '98: SPOT IMAGE S.A. (France), for its uniquely robust commercial imagery architecture including two satellites and seventeen ground stations, an offering that was of enormous value during the Gulf War.

Mr. Jurgen Storbeck and Mr. Frans-Jan Mulschlegel, EUROPOL Drugs Unit

EuroIntel '98: EUROPOL Drugs Unit, under Mr. Jurgen Storbeck as implemented by Mr. Frans-Jan Mulschlegel, for its establishment of a broad open source intelligence exploitation program.

Madame Danielle Cailloux, Comite Permanent de Controle des Services de Renseignements, Belgium

EuroIntel '98: Madame Judge Danielle Cailloux, Member of the Comite Permanent de Controle des Services de Renseignements, for her leadership in introducing open source intelligence into Belgian legislation on intelligence reform, and promulgating understanding of open sources of intelligence among senior leaders in the European community.

Commission on Secrecy, United States of America

OSS '97: Commission on Secrecy for its examination of relative transaction costs between classified and open sources. Note: Senator Daniel Patrick Moynihan (D-NY) served as sponsor and chairman. Mr. Eric Beal, Staff Director.

Maritime Administration, Department of Transportation, USA

OSS '97: Maritime Administration, Department of Transportation, for publication of the Maritime Security Report series using open sources

Loyola College, Maryland, USA

OSS '97: Loyola College in Maryland for the Strategic Intelligence web site that serves as a model for a voluntary but substantive web-based resource useful to all students of the intelligence profession.

Monterey Institute of International Studies, United States of America

OSS '97: Monterey Institute of International Studies, for its open source research model using graduate students with native language fluency to screen and extract multi-lingual open source information on proliferation.

Intelligence Community Librarians Committee, United States of America
OSS '97: Intelligence Community Librarians Committee, for innovation in open source exploitation in the face of institutional resistance.

Sergeant Elliot Jardines, United States Army Reserve
OSS '97: Sgt Elliot Jardines, U.S. Army Reserve, for the publication of Open Source Quarterly and his individual attempts to popularize open sources.

Mr. Maurice Botbol, Intelligence Newsletter
OSS '97: Mr. Maurice Botbol, founder and managing editor of the Intelligence Newsletter, the best open source on global intelligence organizations.

Mr. Stephen Aftergood and Mr. John Pike, Federation of American Scientists
OSS '97: Mr. Stephen Aftergood and Mr. John Pike, Federation of American Scientists, for the Secrecy Bulletin and the Intelligence Reform web site.

Dr. Vipin Gupta and Mr. Frank Pabian, Sandia National Laboratory
OSS '97: Dr. Vipin Gupta and Mr. Frank Pabian, for their extraordinary paper on using commercial imagery to study Indian nuclear testing

Ms. Alice Cranor, Defense Intelligence Agency
OSS '97: Alice Cranor, DIA OSINT program manager and innovator, for her constant advocacy of open source intelligence in support of science and technology collection requirements.

Aspin-Brown Commission, United States of America
OSS '96: Commission on the Roles and Missions of the U.S. Intelligence Community, for its documented findings that U.S. Intelligence Community access to open sources is severely deficient and should be a top priority for funding and a top priority for DCI attention. Note: The Honorable Les Aspin and then, upon his death, The Honorable Harold Brown, served as Chair. Mr. Britt Snider, Staff Director. Ms. Phyllis Provost-McNeil orchestrated the testimony and edited the findings on open source intelligence.

Swedish Open Source Cooperation Forum, Sweden
OSS '96: Swedish Open Source Cooperation Forum, for informally bringing together the civilian, military, business, and academic open source intelligence

coordinators, and creating the first national-level coordinating body for the collection of open sources.

Ministry of Defence, United Kingdom
OSS '96: Ministry of Defence, United Kingdom, for the establishment of the Open Source Information Centre in Whitehall.

Canadian Security and Intelligence Service, Canada
OSS '96: Director General, Canadian Security and Intelligence Service, for publishing unclassified intelligence and attempting to make optimal use of international open sources of information.

Community Open Source Program Office, Office of the Director of Central Intelligence
OSS '96: Community Open Source Program Office, Office of the Director of Central Intelligence, for establishing the Open Source Information System.

Captain Patrick George, Central Bureau of Investigation, Belgium
OSS '96: Captain Patrick George, Head, Criminal Analysis Bureau, Central Bureau of Investigation, Belgium, for establishing an open source intelligence analysis unit and an open source intelligence network across all of Belgium.

Mr. Abram Hoebe, Criminal Intelligence Division, The Netherlands
OSS '96: Mr. Abram Hoebe, Criminal Intelligence Division, The Netherlands, for innovative exploitation of open sources in countering transnational crime in and around the port of Rotterdam.

Mr. Robert Heibel, Mercyhurst College
OSS '96: Mr. Robert Heibel, founding Director, Research and Intelligence Analysis Program, Mercyhurst College, for getting international law enforcement organizations interested in open source intelligence, and for training students in open sources and methods.

Mr. John W. Fisher III, Defense Intelligence Agency
OSS '96: Mr. John W. Fisher III, COTR for Open Source Intelligence Training, Joint Military Intelligence Training College, for his sponsorship of the OSINT HANDBOOK.

Col James "Snake" Clark, USAF, United States Air Force
OSS '96: Colonel (Select) James "Snake Clark, Project Manager for EAGLE VISION, for working around the bureaucracy and delivering a C-130 transportable ground station through which commercial imagery could be immediately exploited by tactical commanders and air crews.

SPOT Image Corporation, United States of America
OSS '95: SPOT Image Corporation (USA), for its extraordinary overnight support of "The Burundi Exercise" that was instrumental in persuading the Aspin/Brown Commission that open source intelligence is a discipline in its own right.

LEXIS-NEXIS, United States of America
OSS '95: LEXIS-NEXIS, for its extraordinary overnight support of "The Burundi Exercise" that was instrumental in persuading the Aspin/Brown Commission that open source intelligence is a discipline in its own right.

Institute for Scientific Information, United States of America
OSS '95: Institute for Scientific Information, for its extraordinary overnight support of "The Burundi Exercise" that was instrumental in persuading the Aspin/Brown Commission that open source intelligence is a discipline in its own right.

Jane's Information Group, United Kingdom
OSS '95: Jane's Information Group, for its extraordinary overnight support of "The Burundi Exercise" that was instrumental in persuading the Aspin/Brown Commission that open source intelligence is a discipline in its own right.

Ms. Helen Burwell, Association of Independent Information Professionals
OSS '95: Ms. Helen Burwell, Publisher, Burwell World Directory of Information Brokers, for her pioneering role in creating the Association of Independent Information Professionals and the international network of professional information brokers.

Mr. Chris Goggans, Electronic Security Engineer
OSS '95: Mr. Chris Goggans, Electronic Security Engineer, for "stuff".

177

Col Mike Pheneger, U.S. Army (Ret.), U.S. Special Operations Command
OSS '95: Col Mike Pheneger, USA (Ret.), former J-2 U.S. Special Operations Command, for his paradigm-shattering unclassified exposures of our lack of tactical military maps for 90% of the world, and our enormous over-investment in duplicative and contradictory orders of battle.

National Technical Information Service, United States of America
OSS '95: National Technical Information Service, for is development of both a web-based electronic access capability and a distributed remote printing agreement with Kinko's.

Mr. Winn Schwartau, Interpact and InfoWarCon
OSS '95: Mr. Winn Schwartau, Author, INFORMATION WARFARE: Chaos on the Electronic Superhighway, for being the first person in America to brief Congress on the possibility of an electronic "Pearl Harbor", and for his sustained efforts to create concepts and doctrine for asymmetric conflict. »

Dr. Stevan Dedijer, Office of Strategic Services and University of Lund
OSS '94: Dr. Stevan Dedijer, Office of Strategic Services in Yugoslavia, originator of the field of business intelligence as a discipline, and over-all "wild man" of open source intelligence.

Dr. Douglas Englebart, Pioneer (Internet, Desktop Tools, Collaborative Work)
OSS '94: Dr. Douglas Englebart, Inventor, for creating the tools that made possible the Internet and all that followed from electronic mail, graphics, hyper-links, and mice; and for his current commitment to distributed online collaborative work.

Mr. Emmanuel Goldstein (P), 2600: The Hacker Magazine, and Hackers on Planet Earth
OSS '94: Emmanuel Goldstein, Leader of 2600 hacker community, for his creation of a hacker journal and his sponsorship of the Hackers on Planet Earth conference in New York City that brought over 750 phreakers out in the open.

Dr. James Holden-Rhodes, Los Alamos National Laboratory and University of New Mexico
OSS '94: Dr. James Holden-Rhodes, author of SHARING THE SECRETS: Open Source Intelligence and the War on Drugs, for his extraordinary development of the early open source intelligence techniques applied to foreign language materials and contributing to the strategic and tactical success of both the U.S. Southern Command and the Drug Enforcement Agency.

Dr. Ross Stapleton-Gray, Central Intelligence Agency
OSS '94: Dr. Ross Stapleton-Gray, CIA Internet guru and policy entrepreneur, recognized by the National Science Foundation as one of America's premier cyber-nauts.

Mr. Tim Hendrickson and PATHFINDER, National Ground Intelligence Center, U.S. Army
OSS '94: U.S. Army Project PATHFINDER, under the leadership of Mr. Tim Hendrickson of the National Ground Intelligence Center, for moving forward with the objective of creating a useful analyst's toolkit.

434th Military Intelligence Detachment, United States Army

OSS '94: U.S. Army 434th Military Intelligence Detachment, for its creation of the first general overview of the utility of open sources to the military. LtCol Rob Simmons, Commanding. [Today Congressman Rob Simmons (R-CT-02)]

Ministry of the Interior, The Netherlands
OSS '94: Ministry of the Interior, The Netherlands, for its establishment of an official open source intelligence unit, the first known unit to exist in Europe, and for its development of the centralized discovery, decentralized exploitation model for Internet data mining.

Dr. Loch Johnson, Regent Professor, University of Georgia
OSS '94: Dr. Loch K. Johnson, dean of the intelligence reform movement, for his lifetime of achievement but especially for his seminal article, "The Seven Sins of Strategic Intelligence".

Mr. David Young, Oxford Analytica
OSS '94: Mr. David R. Young, founder of Oxford Analytica, for creating a viable variation of the President's Daily Brief using only open sources of

information and addressing the needs of Chief Executive Officers and Prime Ministers.

Mr. Rop Gonggrijp, Hac-Tic and Internet Service Provider <xs4all>
OSS '93: Mr. Rop Gonggrijp, Dutch leader of the Hac-Tic group, founder of <xs4all>, for his role as one of the leaders of the movement to both open and protect international networks.

Mr. William McDonald, Hacker-Engineer
OSS '93: Mr. William McDonald, Hacker-Engineer, for "stuff".

Mr. Roger Karraker, "Highways of the Mind" in *Whole Earth Review*
OSS '93: Mr. Roger Karraker, Author of "Highways of the Mind" in *Whole Earth Review*, the seminal work inspiring the grass roots hijacking of the National Information Infrastructure.

Mr. Samuel Mercier, France
OSS '93: Mr. Samuel Mercier, advocate for open source intelligence in France and contributor to an understanding of open sources by key French military generals and admirals.

Mr. Paul Hoffman, Earthseal Entrepreneur
OSS '93: Mr. Paul Hoffman, EarthSeal Entrepreneur, for creating an affordable sticker of the NASA photograph of the Whole Earth that inspired an entire generation of environmentalists and others committed to openness.

Mr. John Berbrich, Defense Intelligence Agency
OSS '93: Mr. John Berbrich, Director for Science & Technology, Defense Intelligence Agency, for his attempts to sponsor improved open source exploitation within the defense intelligence community.

Mr. Alessandro Politi, Western European Union
OSS '93: Mr. Alessandro Politi, developer of "Intelligence Minuteman" concept and one of the leading advocates of open source intelligence within the Western European Union.

MajGen Ken Minihan, USAF, U.S. Air Force
OSS '93: MajGen Ken Minihan, Assistant Chief of Staff for Intelligence, U.S. Air Force, for his attempts to sponsor improved open source exploitation with respect to Chinese telecommunications and other matters.

Mr. William Ruh, The MITRE Corporation
OSS '93: Mr. William Ruh, The MITRE Corporation, for his work on advanced information technology processing initiatives with enormous potential for improving our ability to exploit open sources.

Ms. Bonnie Carroll, Information International Associates, Inc.
OSS '92: Ms. Bonnie Carroll, President, Information International Associates, Inc. for pioneering efforts with the National Federation of Abstracting and Indexing Services, and her role as Secretariat to the CENDI (Commerce, Energy, NASA, Defense, Interior) Working Group on Information .

Ms. Diane Webb, Central Intelligence Agency
OSS '92: Ms. Diane Webb, Analyst, Office of Scientific & Weapons Research, CIA, for developing the functional requirements for CATALYST (Computer Aided Tools for the Analysis of Science & Technology).

Mr. George Marling, U.S. Intelligence Community Staff
OSS '92: Mr. George Marling for his earlier role in developing the HUMINT Committee Open Source Study for the U.S. Intelligence Community.

Chapter 11:
OSINT References

This document, with hot links, is available at www.oss.net/LIBRARY.

Year	Country	Focus	Speaker/Author	Description
9999	ZZ	AAAwards	Steele	Golden Candle Awards & Lifetime Achievement Awards
2006	US	AABiography	Steele	Two-Page Biography for OSS CEO Robert Steele
9999	ZZ	AABook Lists	Steele	Steele's Lists of Books Re Info, Intel, Threat, Strategy, Blowback, etc.
9999	ZZ	AABook Reviews	Steele	Steele's Non-Fiction Reviews Relevant to National Security
2005	US	AABook Top	Steele	Top Books on Intelligence Reform
2003	US	Academic	Andregg	State of the Academic Tribe (Slides)
2003	US	Academic	Andregg	State of the Academic Tribe (Text)
1998	FR	Academic	Baumard	Learned Nations & Knowledge Strategies
1995	US	Academic	Bender	The Information Highway: Will Librarians Be Left by the Side of the Road?
1998	FR	Academic	Bonthous	Culture: The Missing Intelligence Variable
1993	US	Academic	Etheredge	National Knowledge Strategies in the IC and the Library of the Future
1995	US	Academic	Heibel	Research and Intelligence Analyst Program (RIAP) at Mercyhurst College
1993	US	Academic	Jacso	A Proposal for Database 'Nutrition and Ingredient' Labeling
1994	US	Academic	Kahin	New Laws for Government & Business Operations in Cyberspace
1999	US	Academic	Lepingwell	Center for Nonproliferation Studies, MIIS (Briefing Slides)

183

1994	US	Academic	Liddy	An Intelligent Digital Librarian
1997	GE	Academic	Mayer-Kress	The World Brain
1999	UK	Academic	Ostle et al	Oxford Analytica Contact Information of Special Study on Islam
2003	US	Academic	Pak & Zadanowicz	Estimate of Lost Tax Revenues (Text)
2003	US	Academic	Pak & Zadanowicz	Transfer Pricing Import-Export Tax Avoidance Fraud ($50B/Year in US)
1993	US	Academic	Toffler	Keynote Address to OSS '93 (Transcript)
2002	US	Analysis	Andregg	Intelligence-Academia Relationship
2003	US	Analysis	Andregg	Wisdom versus Intelligence
2005	SE	Analysis	Bjore	Sample SILOBREAKER Slides
2003	US	Analysis	Davis	Analytic Paradoxes: Can OSINT Help?
1999	US	Analysis	Hueur	The Psychology of Intelligence Analysis
1999	US	Analysis	Madison	OSINT and Analysis (One Slide)
2003	US	Analysis	Medina	21st Century Analysis
2003	US	Analysis	Moore	Analytic Competencies
1955	US	Analysis	NA	Discovering and Understanding Elites
2005	US	Analysis	OSS	Menopause Memo
1992	US	Analysis	Shepard	Intelligence Analysis in the Year 2002
1999	US	Analysis	Steele	Future of Analysis (Two Slides)
1993	US	Analysis	Whitney-Smith	Analysis for Information Revolutions: Dynamic Analogy Analysis
2003	US	Article	Aviram & Tor	Overcoming Impediments to Information Sharing
1997	US	Article	Dearth	The Future of Intelligence: Global to National, Civic & Technical
2005	US	Article	Gordon	Nothing to Fear from Europe
2005	US	Article	Gordon	Letter to Europe
2004	US	Article	Grossman	Col GI Wilson in Iraq
1993 ?	US	Article	Steele	AFIO: Reinventing Intelligence: From Truth, Power
1998	US	Article	Steele	Asymmetric Warfare: The Big Picture (published in JFQ)
1998	US	Article	Steele	JFQ/AWC: TAKEDOWN: The

184

				Asymmetric Threat to the Nation
1999	US	Article	Steele	Colloquy: Reflections on Intelligence and the End of the Cold War
1999	US	Article	Steele	Muddy Waters, Rusty Buckets, the USN in 21st Century
1999	US	Article	Steele	Reinventing Intelligence: From Truth, Power
1999	US	Article	Steele	Muddy Waters, Rusty Buckets: Skeptical Assessment of Naval Future
1999	US	Article	Steele	SASA: Reflections on Intelligence and the End of the Cold War
2003	US	Article	Steele	TIME: The New Craft of Intelligence, Need for Open Source Agency
2005	US	Article	Steele	Interview with AMU Student
2005	US	Article	Steele	Response to Senator Chambliss in Parameters
2006	US	Article	Steele	National Security in the 21st Century: An Alternative to Idiocy
2006	US	Article	Steele	Interview Questions & Answers for Military Review
2006	US	Article	Steele	Theory and Practice of Intelligence: Challenging the DNI to a Duel
2006	US	Article	Steele	Intelligence Affairs: Reactionary, Evolutionary, or Revolutionary?
2006	US	Article	Steele	Intelligence in Denial 1.9
2006	US	Article	Steele	Re-Inventing Intelligence (3 pages with illustrations)
2006	US	Article	Steele	FORBES: Reinventing Intelligence with Sidebar 1, Print Version
2006	US	Article	Steele	FORBES: Sidebar 2 10 Threats DNI 17.5% (Not Published by Forbes)
2006	US	Article	Steele	FORBES: Sidebar 3 12 Steps to Collective Intelligence (Not Published)
1995 ?	US	Article	Steele & Horowitz	The Dark Side of OSINT (Threat to Operations Security)
2004	US	Article	Wilson	Col GI Wilson on Iraq
2006	US	Book	Steele	Free Full Text of Book, *NEW CRAFT OF INTELLIGENCE*
2002	US	Book Review	Steele	NONE SO BLIND by George Allen

185

2002	US	Book Review	Steele	SECRETS by Daniel Ellsberg
2006	US	Book Review	Steele	Who the Hell Are We Fighting? By Michael Hiam
2006	US	Book Reviews	Steele	Reflections on Poverty and Collective Intelligence (Assorted Reviews)
2006	US	Book Reviews	Steele	Reflections on Poverty and Collective Intelligence
2002	US	Books	Steele	Top Twenty Intelligence Books as of 2002
2004	US	Books	Steele	Overview of Books on Information Society
2004	US	Books	Steele	Overview of Books on Politics, Leadership, and Future
2004	US	Books	Steele	Overview of Books on Strategy & Force Structure
2004	US	Books	Steele	Overview of Books on Intelligence as Process and Profession
2004	US	Books	Steele	Overview of Books on Emerging Threats
2004	US	Books	Steele	Overview of Books on Blowback, Dissent, Anti-Americanism
1992	US	Budget	Donahue	National Funding Directions for Open Source Intelligence
1999	UK	Budget	Steele	Observations on the Intelligence Budget
2003	US	Budget	Steele	SASC One-Pager on Recommended DoD OSINT Investment Strategy
2005	US	Budget	Steele	$2 Billion a Year Obligation Plan for Open Source Agency
2006	US	Budget	Steele	Open Source Agency Budget of $2 Billion a Year
2006	US	Budget	Steele	Commercial Imagery Spending Plan
2000	US	Business		Technology Intelligence from Patents
1994	US	Business	Basch	Secrets of the Super-Searchers: A Personal and Practical Perspective
1996	US	Business	Bates	Recent and Emerging Trends in Information Brokering
1998	FR	Business	Baumlin	Black, White, Gray, Realities of the Investigative Marketplace
1999	FR	Business	Baumlin	Espionage or Business Intelligence:

186

				Nuances of Gray
1994	Switz	Business	Bernhardt	Tailoring Competitive Intelligence to Executive Needs
2003	SE	Business	Bjore	Reinventing Commercial Intelligence
2004	SE	Business	Bjore	Commercial Intelligence
1997	BE	Business	Borry & Sohl	Electronic Sources & Methods: A Belgian Business Perspective
1998	US	Business	Boyer	Assessing US and Other Space Imaging Options for European Needs
1998	GE	Business	Bruckner	Information and Knowledge Management in Intelligence Situations
1998	US	Business	Burwell	Commercial Online Source Validation Methods
1993	US	Business	Caldwell	International Investigative Market (Slides)
1993	US	Business	Caldwell	International Investigative Market (Text)
1996	US	Business	Call	Realities & Myths Regarding Financial Research Using Open Sources
1994	UK	Business	Collier	Global Information Industry and a New Information Paradigm
1998	UK	Business	Collier	The Pricing of Electronic Information
1999	UK	Business	Collier	Overview of New Horizons in OSINT Sources, Softwares, Services
1993	SE	Business	Dedijer	Europe's To BI or not to BE: Inventory of a New Business Innovation
1998	US	Business	Dunn	Confronting the Future of the Information Industry
1993	US	Business	Elias	An Overview of the Information Industry in 1993
1998	Israel	Business	Feiler	Open and Personal: Economic Intelligence in the Middle East
1993	AU	Business	Fraumann	Business is War
1993	US	Business	Herring	Business Intelligence: Some Have It, Some Don't--How They Do It
1995	US	Business	Herring	Business Intelligence in Japan and Sweden: Lessons for the US
1995	US	Business	Herring	Intelligence to Enhance American

187

				Companies' Competitiveness
1995	US	Business	Herring	Using the Intelligence Process to Create Competitive Global Advantage
1993	US	Business	Himelfarb	Intelligence Requirements for Executives
1994	US	Business	Himelfarb	Introduction to Competitive and Business Intelligence
1992	US	Business	Hlava	Information Industry Corporations (Partial Listing)
1992	US	Business	Hlava	Selected Professional and Trade Associations in Information
1992	US	Business	Hlava	The Information Industry: Impact of Globalization
1998	US	Business	Horowitz	Economic Espionage and OSINT: Legal and Security Implications
1994	US	Business	Kelly	ASIDIC Perspectives & Its Contributions to National Competitiveness (S)
1994	US	Business	Kelly	ASIDIC Perspectives & Its Contributions to National Competitiveness (T)
2002	US	Business	Klavans	Identifying Commercial Opportunities from Emerging Science
1996	US	Business	Kolb (SCIP)	Sales Pitch for the Society of Competitive Intelligence Professionals
1994	US	Business	Marcinko	Association of Information and Dissemination Centers, Case Studies
1992	US	Business	Meyer	Business Intelligence at the Cutting Edge
1999	US	Business	Miller	The Year the Information Industry Hit Bottom
1993	US	Business	Monaco & Gerliczy	Economic Intelligence and Open Source Information
1992	US	Business	Nobel	From A to Z: What We've Done with Open Sources
1999	US	Business	Robinson	How Mobil Uses Open Sources & Services
1994	US	Business	Shaker	Beating the Competition: From Boardroom to War Room
1992	US	Business	Shaker &	Intelligence Support to U.S. Business

188

			Kardulias	
1994	US	Business	Shaker & Rice	From War Room to Board Room
1994	US	Business	Sharp	How to Identify Changes that Threaten Your Business Activity, In Advance
1993	JP	Business	Shima	Overview of Japanese Media and Information Systems
1996	US	Business	Sibbit	Emerging Business Models for Commercial Remote Sensing
1995	US	Business	Simon & Blixt	Emerging Issues in Competitive Intelligence
1993	US	Business	Splitt	The U.S. Information Industry: Changing the 21st Century
1994	US	Business	Stanat	The Power of Global Business Information
1998	US	Business	Stara	Valuing Competitive Intelligence
1993	US	Business	Steele	Corporate Role in National Competitiveness
1993	US	Business	Steele	The Intelligence Community as a New Market
1994	US	Business	Steele	Germany: ACCESS: Theory and Practice of Competitor Intelligence
1994 ?	US	Business	Steele	ASIDIC: Intelligence Community as a New Market
1996	US	Business	Steele	Concise Directory of Selected International Open Sources & Services
1996	US	Business	Steele	Open Source Intelligence Handbook, Chapter 1, Overview
1997	US	Business	Suggs	International Trade & Commerce Intelligence Search Strategies (Slides)
1997	US	Business	Suggs	International Trade & Commerce Intelligence Search Strategies (Text)
2000	US	Business	Sullivan	Business Perspective on Essential Overseas Information
1992	US	Business	Williams	OSINT to Create Intelligence in a Commercial Environment
1998	US	Business	Yankeelov	Pushing the Assets of Time and Knowledge
2000	US	Chapter	Steele	Presidential Intelligence: Specifics on Intelligence Reform

189

2001	US	Chapter	Steele	AWC: Threats, Strategy, & Force Structure: An Alternative Paradigm
2001	US	Chapter	Steele	Alternative Paradigm for National Security
2002	US	Chapter	Steele	New Rules for the New Craft of Intelligence
2003	US	Chapter	Steele	Information Peacekeeping & The Future of Intelligence
2004	US	Chapter	Steele	Peacekeeping Intelligence 1.2 (for Swedish Conference on PKI)
2006	US	Chapter	Steele	Strategic Intelligence: Open Source Intelligence (Edited by Loch Johnson)
2006	US	Chapter	Steele	Handbook on Intelligence: OSINT (Edited by Loch Johnson)
2004	US	Collective Intel	Atlee	Definitions of Collective Intelligence
2004	US	Collective Intel	Atlee	National Collaboration Wiki (on Any Topic)
2005	US	Collective Intel	Atlee	Great Quotes on Collective Intelligence
2005	US	Collective Intel	Atlee	Strands of Collective Intelligence
2005	US	Collective Intel	Atlee	World Café Process
2005	US	Collective Intel	Atlee	World Café Book Reivew
2005	US	Collective Intel	Atlee	Update of June 2005
2005	US	Collective Intel	Atlee	On Public Engagement
1995	US	Comments	Steele	National and Corporate Security in the Age of Information
1997 ?	US	Comments	Steele	HUMINT Successes, Failures, and Possibilities
2001	US	Comments	Steele	National Intelligence: Are We Getting Our Money's Worth? NO!
2001	US	Comments	Steele	National Intelligence: Are We Getting Our Money's Worth?
2003	US	Comments	Steele	Alternative State of the Union Address

2005	US	Comments	Steele	On Collective Intelligence and the Denmark Initiative
2006	US	Comments	Steele	Greater Democracy: Citizens Party Parts I and II
2006	US	Comments	Steele	Greater Democracy.org: Citizens Party I & II
2002	US	Community	Steele	Outline for Ten Books on Seven Intelligence Communities of Interest
2003	US	Fantasy	Steele	Alternative State of the Union Address
2003	US	Geospatial	East View	Iraq Post-Conflict Map Availability
2004	US	Geospatial	East View	Aceh Indonesia 1:50,000 Tactical Map Availability
2004	US	Geospatial	East View	Aceh Indonesia 1:250,000 Large Scale Map Availabiility
2005	US	Geospatial	East View	Sudan Tactical Map Availability
2005	US	Geospatial	East View	Liberia Tactical Map Availability
2005	US	Geospatial	East View	Ivory Coast Tactical Map Availability
2005	US	Geospatial	East View	DRC Congo Russian Map Availability
2005	US	Geospatial	East View	DRC Congo Large Scale Map Availability
2005	US	Geospatial	East View	DRC Congo NIMA 250K Map Availability
2005	US	Geospatial	East View	DRC Congo National 200K Map Availability
2005	US	Geospatial	East View	Burundi Tactical Map Availability
2005	US	Geospatial	East View	Afghanistan Military Maps
2005	US	Geospatial	East View	Eastern Congo Priority Tactical Map Deficiencies
2003	US	Geospatial	NAPA	Geographic Information for the 21st Century
1999	US	Geospatial	Steele	Real-World Mapping Shortfalls (Two Slides)
1997	UK	Government	Andrew	Presidents, Secret Intelligence, and Open Sources
1998	NL	Government	BVD	Annual Report of the National Security Service
1998	BE	Government	Cailloux	Belgian Observations on Intelligence Oversight
1998	BE	Government	Cailloux	Report of the Intelligence Oversight

191

				Committee
1994	US	Government	Carroll	Harsh Realities: S&T Acquisition Costs, Obstacles, and Results
1997	US	Government	Carroll	CENDI Information Managers Group
1994	AU	Government	Chantler	Producing Intelligence in Australia: H National Open Source Foundation?
1998	FR	Government	Clerc	Economic Intelligence
1999	US	Government	Coile	Information Overlay for Preparing & Coping with Local Disasters
1992	US	Government	Cotter	NASA Open Source Intelligence Requirements & Capabilities (Slides)
1992	US	Government	Cotter	NASA Open Source Intelligence Requirements & Capabilities (Text)
1998	US	Government	Dearth	Government and the Information Marketplace
1994	US	Government	Devost	Digital Threat: United States National Security and Computers
2002	US	Government	FSMO	Foreign Military Studies Office
1999	CA	Government	George	OSINT: Islamic Unrest in China
1997	US	Government	Haakon	Commercial Imagery Options and Trade-Offs
1993	SE	Government	Heden & Dedijer	The State of the National Intelligence and Security Community of Sweden
1999	US	Government	Heidenrich	Genocide Web Sites (At the Time)
1999	US	Government	Heidenrich	Sample Daily Briefing on Genocide
1997	US	Government	Hodge	CENDI: Help! Impact of the Internet on the Consumer
1998	US	Government	Hughes	FBIS 1995-1998: Transition and Transformation
1992	US	Government	Johnson	NTIS Open Source Intelligence Requirements & Capabilities
1997	US	Government	Johnson	National Technical Information Center
1996	US	Government	Kalil (NEC)	Leveraging Cyberspace
1997	US/ UK	Government	Kerr & Herman	Does the Intelligence Community Have a Future? (Two Items in One)
1992	US	Government	Keyworth	Government as a Customer in the Digital Age
1998	US	Government	Lee	Letter to HPSCI Urging Attention to Commercial Mapping Technology
1998	SE	Government	Leijonhelm	OSINT and Information Sharing

				Between Government & Industry
1996	US	Government	Lucas (COSPO)	The Open Source Information System
1995	US	Government	Markowitz	Community Open Source Program Office (COSPO), Report on the Program
1999	UN	Government	Marks	Proposal for Integrated Regional Information Networks (IRIN)
1992	US	Government	McConnell	Planned Revisions to Circular No. A-130
1992	US	Government	Molholm	The CENDI Paradigm: How Some Federal Managers Have Organized
1992	US	Government	Mortimer	LC FRD Open Source Intelligence Requirements & Capabilities
1998	S. Africa	Government	Mti	OSINT, the African Renaissance, and Sustainable Development
1999	US	Government	OSS	Proliferation Web Sites (At the Time)
1999	US	Government	OSS	Sample Daily Briefing on Proliferation
1995	US	Government	Peters	INADEQUATE ANSWERS: Bureaucracy, Wealth, & Mediocrity (US IC)
1999	NL	Government	Reserved	OSINT: Foundation for Co-Ordination and Information Sharing
1992	US	Government	Riddle	FBIS Open Source Intelligence Requirements & Capabilities
1997	US	Government	Robideau	Department of Energy Technical Information Program
1999	US	Government	Sanz	Nuclear Terrorism Literature Since 1992
1998	GE	Government	Schlickman	Ensuring Trust and Security in Electronic Communications
1999	US	Government	Sovereign	Information Sharing for the Lower End of the Spectrum
1992	US	Government	Steele	Information Concepts & Doctrine for the Future
1998	US	Government	Steele	INFORMATION PEACEKEEPING: The Purest Form of War
1998	US	Government	Steele	Strategic Issues in National and Regional Intelligence & Security

193

1998	US	Government	Steele	Clandestine Human Intelligence Successes, Failures, Possibilities
1999	US	Government	Steele	Relevant Information: New Approach to Collection, Sharing, Analysis
1999	US	Government	Steele	Web-Based Concept for a Global Information Sharing Environment
2000	US	Government	Steele	Spies and Secrecy in an Open World
1998	US	Government	Steele (in French)	Strategic Intelligence in the USA: Myth or Reality?
1999	CA	Government	Stout & Quiggin	OSINT: High Resolution Imagery for Anyone
1992	US	Government	Studeman	Teaching the Giant to Dance
1994	US	Government	Wiener	The Intelligence Community: An Outsider's View
1999	AU	Government	Wing	Optimizing Open Source Information Sharing in Australia
1999	AU	Government	Wing	OSINT in Australia: The Report
2006	SA	Government	Yekelo	African Early Warning
1997	US	Handbook	Admin	Cover, Appreciation, Foreword, Contents
1997	US	Handbook	Horowitz	Appendix G: Open Source OPSEC: Selected References and Information
1997	US	Handbook	Horowitz	Chapter 6. Open Sources and Operational Security--The Dark Side
1997	US	Handbook	OSS	Appendices (List of)
1997	US	Handbook	OSS	Appendix B-3: Glossary of Open Source Acronyms
1997	US	Handbook	OSS	Appendix E-2: Internet: Intelligence-Oriented List of Useful Internet Sites
1997	US	Handbook	PC Magazine	Appendix E-3: Internet: Intel Sites from PC Magazine's Top 100 Web Sites
1997	US	Handbook	Stapleton-Gray	Appendix E-1 Internet: Self-Guided Tour
1997	US	Handbook	Stapleton-Gray	Chapter 4. The Internet as a Tool for All-Source Analysis
1997	US	Handbook	Steele	Appendix A: White Paper on Open Source Intelligence & the Military
1997	US	Handbook	Steele	Appendix B-1: Talking Points on Private Enterprise Intelligence
1997	US	Handbook	Steele	Appendix B-2: Complete Paper on

194

				Private Enterprise Intelligence
1997	US	Handbook	Steele	Appendix B-4: Core Open Source References
1997	US	Handbook	Steele	Appendix C: Access: Theory and Practice of Intel in the Age of Information
1997	US	Handbook	Steele	Appendix D: Concise Directory of Selected Int'l Open Sources & Services
1997	US	Handbook	Steele	Chapter 1. Overview of Open Sources & Services
1997	US	Handbook	Steele	Chapter 2. Access: Intelligence in the Age of Information
1997	US	Handbook	Steele	Chapter 3. International Open Sources and Services
1997	US	Handbook	Steele	Chapter 5. Open Sources and Military Capabilities
1997	US	Handbook	Steele	Chapter 7. Conclusion: Collection and Processing Open Source
1997	US	Handbook	USMC & Steele	Appendix F-1: Expeditionary Environment R&A Framework & Model
1997	US	Handbook	USMC & Steele	Appendix F-2: Mission Area Factors Summary
1997	US	Handbook	USMC & Steele	Appendix H: Expeditionary Factors Study: List of Countries
1997	US	Handbook	Wouters	Appendix E-4: Internet: How to Find an Interesting Mailinglist
1989	US	History	CIA/OSWR, Webb	CATALYST (Computer Aided Tools for the Analysis of S&T)
1991	US	History	Harvard JFK Panel	US Intelligence and American Enterprise
1992	US	History	IC	IC Task Force Vision for OSINT
1995	US	History	Los Alamos	Los Alamos Lab on OSINT
1995	US	History	Simmons	Congressman Simmons (then Major) on OSINT and DIA
1989	US	History	Steele	Operationalization Portion of Steele Thesis on Revolution
1992	US	History	Steele	CIM and Transformation (to Paul Strassman, DirInfo DoD)
1993	US	History	Steele	God, Man, and Information: Invited

				Rant to INTERVAL
2004	US	History	Steele	The OSINT Story 2.1 in RTF
2004	US	History	Steele	The OSINT Story 2.1 in Word Doc
1992	US	History	Steele & USMC	Derogatory Comments, Line by Line, on Decrepit IC Vision for OSINT
1992	US	History	STIC	STIC on OSINT
1989	US	History	USMC	USMC Response to IC Data Call on OSINT
1989	US	History	USMC	Core Documents on OSINT (186 Pages)
1992	US	History	USMC	USMC on OSINT
1992	US	History	USMC	USMC on IC Survey re OSINT
1992	US	History	USMC	USMC Comments on IC Task Forces
1992	US	History	USMC	USMC Comment on IC OSINT
1992	US	History	Wallner	OSINT Requirements Memo
2006	US	Illustration		Pentagon of Influence Emergent Around Free Universal Access to Info
2000 ?	US	Illustration	French TV	Steele Head and Shoulder Photograph (GIF)
2004	US	Illustration	Hayden & Steele	Connecting the Dots from Bottom Up Instead of Top Down
1976	US	Illustration	Steele	Revolutionary Prediction & Analysis Matrix
1979	US	Illustration	Steele	Great Ideas (144) Illustration in Context with One Another
2002	US	Illustration	Steele	Best available current photograph, courtesy of French television
2006	US	Illustration	Steele	Stoplight Chart on Ten Threats, Twelve Polcies, Eight Challengers
2006	US	Illustration	Steele	Levels and Domains of Analysis
2000	GE	Imagery	Asbeck	Western European Satellite Centre
2006	US	IO Analysis	Steele	IO Analysis 101 (Five Slides with Notes)
2006	US	IO Conepts	Corman et al	Strategic Communications Concepts for Dealing with Jihadists
2006	US	IO Intel	Stewart	InfoOps and Intelligence
2006	US	IO Multination	Steele	Multinational Information Operations Center (Brief to Coalition CENT)
2006	CA	IO Technical	Garigue	Technical Preface to IO Book by Steele
2006	US	IO The	Steele	Information Operations: The Book

196

		Book		Briefing
2005	US	Iraq	Anon	Gates of Fire: Photographs from Iraq
2004	US	Iraq	Cordesman	Post Conflict Lessons for Iraq (Premature Assumption Conflict Over)
2003	US	Iraq	Lind	Bill Lind on Three Possible Outcomes in Iraq
2006	US	Iraq	McCaffrey & Steele	General McCaffrey's Report on Iraq, with Steele Comments
2002	CA	Issues	Fyffe	A Canadian Perspective on Global Issues
1999	US	Issues	Heidenrich	Early Warning of Genocide:The Utility of Open Sources
2001	NL	Issues	Jongman	World Conflict & Human Rights Map 2000-2001
2004	US	Issues	Ray	The New Political Compass
2004	US	Issues	Spinney	Israel's Theft of Arab Water and Need for Regional Water Authority
2001	US	Issues	Wallach	FP Interview with Lori Wallach on Immoral Capitalism
2004	US	Knowledge	Scheitle	Knowledge Management
1995	US	Law Enforcement	Campen	National Drug Intelligence Center (NDIC), NDIC Open Source Summary
1996	US	Law Enforcement	Campen (NDIC)	Open Source Connection and Processing in Support of Law Enforcement
1996	US	Law Enforcement	Cascallar (FBI)	Foreign Language Operational and Training Issues for Law Enforcement
2000	UK	Law Enforcement	Crow	International Open Source Realities in Law Enforcement
1998	IT	Law Enforcement	Cucuzza	Globalization: Consequences and Risks
1999	UK	Law Enforcement	Edwards	Scotland Yard OSINT (Text)
2000	UK	Law Enforcement	Edwards	Information Overload (Slides)
2000	UK	Law Enforcement	Edwards	Information Overload (Text)
2000	UK	Law Enforcement	Edwards	Information Overload (Viewgraphs)

197

2003	UK	Law Enforcement	Edwards	OSINT at Scotland Yard (Slides)
2003	UK	Law Enforcement	Edwards	OSINT at Scotland Yard (Text)
1995	US	Law Enforcement	Farwell	Brain Fingerprinting (Article)
1995	US	Law Enforcement	Farwell	Brain Fingerprinting (Patent)
1998	US	Law Enforcement	FBI	Innocent Images: Child Pornography & Sexual Exploitation Online
1998	UK	Law Enforcement	Fry	OSINT & Law Enforcement: Learning Curves & Pain Barriers
2000	BE	Law Enforcement	George	OSINT in the Belgian Gendarme
1992	US	Law Enforcement	Holden-Rhodes	Open Source Intelligence in the War on Drugs
1997	UN	Law Enforcement	IALEIA	Intelligence-Led Policing: International Perspectives
1999	BE	Law Enforcement	Lejeune	INTERPOL OSINT
1996	US	Law Enforcement	Lodge (FINCEN)	OSINT Measures Against Financial Crime Targets
2000	EU RO POL	Law Enforcement	Mulschlegel	OSINT in EUROPOL
1995	US	Law Enforcement	Oehler	NPC: Intelligence Support to Domestic and Translational Law Enforcement
1999	US	Law Enforcement	OSS	Sample Daily Briefing on Transnational Crime
1999	US	Law Enforcement	OSS	Transnational Crime Web Sites
1997	US	Law Enforcement	Peterson & Dolan	OSINT in Fighting Transnational Crime: Obstacles and Solutions
1998	US	Law Enforcement	Rodriguez Jr.	The Internet and Missing Children: Summary of Video
1996	AU	Law Enforcement	Roger (QJC)	Open Source Strategies for Law Enforcement
1995	US	Law Enforcement	Schneider	The Criminal Intelligence Function: Toward a Model
1995	CA	Law Enforcement	Schnittker	Open Sources in the Criminal Intelligence Program of the RCMP

198

				(Slides)
1995	CA	Law Enforcement	Schnittker	Open Sources in the Criminal Intelligence Program of the RCMP (Text)
1999	CA	Law Enforcement	Schnittker	RCMP Lessons Learned in OSINT
1995	US	Law Enforcement	Smith	Critical Comments on the US IC Approach to OSINT
1994	US	Law Enforcement	Steele	Recommended Reading About Hackers
1994	US	Law Enforcement	Steele	Talking Points About Hackers
1997	US	Law Enforcement	Steele	Open Source Intelligence and the War on Drugs
1998	US	Law Enforcement	Steele	OSINT: Orientation for Law Enforcement Professionals
2004	US	Law Enforcement	Steele	Keynote Presentation to Texas Law Enforcement Conference
2004	US	Law Enforcement	Steele	DHS: The Future of Intelligence (not secret, not federal, not expensive)
1999	EU RO POL	Law Enforcement	Storbeck	OSINT: Foundation for Regional Cooperation in Crime-Fighting
2004	US	Legilslation	9-11 Commission	Page 413 showing Open Source Agency independent of CIA under DNI
1992	US	Legislation	Cheney	Two Letters Destroying Hope for National Security Act of 1992
1992	US	Legislation	Cheney	SecDef Letter Destroying the National Security Act of 1992
2005	US	Legislation	Congress	Congressional Record of DNI Negroponte Nomination
2005	US	Legislation	Congress	DHS Act with Open Source Strategy
2005	US	Legislation	Defense Daily	Congress Wants DoD to Focus on OSINT
2006	US	Legislation	HASC	House Section 931 Defense Authorization, on DoD OSINT
2004	US	Legislation	OSS	108th Congress Ugly Draft Bill Creating Open Source Agency
2004	US	Legislation	Senate Govt Af Com	Excerpts and Comments on Hearings on Open Source Agency

199

2004	US	Legislation	Simmons	Exchange of Correspondence with General Schoomaker
2006	US	Legislation	Simmons	Political and Policy Preface to IO Book by Steele
1994	US	Legislation	Steele	Draft Legislation: National Information Strategy Act of 1994
2003	US	Legislation	Steele	SASC Two-Page Brief on OSINT
2003	US	Legislation	Steele	Smart Nation Act for the 108th Congress (Version 1.3)
2004	US	Legislation	Steele	108th Congress Lame Duck Smart Nation Act (Short Version)
2004	US	Legislation	Steele	SASC Two Page Brief and One Page Budget Integrated
2005	US	Legislation	Steele	Smart Nation Act for 108th Congress
2006	US	Legislation	Steele	Core Questions for the Director of National Intelligence
2004	US	Legislation	Steele for Simmons	108th Congress Bill for Independent Open Source Agency with OSIS-X
1995	US	Legislation	Straub	View from the Hill: Members View OSINT as Free, Are Skeptical
2005	US	Legislation	Studeman	Testimony on Hill 22 Sep 05
2004	US	Librarians	Marlatt	Librarianship
2005	UK	Link	Collier	Google Legacy Book
2003	Global	Links	OSS	Internet Links on Citizen Oversight
2006	US	Links	OSS	Information Operations Links
2006	US	Links	OSS	Open Source Intelligence Links
2006	US	Links	OSS	Strategic Peace Operations & Peacekeeping Intelligence Links
2006	US	Links	OSS	Intelligence Reform Links
2006	US	Links	OSS	Collective Intelligence Links
1993	US	Media		Definitive Guide to the Zine Revolution: Factsheets
1993	US	Media		Illustrative Extracts from Alternative Press Index
1993	US	Media		Illustrative Extracts from Alternative Press Review
1998	US	Media	Bianco	Journalist's Low-Tech Approach to Overt Collection in Third World
1999	US	Memo	Allison et al	Memo on Defending USA from Nuclear Terrorism

2005	US	Memo	Profaca	Compiled Quotes on OSINT
1991	US	Memo	Steele	Defense Intelligence Productivity in the 1990's
1991	US	Memo	Steele	Defense Intelligence Productivity in the 1990's
2001	US	Memo	Steele	AWC: Streamlining National Security
2001	US	Memo	Steele	Decision Paper for the Vice President Elect
2001	US	Memo	Steele	Invited One-Pager on Intelligence and Homeland Security to Condi Rice
2001	US	Memo	Steele	OMB: Open Source Intelligence & Government Operations
2001	US	Memo	Steele	SASC: One-Pager Proposed Budget for National OSINT Program
2001	US	Memo	Steele	Unsolicited One-Pager on National Intelligence Reform to Condi Rice
2001	US	Memo	Steele	To Condi Rice: One-Pager on National Security Reform
2001	US	Memo	Steele	To Condi Rice: One-Pager on Homeland Security Intelligence
2001	US	Memo	Steele	AWC: Streamlining National Security: A Personal Perspective
2001	US	Memo	Steele	To Dick Cheney: Decision Support From Open Source Intelligence
2003	US	Memo	Steele	To Condi Rice on Calling Dissent Treason
2003	US	Memo	Steele	To Condi Rice: Resign or Respect Dissent on Iraq War
2004	US	Memo	Steele	Citizen in Search of a Leader (Updated): The Four Reforms
2004	US	Memo	Steele	Response to DIA Call for Data Inputs on OSINT
2005	US	Memo	Steele	Status of OSINT in USG and DoD, Memo for the CG
2006	US	Memo	Steele	Letter to All Ambassadors of 28 July 2006
1996	US	Memo	Steele & Horowitz	Summary of the Dark Side of OSINT
1997	US	Military	Alger	IATAC: Building a Knowledge Base of Emerging IAT

201

1998	US	Military	Beavers & Shanahan	Operationalizing IO in Bosnia-Herzegovina (Book Chapter)
1995	SE	Military	Bjore	Six Years of Open Source Information (OSI): Lessons Learned
1998	SE	Military	Bjore	Open Sources and Methods for the Military
1998	SE	Military	Bjore	OSINT Lessons Learned
1994	US	Military	Brooks & McKeeyer	Split-Based Ops in DESERT STORM: Glimpse of the Future Digital Army
1997	US	Military	Clark	EAGLE VISION: Tactical Downlink Station for Imagery
1999	US	Military	Clark	EAGLE VISION: USAF Initiative for Tactical Receipt of Imagery
1992	US	Military	Clift	Military OSINT Requirements, Capabilities, and Contracting Directions
1997	US	Military	Clinton	Managing Complex Contingency Operations
1999	US	Military	Connors	PACOM Additional Slides on VIC
1999	US	Military	Connors	U.S. Pacific Command's Virtual Information Center (VIC)
2000	CA	Military	Cox	OSINT at SHAPE…Some Musings
1995	US	Military	Dandar	Army Intelligence XXI, Open Source Status Report
1995	US	Military	Dandar	OSIF Exploitation for Army Intelligence XXI: Summary
1999	US	Military	Dearth	Intelligence in the 21st Century
2000	FR	Military	Debat	The Challenge of Informing European Defence Decisions
1995	UK	Military	Garfield	Update on the UK MoD OSINT Programme (Slides)
1995	UK	Military	Garfield	Update on the UK MoD OSINT Programme (Text)
2002	US	Military	Hardee	Growing an Open Source Intelligence Program
2003	US	Military	Hardee	OSINT in Support of Special Operations
2003	US	Military	Harrison	OSINT Requirements, Collection, & Production Management
2000	US	Military	Hughes	Open Sources and Intelligent

				Solutions
1999	US	Military	Lee	Summary of Military Map Availibililty for Iran
1997	US	Military	Molholm	DTIC: Building a Virtual Knowledge Warehouse
2000	Austria	Military	Mueller	Austrian Military Intelligence Thoughts on OSINT
1994	US	Military	Munro	INFORMATION WARFARE: Snake Eaters Meet Net-Heads
1999	US	Military	Myers & Madison	Virtual Information Center Concept Refinement
1997	US	Military	Necoba	The Marines and OSINT
1994	US	Military	Pedtke	NAIC & The Intelligence Community Open Source Architecture
1997	US	Military	Pedtke	National Air Intelligence Center Science & Technology OSINT
1992	US	Military	Pedtke et al	NAIC S&T Open Source Intelligence Requirements & Capabilities
1992	US	Military	Petersen	New Roles for the U.S. Military
1999	US	Military	Prinslow & Bond	Information Sharing in Humanitarian Emergencies
1998	UK	Military	Rathmell	Assessing the IW Threat from Sub-State Groups
2000	UK	Military	Regan	The UK Ministry of Defence OSINT Program
2000	US	Military	Reynolds	U.S. Transportation Command OSINT
1995	US	Military	Ricardeli	OSINT in Support of Haiti Invasion (Slides)
1995	US	Military	Ricardeli	OSINT in Support of Haiti Invasion (Text)
1992	US	Military	Schwartau	Introduction to Information Warfare
2004	US	Military	Simmons	Foreword to the Draft SOF OSINT Handbook
1996	US	Military	Smith	Defense Mapping Agency and the Commercial Sector
1991	US	Military	Steele	Defense Intelligence Productivity in the 1990's
1992	US	Military	Steele	Intelligence Lessons Learned from Recent Expeditionary Operations
1992	US	Military	Steele	Comments Prepared for Future War

203

				Roundtable
1994	US	Military	Steele	DIA/JMITC: NS via the Reinvention of National & Defense Intelligence
1995	US	Military	Steele	The Military Perspective on Information Warfare: Apocalypse Now
1995	US	Military	Steele	AWC: Open Source Intelligence for the Military
1996	US	Military	Steele	Open Source Intelligence Handbook, Chapter 5, OSINT and Military
1996	US	Military	Steele	DIA/JMITC: National Knowledge Strategy & Revolution in Intelligence
1997	US	Military	Steele	CINC Brief: The One that Got CINCSOC (Now CSA) to Buy In
1997	US	Military	Steele	Creating a Bare Bones OSINT Capability (Slides)
1997	US	Military	Steele	Creating a Bare Bones OSINT Unit for DIA
1997	US	Military	Steele	CINCSOC 10 Minute Brief on OSINT
1998	US	Military	Steele	INFORMATION PEACEKEEPING: Purest Form of War (Outline)
1998	US	Military	Steele	Skeptical Assessment of USN-USMC Based on Real-World OSINT
1998	US	Military	Steele	TAKEDOWN: The Asymmetric Threat to the Nation
1999	US	Military	Steele	Overview of OSINT Issues & OSINT Utility to DoD
1999	US	Military	Steele	Setting the Stage for Information Sharing in the 21st Century: 3 Issues
1999	US	Military	Steele	What Do We Need to Know and Where Do We Get It? (Slides)
1999	US	Military	Steele	Expeditionary Environment in the 21st Century
2000	US	Military	Steele	Briefing to NATO/PfP: One World Ready or Not
2001	US	Military	Steele	AUSA: Intelligence Support to a Transforming Army
2001	US	Military	Steele	AWC: Welcome to the Real World: Force Structure Trade-Offs
2003	US	Military	Steele	SOUTHCOM: Strategic Threat

				Assessment
2003	US	Military	Steele	AFCEA Texas: C4I Revolution and National Security
2003 ?	US	Military	Steele	To SecDef: Force Structure Trade-Offs and the Real World
2005	US	Military	Steele	US Army Conference: E3i: Making the Revolution
1996	US	Military	Stein	Mapping, Charting, and Geodetic Needs for Remote Sensing Data
1992	US	Military	Strassmann	Forcing Innovation, Cutting Costs, and Increasing Defense Productivity
1998	UK	Military	Tyrrell	OSINT: The Challenge for NATO
2005	US	Military	USA	Army Modernization Briefing
1990	US	Military	USMC & Steele	Expeditionary Environment Research & Analysis Model
1990	US	Military	USMC & Steele	Expeditionary Mission Area Factors Summaries
1997	US	Military	Vesely	Striking A Balance: National, Operational, & Tactical Acquisition
2004	NL	Military	Wiebes	SIGINT in Bosnia
1999	US	Military	Wirtz	Bridging the Culture Gap: OSINT and the Tet Offensive
2006	US	Mind-Set	Andregg	Why US Intelligence Community Makes You Crazy
1994	Switz	NGO	Fuchs	Complete Remarks of the Director General of the Red Cross
1994	Switz	NGO	Fuchs	Handling Information in Humanitarian Operations Within Armed Conflicts
1999	Switz	NGO	Fuchs	Summary of 1994 Remarks on Red Cross OSINT
1999	UN	NGO	GDIN	Global Disaster Information Network Participants
2005	NA	None	None	Conference Delayed to 2006 While Awaiting IC and DoD Actions
2000	UN	Nuclear	Chitumbo et al	Nuclear Transparency through Open Source Intelligence (Slides)
2000	UN	Nuclear	Chitumbo et al	Nuclear Transparency through Open Source Intelligence (Text)
1996	US	Peace	Air Force	Peacespace Dominance
2003	AF	Peace	Brahimi	Brahimi Report Extracts Relevant to

				UN/NGO Intelligence Function
2003	NL	Peace	Cammaert	Comments on Intelligence and Peacekeeping
2000	CA	Peace	Charters	OSINT for Peace Operations: Perspectives from UN Operations
1999	US	Peace	Dearth	Peacekeeping in the Information Age
1998	US	Peace	GDIN	Background on Meeting of Disaster Relief Experts
1998	US	Peace	GDIN	Global Disaster Information Network Conference Concept Paper
1999	US	Peace	GDIN	Global Disaster Information Network Background Paper
1999	US	Peace	GDIN	Proposal to Increase Information Sharing Through ReliefWeb
2006	US	Peace	None	Draft Legislation to Establish Department of Peace
1999	US	Peace	Rhoader	Peace Wing
2006	SE	Peace	Salin	Peacekeeping Intelligence Training
2004	US	Peace	Schell	Review of Unconquerable World by Richard Falk
1999	AU	Peace	Smith	Intelligence and UN Peacekeeping
1993	US	Peace	Steele	Information Peacekeeping: A Note
2002	US	Peace	Steele	Netherlands: Information Peacekeeping & The Future of Intelligence
2003	US	Peace	Steele	Peacekeeping Intelligence Leadership Guidance 1.0
2003	US	Peace	Steele	Information Peacekeeping & The Future of Intelligence
2004	US	Peace	Steele	PKI III: Peacekeeping Intelligence & Information Peacekeeping
2004	US	Peace	Steele	Sweden: Peacekeeping Intelligence & Information Peacekeeping
2006	US	Peace	Steele	Peacekeeping Intelligence & Information Peacekeeping 1.3
2003	US	Peace	Steele et al	Peacekeeping Intelligence Leadership Digest 1.0
2006	SE	Peace	Svensson	Swedish Peacekeeping Intelligence Curriculum
2006	SE	Peace	Svensson	Swedish Peacekeeping Intelligence Course Description

2006	US	Peace	Tillman	Department of Peace (Kucinich Supports)
2006	US	Peace	Tillman	Peace Trip
1993	US	Peace	Whitney-Smith	Toward an Epistemology of Peace
2002	US	Peaee	Steele	Netherlands Keynote on Information Peacekeeping
2004	US	Policy	Alexander	Army G-2 Accepts OSINT as Separate Discipline
1999	US	Policy	Allen (ADCI/C)	OSINT as a Foundation for All-Source Collection Management
2004	US	Policy	Andregg	Insanity of Planned Intelligence "Reforms"
2005	US	Policy	Andregg	Ethics and the IC: Breaking the Laws of God and Man
2004	AU	Policy	Anon & Steele	Update on OSINT in Australia
1992	US	Policy	Barlow	EFF and the National Public Network (NPN)
2005	UK	Policy	BASIC	Think Tank Report on US Intelligence Incompetence
1993	FR	Policy	Beaumard	France: Think-tank to Anticipate & Regulate Economic Intelligence Issues
1993	FR	Policy	Beaumard	Learned Nations: Competitive Advantages Via Knowledge Strategies
2000	US	Policy	Berkowitz	An Alternative View of the Future of Intellligence
1997	FR	Policy	Botbol	The OSINT Revolution: Early Failures and Future Prospects
1993	US	Policy	Brenner	Law and Policy of Telecommunications and Computer Database Networks
2000	RU	Policy	Budzko	Russian View of Electronic Open Sources and How to Exploit Them
1992	US	Policy	Castagna	Review of Toffler's *PowerShift*
1993	US	Policy	Castagna	Review of Reich, *The Work of Nations*
1993	AU	Policy	Chantler	Need for Australia to Develop a Strategic Policy on OSI
1993	US	Policy	Cisler	Community Computer Networks

1993	US	Policy	Civille	The Spirit of Access: Equity, NREN, and the NII
1996	FR	Policy	Clerc	Economic and Financial Intelligence: The French Model
2004	FR	Policy	Clerc	Cognitive Knowledge for Nations
2004	US	Policy	Cordesman	Questions & Answers on Intelligence Reform
2004	US	Policy	Cordesman & Steele	Questions & Answers on Intelligence Reform
2003	US	Policy	Czech	Steady State Revolution and National Security
1992	SE	Policy	Dedijer	Open Source Solutions: Intelligence and Secrecy
2006	US	Policy	DoD	QDR Shift in Focus 18 Years After Gray and Steele Recommended Same
1998	US	Policy	Donahue	Balancing Spending Among Spies, Satellites, and Schoolboys
2000	US	Policy	Ermarth	OSINT: A Fresh Look at the Past and the Future
2005	EU	Policy	EU	European Union Proposed Multi-National Intelligence Service
1993	US	Policy	Fedanzo	A Genetic View of National Intelligence
1997	US	Policy	Felsher	Viability & Survivability of US Remote Sensing as Function of Policy
2003	CA	Policy	Fyffe	Intelligence Sharing and OSINT
2003	CA	Policy	Fyffe	Intelligence Sharing and OSINT (Summary)
1992	US	Policy	Gage	Open Sources, Open Systems
2005	US	Policy	Godson	Culture of Lawfullness
1992	US	Policy	Greenwald	Unrepresented Nations & Peoples Organization: Diplomacy's Cutting Edge
1993	US	Policy	Haver	Intelligence Aim Veers to Amassing Overt Information
2001	US	Policy	Heibel	Intelligence Training: What Is It? Who Needs It?
2001	US	Policy	Heibel	Value of Intelligence & Intelligence Training to Any Organization
1992	US	Policy	Hughes	An Affordable Approach to

				Networking America's Schools
1991	US	Policy	JFK Working Group	National Intelligence and the American Enterprise: Possibilities
1992	US	Policy	Kahin	New Legal Paradigms for Multi-Media Information in Cyberspace
1996	US	Policy	Kahin	What Is Intellectual Property?
1992	US	Policy	Kahn	Outline of a Global Knowledge Architecture, Visions and Possibilities
1991	US	Policy	Karraker	Highways of the Mind
1993	JP	Policy	Kumon	Japan and the United States in the Information Age
1993	SE	Policy	Leijonhelm	Economic Intelligence Cooperation Between Government Industry
2003	UN	Policy	Lewis	Creating the Global Brain
1993	US	Policy	Love	Comments on the Clinton Administration's 'Vision' Statement for the NII
2003	US	Policy	Markowitz	OSINT in Support of All Source
2003	US	Policy	Markowitz	Open Source Intelligence Investment Strategy
2006	US	Policy	Markowitz	Defense Science Board Report on Transitions (NGO, OSINT)
2001	US	Policy	Oakley	Use of Civilian & Military Power for Engagement & Intervention
1994	US	Policy	Ogdin & Giser	Cyber-Glut, and What To Do About It
2006	US	Policy	Peters	Counterrevolution in Military Affairs
1993	US	Policy	Petersen	A New Twenty-First Century Role for the Intelligence Community
2000	IT	Policy	Politi	The Birth of OSINT in Italy
2002	Italy	Policy	Politi	11th of September and the Future of European Intelligence
1995	US	Policy	Prusak	Seven Myths of the Information Age
1999	UK	Policy	Rolington	Changing Messages in Western Knowledge Over 400 Years (Slides)
1999	UK	Policy	Rolington	Changing Messages in Western Knowledge Over 400 Years (Text)
1993	GE	Policy	Schmidt	History of Failure, Future of Opportunity: Reinventions and Deja Vu

1994	FR	Policy	Schmidt	Open Source Solutions 1994: The State of Intelligence
1994	US	Policy	Schwartau	Letter on NII Security
1994	US	Policy	Schwartau et al	Cross-Walk of 3 Experts' Spending $1 Billion per Year for NII Security
2004	US	Policy	Simmons	Congressman Simmons Letter to General Schoomaker on OSINT
1990	US	Policy	Steele	Recasting National Security in a Changing World
1991	US	Policy	Steele	How to Avoid Strategic Intelligence Failures in the Future
1992	US	Policy	Steele	E3i: Ethics, Ecology, Evolution, and Intelligence
1992	US	Policy	Steele	Inaugural Remarks Opening 1st International Conference
1992	US	Policy	Steele	Information Concepts & Doctrine for the Future
1992	US	Policy	Steele	OSINT Clarifies Global Threats: Offers Partial Remedy to Budget Cuts
1992	US	Policy	Steele	Review Strassmann, *Information PayOff*
1993	US	Policy	Steele	A Critical Evaluation of U.S. National Security Capabilities
1993	US	Policy	Steele	ACCESS: Theory and Practice of Intelligence in the Age of Information
1993	US	Policy	Steele	Executive Order 12356, 'National Security Information'
1993	US	Policy	Steele	Reinventing Intelligence in the Age of Information (TP for DCI)
1993	US	Policy	Steele	Reinventing Intelligence: The Advantages of OSINT
1993	US	Policy	Steele	Role of Grey Lit & Non-Traditional Agencies in Informing Policy Makers
1994	US	Policy	Steele	Communications, Content, Coordination, and C4 Security: Talking Points
1994	US	Policy	Steele	Correspondence to Mr. Marty Harris, NII Commission
1994	US	Policy	Steele	DATA MINING: Don't Buy or Build Your Shovel Until You Know What...
1994	US	Policy	Steele	Expansion of Questions Posed by

				Senator John Warner to Aspin-Brown
1994	US	Policy	Steele	Letter to the Open Source Lunch Club on PFIAB Being Useless
1994	US	Policy	Steele	National and Corporate Security in the Age of Information
1994	US	Policy	Steele	Private Enterprise Intelligence: Its Potential Contribution to Nat'l Sec.
1995	US	Policy	Steele	Conference Executive Summary C/HPSCI and former DCI Colby
1995	US	Policy	Steele	Creating a Smart Nation: Strategy, Policy, Intelligence, & Information
1995	US	Policy	Steele	SMART NATIONS: NI Strategies and Virtual Intelligence Communities
1996	US	Policy	Steele	Creating a Smart Nation (Govt Info Q and also CYBERWAR Chapter)
1996	US	Policy	Steele	InfoPeace: OSINT as a Policy Option & Operational Alternative
1996	US	Policy	Steele	Open Sources and the Virtual Intelligence Community
1996	US	Policy	Steele	Protecting the Civilian Infrastructure as an Aspect of Information Warfare
1997	US	Policy	Steele	Intelligence in the Balance: Opening Remarks at OSS '97
1999	UK	Policy	Steele	Snakes in the Grass: Open Source Doctrine
2003	US	Policy	Steele	Open Letter to Ambassadors Accredited to the USA
2004	US	Policy	Steele	DoD OSINT Program: One Man's View of What Is Needed
2004	US	Policy	Steele	Transcript of Steele at Secretary of State's Open Forum 24 March 2004
2005	US	Policy	Steele	ON INTELLIGENCE: Overview in Aftermath of 9-11
2005	US	Policy	Steele	Op-Ed on Condi Rice's Active Deception
2005	US	Policy	Steele	Cease and desist letter on Naquin
2006	US	Policy	Steele	Terms of Reference for Intelligence Reform 1.1
2006	US	Policy	Steele	In Search of a Leader (Four Essential Reforms)
2006	US	Policy	Steele	Electoral Refrom as Precursor to

				Intelligence Reform
1997	US	Policy	Sutton	Global Coverage ($1.5B/Year Needed for Lower Tier OSINT)
2005	US	Policy	Tama	Princeton Review on Intelligence Reform
1993	US	Policy	Toffler (Both)	Knowledge Strategies, Intellience Restructuring, Global Competitiveness
2004	NL	Policy	Tongeren (van)	Need for Global Alliance for Human Security (Complete)
2004	NL	Policy	Tongeren (van)	Need for Global Alliance for Human Security (Overview)
2003	BE	Policy	Truyens	Intelligent vs. Intelligence: That Is The Question
1997	US	Policy	Tsuruoka	Asian Perceptions of What Is and Is Not Legal in Economic Intelligence
2006	US	Policy	Tsuruoka	Managing for the Future: Interview with Alvin Toffler
1997	UK	Policy	Tyrrell	Proposals to Develop a NATO/PfP OSINT Capability
1993	US	Policy	Wallner	Overview of IC Open Source Requirements and Capabilities
1992	US	Policy	Wood	Remarks, Don't Be Suspicious of Contractors
1993	US	Policy	Wood	The IC and the Open Source Information Challenge
1957	US	Policy	Wright	Project for a World Intelligence Center
1996	US	Policy	Zuckerman	The Central Role of Open Source Economic Intelligence
1993	US	Presentation	Steele	INTERVAL: God, Man, and Information
1993	US	Presentation	Steele	OSS '93: Reinventing National Intelligence—Advantages of OSINT
1993	US	Presentation	Steele	California: Comments to INTERVAL In-House (God, Man, and Info)
1994	US	Presentation	Steele	Australia: Practical Overview of Open Sources, Softwares, & Services
1994	US	Presentation	Steele	Intelligence Community as a New Market
1994	US	Presentation	Steele	6th National Threat Symposium:

				Advantages of OSINT for Nat'l Sec
1994	US	Presentation	Steele	Australia: Practical Overview of Open Sources, Softwares, & Services
1994	US	Presentation	Steele	Advantages of OSINT for National and Corporate Security
1995	US	Presentation	Steele	CENDI & COSPO As Catalysts for National Security & Competitiveness
1995	US	Presentation	Steele	France: Flag Conference on War and Peace in the 21st Century
1997	US	Presentation	Steele	DIA/JMITC: The Future of Intelligence
1999	US	Presentation	Steele	SASA at DIA: Tough Love
2001	US	Presentation	Steele	The New Craft of Intelligence: Personal, Public, & Political
2001	US	Presentation	Steele	Strategic Advisory Group Briefing on New Craft of Intelligence
2004	US	Presentation	Steele	Austria: New Craft of Intelligence, Europe as Victim, Europe as Leader
2004	US	Presentation	Steele	Typical Q&A After 9-11 Presentation
2004 ?	US	Presentation	Steele	Austria: Europe as Victim, Europe as Leader
2005	US	Presentation	Steele	Hackers in California: The Googlization of Intelligence
2005	US	Presentation	Steele	MALAS in MO: On Intelligence
2005	US	Presentation	Steele	AWC: E3i, Making Revolution (Moral, Conceptual, Technical, Cultural)
2005	US	Presentation	Steele	The Googleization of Intelligence: Brief to Hackers in Silicon Valley
2005	US	Presentation	Steele	Eight-Slide Transformation Briefing
2006	US	Presentation	Steele	National Press Club: New Rules for the New Craft of Intelligence
2006	US	Presentation	Steele	World Affairs Council: Bin Laden, Intelligence & National Security
2006	US	Presentation	Steele	National Press Club: Failure of U.S. Intelligence
2006	US	Presentation	Steele	National Press Club: Overview of the Real World
2006	US	Presentation	Steele	HOPE6: Bin Laden, US Intelligence, & How NOT to Spend Treasure
2006	US	Presentation	Steele	HOPE6: Failure of 21st Century

213

				Intelligence, Updated
2006	US	Presentation	Steele	Staff Briefing on Smart Nation Act
1997	US	Presentation	Sutton	Global Coverage Slides
2001	US	Press Release	2001-09-13	Winning WWIII: Not A War Than Can Be Won By Military Means
2002	US	Press Release	2002-00-00	ACFR Across America: 9-11, US Intelligence, & the Real World
2002	US	Press Release	2002-12-13	Intelligence Reform Basics
2003	US	Press Release	2003-02-15	National Counterterrorism Center Will Fail
2003	US	Press Release	2003-08-17	Networked Open Model for National Security
2003	US	Press Release	2003-08-19	Fifth Generation Warfare
2004	US	Press Release	2004-02-05	The Facts on Intelligence Policy Failure
2004	US	Press Release	2004-04-02	Revitalizing National Security and National Intelligence
2004	US	Press Release	2004-05-05	Fixing the Clandestine Service with Five Tracks
2004	US	Press Release	2004-07-12	Missing Elements of the Senate Intelligence Report
2004	US	Press Release	2004-07-16	Projected Failure of the Global War on Terror Game
2004	US	Press Release	2004-07-20	Actual Failure of Global War on Terror Game
2004	US	Press Release	2004-07-22	Four Deficiencies in the 9-11 Commission Report
2004	US	Press Release	2004-07-28	On Need for an Independent Open Source Agency Not Under DNI
2004	US	Press Release	2004-07-29	Open Source Agency Need for Independence from DNI & Secret Agencies
2004	US	Press Release	2004-07-30	OSINT, GWOT, and National Security Transformation
2004	US	Press Release	2004-08-12	Four Conditions for any New DCI
2005	US	Press Release	2005-04-13	Questions Congress Must Ask the DNI Designate, Who Must Answer
2005	US	Press	2005-10-09	OSINT Team Formation

		Release		
2005	US	Press Release	2005-10-11	NORTHCOM & National Guard Good for Stabilization/Reconstruction
2005	US	Press Release	2005-10-26	JIOC and OSINT a $5 Billion a Year Marketplace
2005	US	Press Release	2005-10-31	Breakaway Games as IO and OSINT Channel for Decision Support
2005	US	Press Release	2005-11-01	Ambassador Joseph Wilson Sets the Record Straight
2005	US	Press Release	2005-11-02	OSS CEO Denounces Torture as Treason
2005	US	Press Release	2005-11-02	OSS Distributes Book on "The Google Legacy" by Steve Arnold
2005	US	Press Release	2005-11-03	Posting of Draft Legislation to Create Open Source Agency
2005	US	Press Release	2005-12-11	Op-Ed on Condi Rice Deception
2005	US	Press Release	2005-12-14	Intelligence for the Poor
2006	US	Press Release	2006-01-10	OSS CEO on Future Directions of OSINT and IO
2006	US	Press Release	2006-01-14	OSINT Lifetime Awards (in 2006)
2006	US	Press Release	2006-01-15	Iran and Pakistan Now Have One-Two Punch on US Carriers
2006	US	Press Release	2006-02-28	Information Operations Book Now at Amazon
2006	US	Press Release	2006-03-01	Google, OSINT, and Information Operations
2006	US	Press Release	2006-03-02	Exxon Mis-Information
2006	US	Press Release	2006-03-02	Open Letter to Exxon CEO
2006	US	Press Release	2006-03-15	OSINT Familiarization Link List
2006	US	Press Release	2006-03-24	Lockheed Craps Out
2006	US	Press Release	2006-03-27	OSINT Chiefs of Station in 40 Countries
2006	US	Press Release	2006-04-06	US Dollar Tanking, Gold, Chinese Implications

2006	US	Press Release	2006-04-13	Public Challenge to DNI for an Intelligence Duel: $60B in Waste vs OSINT
2006	US	Press Release	2006-04-17	Press Conference Challenging DNI to Duel on Day He Speaks at NPC
2006	US	Press Release	2006-04-17	Open Letter Challenging DNI to an Intelligence Duel
2006	US	Press Release	2006-04-19	US Intelligence Upside Down & Inside Out: Challenge DNI to Duel/Debate
2006	US	Press Release	2006-04-21	The Death of U.S. Intelligence (Obituary)
2006	US	Press Release	2006-04-22	Praise for Mary McCarthy, Censure of DNI and DCI
2006	US	Press Release	2006-04-24	People to Cheney: Hit the Road
2006	US	Press Release	2006-04-29	American Independence Party
2006	US	Press Release	2006-05-06	Three Conditions for General Hayden's Success at CIA
2006	US	Press Release	2006-05-08	(Satire) White House Transfers National Agencies Out of Defense
2006	US	Press Release	2006-05-08	(Satire) White House DCI Announcement
2006	US	Press Release	2006-05-08	(Satire) White House Announcement on General Hayden
2006	US	Press Release	2006-06-23	Flunking the Vice President and Government on Ten High Level Threats
2006	US	Press Release	2006-07-02	First Amendment, Need for Public Intelligence
2006	US	Press Release	2006-07-20	Steele at Hackers, Open Source Agency Litmus Test for Congress
2006	US	Press Release	2006-07-20	Free Public Daily Brief & Weekly Summaries Contrast to $60B on Secrets
2006	US	Press Release	2006-07-28	OSS.Net Table of Contents
2006	US	Press Release	2006-09-06	Drivel Award for Times Online (UK)
2006	US	Press Release	2006-09-06	Award for Wiki Foundation and Freedom of Information Pioneers

216

2006	US	Press Release	2006-09-07	Open Letter to Military-Industrial-Congressional Complex
1992	US	Process	Andriole	IT Support for OSINT Analysis & Production (Slides)
1992	US	Process	Andriole	IT Support for OSINT Analysis & Production (Text)
1999	US	Process	Appleby	Feedback: The Missing Link in Information Superiority
1993	US	Process	Bermudez	Letter from a Source
1992	US	Process	Bodansky & Forest	GOP Terrorism Task Force: Research Techniques & Philosophy
1993	FR	Process	Bonthous	Culture: The Missing Intelligence Variable
1993	US	Process	Brodwin & Bernardi	Information Overload
2001	US	Process	Chester	The Atlantic Command's Open Source Intelligence Approach & Future
1993	US	Process	Christian	Area Information Servers (WAIS) and Global Change Research
2005	US	Process	Clapper	Interview
2006	US	Process	CRS	Data Mining and Homeland Security
2005	US	Process	DNI	Press Release on Appointment of ADDNI/OS
2005	US	Process	DNI	Office of the DNI Organization Charts
2001	US	Process	Dziedzic & Wood	Information Technology as Catalyst for Civil-Military Unity of Effort
1992	US	Process	Fedanzo	Implementing OSINT Through a Distributed Collection Model
2005	US	Process	Gerecht	Need for New Clandestine Service
1997	US	Process	Gupta & Pabian	Tricks of the Trade: Analytic Tools and Techniques
1993	US	Process	Halberstadt	Power and Communication in the Information Age
2005	US	Process	Harris	ABLE DANGER Summary
1993	US	Process	Herring	The Role of Intelligence in Formulating Strategy
1993	US	Process	Horowitz	Understanding Sources: The Real Challenge
1993	JP	Process	Ishii	Cross-Cultural Communication &

217

				Computer-Supported Collaboration
2005	US	Process	JHU-APL	Asymmetric Information
2005	US	Process	Kamien et all	Needs Analysis for Information Sharing
1992	US	Process	Kees	Advanced Information Processing and Analysis
2005	US	Process	Liszkiewiez	Reconfiguring the Global System through Mobile Democracy
1993	US	Process	Magee	The Age of Imagination: Coming Soon to a Civilization Near You
1992	US	Process	McIntyre	Competitive Advantage: The Power of Online Systems
1992	US	Process	Ogdin	Words Are Not Enough
1993	US	Process	Pedtke	Putting Functionality in the Open Source Network
2005	US	Process	Peters	On the Soul of Intelligence
1997	US	Process	Pinchot	Beyond Bureaucracy: Intrapreurship
2005	US	Process	Rushkoff	Open Source Democracy
1992	US	Process	Sacks	Using the Telephone as a Research Tool
1992	US	Process	Shepard	Analysis in the Year 2002: A Concept of Operations
1992	US	Process	Sibbet	Commercial Remote Sensing: Open Source Imagery Intelligence
2004	US	Process	Steele	OSS Proprietary Listing of Capabilities Needed by Open Source Agency
1992	US	Process	Tenny	Government Information Wants to be Free
1992	US	Process	Thompson	Ranked Retrieval and Extraction of Open Source Intelligence
1992	US	Process	Tow	Painting the Future: Some Remarks from INTERVAL
2006	US	Process	Turnbull	GSA Collaborative Workshop on Information Sharing
1992	US	Process	Whitney-Smith	Information Revolutions and the End of History
2003	US	Processing	DoD	Defense Intelligence Meta-Tagging
1997	US	Reader	Admin	Cover, Appreciation, Foreword, Contents
1994	US	Reader	Basch	Secrets of the Super-Searchers

1997	US	Reader	Basch	Secrets of the SuperSearchers: A Personal and Practical Perspective
1997	FR	Reader	Baumard	Learned Nations: Competitive Advantages Through Knowledge Strategies
1997	FR	Reader	Bonthous	Culture: The Missing Intelligence Variable
1994	UK	Reader	Collier	Toward a Global Information Industry and New Information Paradigm
1997	UK	Reader	Collier	Toward the Global Information Industry and a New Information Paradigm
1997	US	Reader	Donahue	National Funding Directions for Open Source Intelligence
1994	US	Reader	Englebart	Toward High Performance Organizations
1997	US	Reader	Fedanzo	A Genetic View of National Intelligence
1997	US	Reader	Fedanzo	Implementing OSINT Through a Distributed Contribution Model
1997	US	Reader	Herring	The Role of Intelligence in Formulating Strategy
1997	US	Reader	Hlava	Selected Professional or Trade Associations in Information
1997	US	Reader	Karraker (WIRED)	Highways of the Mind
1997	US	Reader	Kees	Advanced Information Processing & Analysis
1997	SE	Reader	Leijonhelm	Economic Intelligence Cooperation Between Government and Industry
1995	US	Reader	Markowitz	COSPO: Community Open Source Program Office Strategic Plan
1997	US	Reader	Markowitz	Community Open Source Strategic Plan (COSPO)
1993	US	Reader	McGill	Private Sector Role in Collecting, Processing, Disseming Intelligence
1997	US	Reader	McGill	Private Sector Role in Collecting, Processing, & Disseminating Intelligence
1997	US	Reader	MITRE	Open Source Research Processing Initiative

219

1995	US	Reader	Peters	After the Revolution
1997	US	Reader	Peters	After the Revolution
1997	US	Reader	Rheingold	Tools for Thinking--Thinking New Thoughts
1993	FR	Reader	Schmidt	A History of Failure, A Future of Opportunity: Reinvention & Deja Vu
1997	US	Reader	Schmidt	A History of Failure, A Future of Opportunity: Reinventions and Deja Vu
1997	US	Reader	Shepard	Intelligence Analysis in the Year 2002: A Concept of Operations
1997	US	Reader	Sibbit	Commercial Remote Sensing: Open Source Imagery Intelligence
1993	US	Reader	Steele	Reinventing Intelligence: The Advantages of OSINT
1994	US	Reader	Steele	Draft Legislation: National Security Act of 1994
1994	US	Reader	Steele	Private Enterprise Intelligence: Its Potential Contribution to Nat'l Sec
1994	US	Reader	Steele	Talking Point for the Public Interest Summit
1995	US	Reader	Steele	House Appropriations Committee Surveys Open Source Intelligence
1995	US	Reader	Steele	Intelligence Building Blocks
1995	US	Reader	Steele	Lip Service, Great Pretenders, and Open Source Intelligence
1995	US	Reader	Steele	Mapping, Charting, & Geodesy Deficiencies
1995	US	Reader	Steele	National Intelligence: The Community Tomorrow? (At NSA, 1995)
1995	US	Reader	Steele	OSINT: What Is It? Why Is It Important to the Military?
1997	US	Reader	Steele	ACCESS: Theory and Practice of Intelligence in the Age of Information
1997	US	Reader	Steele	Commercial Imagery (OSS Notices Extract)
1997	US	Reader	Steele	Draft Legislation: The National Information Strategy Act of 1994
1997	US	Reader	Steele	E3i: Ethics, Ecology, Evolution, and Intelligence

220

1997	US	Reader	Steele	HAC Surveys Open Source Intelligence (OSS Notices Extract)
1997	US	Reader	Steele	Information Concepts & Doctrine for the Future
1997	US	Reader	Steele	Intelligence Building Blocks (OSS Notices Extract)
1997	US	Reader	Steele	Lip Service, Great Pretenders, & OSINT (OSS Notices Extract)
1997	US	Reader	Steele	Mapping, Charting, & Geodesy Deficiencies (OSS Notices Extract)
1997	US	Reader	Steele	National Intelligence: The Community Tomorrow? (SASA at NSA)
1997	US	Reader	Steele	Open Source Intelligence: What Is It? Why Is It Important to the Military?
1997	US	Reader	Steele	OSINT: Graphical Overviews
1997	US	Reader	Steele	Private Enterprise Intelligence: Its Potential Contribution to Nat'l Security
1997	US	Reader	Steele	Reinventing Intelligence: The Advantages of Open Source Intelligence
1997	US	Reader	Steele	Talking Points for the Public Interest Summit
1997	US	Reader	Steele	Testimony to Commission on Eliminating Excessive Secrecy in Govt
1997	US	Reader	Steele	Toward High-Performance Organizations: A Strategic Role for Groupware
1997	US	Reader	Studeman	Teaching the Giant to Dance: Contradictions & Opportunities within the IC
1997	US	Reader	Toffler	Global Security & Global Competitiveness (OSS '03 Keynote)
2003	CA	Reference	Fyffe	OSS '03 Presentation on Information Sharing
2002	US	Reference	Herz	Harnessing the Hive via Online Games for Networked Innovation
2006	US	Reference	Steele	Open Source Intelligence Familiarization Documents (One Page of Links)

221

2004	US	Reform	Atlee	A Model of Intelligence Systems (Individual to Social)
2004	US	Reform	Atlee	Beyond Intelligence Reform Toward Co-Intelligence
2004	Austria	Reform	Beer	Need for a Theory of Intelligence
2002	Israel	Reform	Crevald van	Twenty Four Theses on Intelligence
2001	US	Reform	Foster	Getting to Tomorrow: A Plea for Strategic Reformation
2001	US	Reform	Gessaman	Summary of Comments on National Security Budget with Slides
2004	US	Reform	Harris	Beautiful Minds: Maverick Minds Needed to Achieve Reform
2004	US	Reform	Marrin	Improving Training for New Analysts
2002	US	Reform	Pinkham	Citizen Advocacy in the Information Age
2001	US	Reform	Treverton	Reshaping National Intelligence for an Age of Information
2004	NL	Reform	Wiebes	Intelligence and the War in Bosnia
2004	US	Report	Metz & Millen	Insurgency & Counterinsurgency in the 21st Century
2004	US	Report	OSS	Pacific Rim Year in Review
2006	US	Report	OSS	Public Daily Brief Weekly Summary Beta
2004	PRC	Report	PRC	Defense White Paper from Peoples Republic of China
2005	US	Report (External)	CRS	DHS Information Sharing
2005	US	Report (External)	PDC	White Paper on Public Diplomacy
2004	US	Requirements	Harrison	U.S. Special Operations Command OSINT Requirements
1992	US	Research	Ruh	Open Source Processing Research Initiative
2006	UK	Search	Morville	Peter Morville on Ambient Findability
1992	US	Security	Anderson	Computer Security Issues in Open Source Databases
1999	US	Sources	Lee	New Developments in Access to Russian Military Maps of Third

				World
1998	UK	Sources	Rathmell & Jasani	Revolution in Space-Based Imaging
1997	US	Strategy	Admin	Cover, Appreciation, Foreword, Contents
1992	US	Strategy	Steele	E3i: Ethic, Ecology, & Evolution: An Alternative Paradigm
1993	US	Strategy	Steele	Comments on Executive Order 12356, National Security Information
1993	US	Strategy	Steele	Testimony to the President's Inter-Agency Commission
1996	US	Strategy	Steele	Clandestine Sources and Methods: Primer on Deception of Congress
1996	US	Strategy	Steele	Secrecy and Openness: Talking Points for a Seminar on the Hill
1997	US	Strategy	Steele	Comments on Executive Order 12356, National Security Information
1997	US	Strategy	Steele	Cover, Appreciation, Foreword, Contents
1997	US	Strategy	Steele	Creating a Smart Nation: Strategy, Policy, Intelligence, Information
1997	US	Strategy	Steele	E3i: Ethics, Ecology, Evolution, and Intelligence
1997	US	Strategy	Steele	Intelligence & Counterintelligence for the 21st Century
1997	US	Strategy	Steele	Secrecy & Openness: Talking Points for Seminar on Intelligence Reform
1997	US	Strategy	Steele	Sources & Methods: A Primer for Congressional Inquiry
1997	US	Strategy	Steele	TESTIMONY to the Pres. Inter-Agency Task Force on National Security
1997	US	Strategy	Steele	VIRTUAL INTELLIGENCE & Information Peacekeeping
1992	US	Technology	`McConnell	The Future Federal Information Infrastructure
2004	US	Technology	Anonymous	Semantic Web Presentation
2004	US	Technology	Anonymous	Semantic Web Architecture and Applications
2004	US	Technology	Anonymous	Semantic Web Non-Memo
1997	US	Technology	Arnold	Technology Vectors: 1998 and

				Beyond
1998	US	Technology	Arnold	The Changing Intelligence Environment
1998	US	Technology	Arnold	The Future of Online
1999	US	Technology	Arnold	Intelligence Management and the Bottom Line
2002	US	Technology	Arnold	Nomadic Computing
2003	US	Technology	Arnold	One Machine…One View
2004	US	Technology	Arnold	The Information Technology Marketplace
2004	US	Technology	Arnold	Table of Contents for Enterprise Search Book
2006	US	Technology	Arnold	The Google Legacy
2005	US	Technology	CISCO	CISCO Application Oriented Network One-Pager
2005	US	Technology	CISCO	CISCO Application Oriented Network Executive IT Overview
1994	US	Technology	Englebart	Toward High-Performance Organizations: A Strategic Role for Groupware
2004	US	Technology	GAO	Report on the Global Information Grid and DoD
2004	US	Technology	Gill	Open Spectrum as the Third Open
2004	US	Technology	Gill	Wireless Grid: The Possibilities
2004	US	Technology	Guest	Comments on GAO Report on DoD Global Information Grid
2003	US	Technology	Hock	The Open-ness of the Internet
1997	US	Technology	Mani	MITRE: Search Engine Technologies
1997	US	Technology	Maybury	MITRE: Knowledge Management
1992	US	Technology	Rheingold	Tools for Thinking & Virtual Reality: Our Info EcoSystem
1996	US	Technology	Ruh	Optimizing Corporate Capital Through Information Technology
1988	US	Technology	Steele	Generic Intelligence Center Production Requirements
2002	US	Technology	Steele	NSA in Las Vegas: New Craft: What Should the T Be Doing to the I in IT?
2002	US	Technology	Steele	NSA in Las Vegas: New Craft (Alternative Copy)
2004	US	Technology	Steele	Comments of GAO Report on DoD Global Information Grid

2005	US	Technology	Steele	GSA Roundtable on IT Innovation
2002	US	Technology	Stratton	In-Q-Tel
2004	NO	Terrorism	Bjorgo	Root Causes of Terrorism
2004	US	Terrorism	Kaplan	The Saudi Connection to Terrorism
2004	US	Terrorism	Knapp	Al Qaeda and the Mass Media (PSYOP Briefing)
2004	US	Terrorism	Knapp	Al Qaeda and the Mass Media (Reference)
2004	US	Terrorism	Knapp	Distortion in Islam and Jihad
2004	US	Terrorism	Knapp	Diversity in Islam
2004	US	Threat	Daly	Globalization & National Defense (Ecological Economics)
2006	US	Threat	Daly	Al Qaeda Against Saudi Oil
2003	US	Threat	Danzip	Countering Traumatic Attacks
2005	US	Threat	Ellis	Scenarios for Next Generation Crises in Latin America
2002	US	Threat	Emerson & Steele	American Jihad Map
2005	US	Threat	GAO	GAO Report: US Not Addressing Islamic Fundamentalism
2006	US	Threat	Johnson	Battle of Algiers and Its Lessons
2004	US	Threat	Louisiana	Pre-Hurricane Katrina Study and Conclusions
2003	PRC	Threat	OSS	PRC Treaty & Trade Penetration of Latin America
2005	US	Threat	OSS	Somalia Piracy Quick Report
2005	US	Threat	OSS	Report on Remote Detonation of Improvised Explosive Devices
2005	US	Threat	OSS	PRC Trade in Latin America
2004	US	Threat	Palmer	The Real Axis of Evil: 44 Dictators
2004	US	Threat	Peters	Early Warning of Disease From Pattern Analysis
2005	US	Threat	Ray & Gross	The Perfect Storm
2004	US	Threat	Seagrave	Transcript of Video on Stolen Gold Held by US Treasury & Citi-Bank
2006	US	Threat	Seagraves	*Gold Warriors*: New Epilogue, Further of US Theft of WWII Gold Loot
2006	US	Threat	Seagraves	*Gold Warriors* New Chapter Seventeen
1994	US	Threat	Steele	6th National Threat Symposium: New

225

				Directions in Information Sharing
1998	US	Threat	Steele	TAKEDOWN: Targets, Tools, & Technocracy
2000	US	Threat	Steele	Georgetown/AWC: Non-Traditional Threats
2002	US	Threat	Steele	ACFR, 19 Cities: 9-11, U.S. Intelligence, & the Real World
2005	US	Threat	Steele	Worksheet for Book Review on *Crossing the Rubicon*
2005	US	Threat	Steele	Mother Nature as Terrorist
2005	US	Threat	Steele	9-11: Who's To Blame? One Man's Opinion
2006	US	Threat	Steele	Who Is to Blamce? The Vice President and Us
2006	US	Threat	Stern	Al Qaeda Approach to US Muslims
2006	UK	Threat	Story	Crunch Time for CIA, Banks, and Related Thieves of $742 Trillion
2005	US	Threat	Thompson	Is the Terrorism Threat Over-Rated?
2004	US	Threat	Vlahos	Attachment to the Muslim Renovatio Memo
2004	US	Threat	Vlahos	The Muslim Renovatio and U.S. Strategy
2004	US	Threat	Vlahos	The Muslims Are Coming
2004	US	Threat	Vlahos	Insurgency Within Islam
1998	US	Threats		Transnational Enemies: Threats Without Names
2002	US	Threats	Betts	The Next Intelligence Failure: The Limits of Prevention
2003	US	Threats	Copeland	Analysis of the New Paradigm for Terrorism
1997	US	Threats	Fialka	War by Other Means: Economic Espionage In (Against) America
1998	US	Threats	Glaebus	Metaphors & Modern Threats: Biological, Computer, Cognitive Viruses
2001	US	Threats	Godson	Governments and Gangs
2001	US	Threats	Heidenrich	Early Warning & Complex Monitoring of Ethnic Genocide (Slides)
2001	US	Threats	Heidenrich	Early Warning & Complex Monitoring of Ethnic Genocide

				(Text)
2002	NL	Threats	Jongman	World Conflict and Human Rights Map 2001-2002
1996	US	Threats	Keuhl	School of Information Warfare Threat and Strategy: Shifting Paradigms
2003	US	Threats	Manwaring	Street Gangs: New Urban Insurgency
2003	US	Threats	Manwaring	War & Conflict: Six Generations
2005	NGO	Threats	NGO	Changing Face of Global Violence
2005	NGO	Threats	NGO	Human Security Audit
1996	US	Threats	O'Malley	Countering the Business Intelligence Threat
2003	US	Threats	Pelton	Summary of Presentation on World's Most Dangerous Places
2004	US	Threats	Pelton	Robert Young Pelton on Dangerous World
1997	US	Threats	Schwartau	Information Warfare: The Weapons of the Information Age
2004	US	Threats	Steele	Three Book Review Relevant to Global War on Terror (GWOT)
1996	US	Threats	Strassmann	U.S. Knowledge Assets: The Choice Target for Information Crime
1997	US	Threats	Tenney	Cyber-Law and Cyber-Crime: Spamming Methods and Costs
2002	US	Threats	Wheaton	Transitions from Authoritarian Rule: A Model
2002	US	Threats	Wheaton	Virtual Afghanistan: Modeling a Transition from Authoritarian Rule
1994	US	Threats	Whitney-Smith	Refugees: Weapon of the Post Cold War World--Counter Offensive: IW
1996	US	Threats	Winkler	Electronic Industrial Espionage: Defining Ground Zero
1998	US	Tools	Arnold	New Trends in Automated Intelligence Gathering Software
2002	US	Tools	Hohhof	Competitive Intelligence Analysis Tools
1998	US	Tools	Maybury	Tools for the Knowledge Analyst
2001	US	Tools	Porter	Tools of the Trade: A Long Way to Go
2006	US	Training	Anon	Source Guidebook for Open Source

227

				Intelligence in the Deep Web
2000	SE	Training	Bjore	PRIMER: How InfoSphere Uses the Internet
2002	SE	Training	Bjore	Sense-Making
2002	US	Training	Black	OSINT 101: Desktop Tools for Smart People
1999	US	Training	Caputo	Commercial Online Databases and the Internet
2002	US	Training	Chester	OSINT 101: NATO Lessons Learned
2000	US	Training	CSM	PRIMER: Top Secret Kodak Moments in Space
2000	US	Training	David	PRIMER: Intelligence Analysis in a New Century
2000	US	Training	Davis	PRIMER: Compendium of Analytic Tradecraft Notes
1996	US	Training	Donnelly	OSINT in the Information Age: Opportunities and Challenges
1999	NL	Training	Dunnink	User-Centric Approach to Tools (Slides)
1999	NL	Training	Dunnink	User-Centric Approach to Tools (Text)
1996	US	Training	Eiblum	Fishing for Free Info with GILS (Government Information Locator Service)
2000	NL	Training	Farace	PRIMER: Gray Literature 2: Finding the Not Easily Found
1999	US	Training	Feldman	The Internet Search-Off
1999	US	Training	Gupta & Bernstein	Remote Monitoring of the Spratley Islands (Commercial Imagery)
2002	US	Training	Henk	Respecting the Cultural Dimension: Intelligence and Africa
2002	US	Training	Hock	OSINT 101: Overview of the World of Information
2002	US	Training	Hohhof	OSINT 101: Competitive Intelligence Analysis Tools & Web-Sites
2002	US	Training	Klavans & Ashton	Technology Mapping with Open Sources of Information
2000	US	Training	Klein	PRIMER: Gray Literature 1: Finding the Needle in the Haystack
2004	US	Training	Koenig	Bibliography of Sources
2004	US	Training	Koenig	List of Organizations

2004	US	Training	Koenig	List of Web Sites
2000	US	Training	Lanza	PRIMER: Beyond the Internet (Slides)
2000	US	Training	Lanza	PRIMER: Beyond the Internet (Text)
2002	US	Training	Lee	OSINT 101: Geospatial Information Sources
1998	US	Training	Lowenthal for OSS	OSINT: New Myths, New Realities
2002	US	Training	Manwaring	Intelligence & Asymmetric Warfare
2002	US	Training	Marshall	OSINT and Global Hotspots
2004	US	Training	Mazzafro	Lessons from Iraq: How OSINT Can Help All-Source
2002	US	Training	Moore & Krizan	OSINT 101: Core Analytic Competencies
1998	NL	Training	Mulschlegel	Internet Search Tools and Search Techniques from User's View
2004	CA	Training	Mutton	Burden Sharing Approach to OSINT
1997	US	Training	Oehler	Example of a World Class OSINT Report on Proliferation
2006	US	Training	OSS	Open Source Intelligence Familiarization Links 2.0
2002	NATO	Training	OSS & SACLANT	NATO Open Source Intelligence Handbook
2003	NL	Training	Reuser	Intelligence Librarian Tradecraft
2006	NL	Training	Reuser	Virtual Open Source Agency
2000	US	Training	Rodriguez	PRIMER: Briefing on DIALOG
2000	US	Training	Rodriguez	PRIMER: Chart Comparing DIALOG to Internet (At the Time)
2000	US	Training	Sacks	PRIMER: Primary Research
2002	NATO	Training	SACLANT	NATO Intelligence Exploitation of the Internet
2002	NATO	Training	SACLANT & OSS	NATO Open Source Intelligence Reader
2000	US	Training	Sandman	Applied Human Intelligence
2002	US	Training	Smith	OSINT 101: Internet and Commercial Online Exploitation
2000	US	Training	Snowden	PRIMER: Geospatial Intelligence Options
2000	US	Training	Soule & Ryan	PRIMER: Gray Literature 3: Technical Briefing
1992	US	Training	Steele	Intelligence Preparation of the

				Battlefield: USMC Viewpoint
1996	US	Training	Steele	Original Open Source Intelligence Handbook Table of Contents
1998	US	Training	Steele	OPEN SOURCE INTELLIGENCE:EXECUTIVE OVERVIEW
1999	US	Training	Steele	Hand-Out of Convenience Center URLs (At the Time)
1999	US	Training	Steele	Hand-Out of OSINT URLs (At the Time)
1999	US	Training	Steele	Overview of Open Source Intelligence
1999	US	Training	Steele	Overview of Selected International Sources & Services (Slides)
2000	US	Training	Steele	PRIMER: A Few Thoughts on the Internet (At the Time)
2002	US	Training	Steele	OSINT 101: Cover and Contents
2002	US	Training	Steele	The New Craft of Intelligence: Personal, Public, & Political
2004	US	Training	Steele	The Future of Intelligence (Seven Tribes, Seven Standards)
2004	US	Training	Steele	The Failure of 21st Century Intelligence
2004	US	Training	Steele	PROCESSING: Make the Most of What You Know
2004	US	Training	Steele	NEW RULES: New Rules for the New Craft of Intelligence
2004	US	Training	Steele	COLLECTION: Know Who Knows
2004	US	Training	Steele	CINC Brief: 10 Minutes in 1997 with CINCSOC (today CSA)
2004	US	Training	Steele	ANALYSIS: All-Source Analysis, Making Magic
2004	US	Training	Steele	OVERVIEW: 9-11, U.S. Intelligence, & The Real World (Original)
2004	US	Training	Steele	OSINT & Strategic Generalizations
2004	US	Training	Steele	OPM Class: Afterthoughts & Additions
2004	US	Training	Steele	SOF Open Source Intelligence Handbook (Draft, Foreword by Simmons)
2004	US	Training	Steele	OSINT Executive Overview

230

				(Contents) in RTF
2004	US	Training	Steele	OSINT Executive Overview (Cover) in RTF
2004	US	Training	Steele	OSINT Executive Overview (Contents) in Word Doc
2004	US	Training	Steele	OSINT Executive Overview (Cover) in Word Doc
2006	US	Training	Steele	Steele on Future of Intelligence (New, Positive)
1998	US	Training	Steele & Lowenthal	OSINT: Executive Overview
1999	US	Training	Steele & Lowenthal	OSINT Private Sector Capabilities To Support DoD Policy, Acq, Ops
2006	US	Training	Sutton	Global Coverage: Review of Needed Funding
2006	US	Training	Turnbull	Information Sharing (GSA Collaboration Working Group)
2002	US	Training	Vickers	Inconvenient Warning
2000	US	Training	Webb & Steele	PRIMER: Integrated Analytic Toolkit Requirements
2001	US	Training	Zullo	The Internet and Premium Commercial Sources of Information
2004	US	Trip Report	Steele	Peacekeeping Intelligence Conference in Europe: Trip Report
2004	US	Trip Report	Steele	Harsh Comments on FBIS Mis-Statements at Intelink Conference
2004	US	Trip Report	Steele	High Praise for Intelink: Trip Report
2004	US	Values	Ray	Values in America
1997	US	Vendor	Blejer	SRA: Intelligence Information Systems
1999	US	Vendor	Boyer	AUTOMETRIC (Now Boeing): High Resolution Imagery
1998	UK	Vendor	Brenton	MEMEX Software
1997	US	Vendor	CORE	CORE SW: Business Plan Summary
1999	NL	Vendor	DataExpert	DateExpert
2004	US	Vendor	Dietz	LEXIS-NEXIS Open Sources on North Korea
2004	US	Vendor	Dietz	Top Ten Stories on North Korea
1996	US	Vendor	Dixon	LEXIS-NEXIS, Online Public Records and Criminal Investigations
1992	US	Vendor	Driver	N-STAR: An Automated Analyst

				Tool for Open Source Data
2006	US	Vendor	Fleming	Icosystem
1993	UK	Vendor	Hall	Jane's Approach to the New Threat Environment
1998	UK	Vendor	Hunter	I2: Creating Intelligence Automatically
1992	US	Vendor	Hutchinson	Jane's RUMOR OF WAR: An Information Vendor's View
1996	UK	Vendor	Hutchinson	Jane's: The Role of Sources in Open Intelligence
1997	US	Vendor	Jacobs	ISOQUEST: Software for Managing Information Overload
1992	US	Vendor	Kovaly	Unique Wire Service Provides Early Intelligence
1996	US	Vendor	Krattenmaker	LEXIS-NEXIS, LEXMAP Demonstration and Discussion
2006	US	Vendor	Lederman	Deep Web Technologies
1995	US	Vendor	McLagan	NewsEdge, Tailored News Alerts for a Competitive Edge
2001	US	Vendor	NA	Bright Planet White Paper on the Deep Web
1996	US	Vendor	Nachmanoff	Oxford Analytica: Economic Intelligence Services for the Private Sector
1995	US	Vendor	Nanz	Commercial Imagery and National Defense (Slides)
1995	US	Vendor	Nanz	Commercial Imagery and National Defense (Text)
1996	US	Vendor	Nanz	SPOT Image: Remarks on Commercial Imagery
1992	US	Vendor	Pincus	METAMORPH: Theoretical Background and Operational Functionality
1999	US	Vendor	Powerize	Powerize Overview
2006	US	Vendor	Proctor	IBM's Text Analytic OS Architecture
1998	US	Vendor	Retrieval Tech.	Real Time News Meets Knowledge Management
1997	US	Vendor	Rodriguez	DIALOG: Targetted Decisions Support versus Generic Internet
1995	UK	Vendor	Rolington	Jane's: A Theory of Open Source Information

2001	UK	Vendor	Rotheray	BBC Views on New Risks of Crisis Seen From Open Sources (Slides)
2001	UK	Vendor	Rotheray	BBC Views on New Risks of Crisis Seen From Open Sources (Text)
2006	US	Vendor	Ruh	CISCO's Application Oriented Network
1994	US`	Vendor	Vajta-Williams	Space Imaging, Commercial Imagery, and You
1992	US	Vendor	Vendor	PERISCOPE, Commercial Open Source
1997	US	Vendor	Weigand	Forecast International: Reducing Risk Via Practical OSINT (Slides)
1997	US	Vendor	Weigand	Forecast International: Reducing Risk Via Practical OSINT (Text)
1988	US	Whole Earth R	Baker, S.	Gossip
1988	US	Whole Earth R	Baker, W.	Gossip
1990	US	Whole Earth R	Barlow	Crime and Puzzlement: The Advance of the Law on the Electronic Frontier
1989	US	Whole Earth R	Berman	The Gesture of Balance
1982	US	Whole Earth R	Brand	Uncommon Courtesy: A School of Compassionate Skills
1988	US	Whole Earth R	Brand	The Information Wants to Be Free Strategy
1990	US	Whole Earth R	Brand	Outlaws, Musicians, Lovers, and Spies: The Future of Control
1992	US	Whole Earth R	Brand	Army Green
1985	US	Whole Earth R	Brand, Kelly, Kinney	Digital Retouching: The End of Photography as Evidence of Anything
1991	US	Whole Earth R	Brilliant	Computer Conferencing: The Global Connection
1991	US	Whole Earth R	Clay	Genes, Genius, and Genocide
1988	US	Whole Earth R	Coate	Tales from Two Communities: The Well and the Farm
1990	US	Whole Earth R	Dodge	Life Work
1987	US	Whole Earth	Donaldson	An Incomplete History of

		R		Microcomputing
1991	US	Whole Earth R	Elgin	Conscious Democracy Through Electronic Town Meetings
1986	US	Whole Earth R	Fend & Gunther	What Have You Got to Hide: Iraq Iran Basra Abadan
1988	US	Whole Earth R	Ferguson	Gossip
1988	US	Whole Earth R	Fields	Gossip
1991	US	Whole Earth R	Garcia	Assessing the Impacts of Technology
1989	US	Whole Earth R	Garfinkle	Social Security Numbers: And Other Telling Information
1991	US	Whole Earth R	Godwin	The Electronic Frontier Foundation and Virtual Communities
1989	US	Whole Earth R	Haight	Living in the Office
1988	US	Whole Earth R	Hardin	Gossip
1988	US	Whole Earth R	Hawkins	Computer Parasites & Remedies--A Catalog of First Sightings
1987	US	Whole Earth R	Henson	MEMETICS: The Science of Information Viruses
1987	US	Whole Earth R	Horvitz	An Intelligent Guide to Intelligence
1989	US	Whole Earth R	Horvitz	The USENET Underground
1985	US	Whole Earth R	Hunter	Public Image
1983	US	Whole Earth R	Illich	Silence is a Commons: Computers Are Doing to Communication What …
1990	JP	Whole Earth R	Ishii	Cross-Cultural Communications & Computer-Supported Cooperative Work
1989	US	Whole Earth R	Jaffe	Hello, Central: Phone Conferencing Tips
1989	US	Whole Earth R	Johnson`	The Portable Office
1990	US	Whole Earth R	Jordon III	Restoration: Shaping the Land, Transforming the Spirit

1992	US	Whole Earth R	Kapor et al	We Need a National Public Network
1991	US	Whole Earth R	Karraker	Highways of the Mind
1982	US	Whole Earth R	Kayes	Force Without Power: A Doctrine of Unarmed Military Service
1988	US	Whole Earth R	Keen	Gossip
1985	US	Whole Earth R	Kleiner	The Health Hazards of Computers: A Guide to Worrying Intelligently
1988	US	Whole Earth R	Kleiner	Gossip
1992	US	Whole Earth R	Kleiner	The Co-Evolution of Governance
1987	US	Whole Earth R	Krause	Bio-Acoustics: Habitat Ambience & Ecological Balance
1990	JP	Whole Earth R	Kumon	Toward Co-Emulation: Japan and the United States in the Information Age
1988	US	Whole Earth R	Leary	Gossip
1991	US	Whole Earth R	Lovins & Lovins	Winning the Peace
1985	US	Whole Earth R	Mander	Six Grave Doubts About Computers
1991	US	Whole Earth R	Marx	Privacy & Technology
1982	US	Whole Earth R	Meadows	Whole Earth Models & Systems
1991	US	Whole Earth R	Meeks	The Global Commons
1986	US	Whole Earth R	Minsky	Society of Mind
1990	US	Whole Earth R	Monschke	How to Heal the Land
1988	US	Whole Earth R	Nelson	Gossip
1988	US	Whole Earth R	Newroe	Distance Learning
1988	US	Whole Earth R	Pert	The Material Basis of Emotions with Inset, Mind as Information
1992	US	Whole Earth	Petersen	Will the Military Miss the Market

		R		
1988	US	Whole Earth R	Rappaport	Gossip
1989	US	Whole Earth R	Rheingold	Ethnobotany: The Search for Vanishing Knowledge
1991	US	Whole Earth R	Rheingold	Electronic Democracy: The Great Equalizer
1987	US	Whole Earth R	Roberts	Electronic Cottage on Wheels
1986	US	Whole Earth R	Sanders	Etiquette for the Age of Transparency
1991	US	Whole Earth R	Schuman	Reclaiming our Technological Future
1986	US	Whole Earth R	Scxhwartz & Brand	The World Information Economy
1990	US	Whole Earth R	Shapard	Observations on Cross-Cultural Electronic Networking
1992	US	Whole Earth R	Staple & Dixon	Telegeography: Mapping the New World Order
1992	US	Whole Earth R	Steele	E3i: Ethics, Ecology, Evolution, and Intelligence
1986	US	Whole Earth R	Thompson	A Gaian Politics
1988	US	Whole Earth R	Thurow & Walsh	Getting Over the Information Economy
1992	US	Whole Earth R	Tibbs	Industrial Ecology: An Environmental Agenda for Industry
1990	US	Whole Earth R	Vidal	Founding Father Knows Best
1991	US	Whole Earth R	Warren & Rheingold	Access to Political Tools: Effective Citizen Action
1991	US	Whole Earth R	White	Earthtrust: Electronic Mail and Ecological Activism
1991	US	Whole Earth R	Whitney-Smith	Information Doesn't Want
1991	US	Whole Earth R	Wittig	Electronic City Hall

Chapter 12:
The Failure of 20th Century Intelligence[1]

---

[1] This briefing, in color, with words in Notes format, is available at www.oss.net/FAILURE. Read from left to right.

OSS.NET®

Global Processing Failure I
No Data Standards

- Data standards (for instance, XML) are vital if we are to be able to exploit modern information technology.
- Microsoft is the enemy of the state! Open source software, and data standards, add value to your work.

OSS.NET®

Global Processing Failure II
No Geospatial Attributes

- Automated "all-source fusion" is not possible unless every datum, in every medium, has both a time *and* a geospatial attribute.
- XML Geo needs to be an international standard--you can lead.

OSS.NET®

Global Processing Failure III
No Interoperability or All-Source Mixing

- Security is the opposite of intelligence.
- Compartmentation is the enemy of knowledge.
- There must be one single processing agency where *everything* can be mixed and evaluated.

OSS.NET®

Global Analysis Failure I
Emphasis on Security Instead of Answers

- Intelligence is about decision-support--about answering the question!
- Must not confuse expertise, foreign languages, and security clearances nor should we require that the *same* person have them all! Mix and match...

OSS.NET®

Global Analysis Failure II
Focused on Threats Instead of Opportunities

- Threats that are here and now represent a strategic warning failure.
- Intelligence is at its best when it makes the case for preventive investments-- anticipatory policy-- opportunities for advantage.

OSS.NET®

Global Analysis Failure III
Emphasis on Local Now Vice Global Future

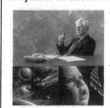

- Greatest intelligence value comes from strategic estimative analysis about *big* issues--*global* issues
- Politicians already know the local nuances--must teach them--and the public-- the global tradeoffs

Global Policy Failure I
Failure to Impact on Budget

- National intelligence has virtually no impact on how the citizen's taxes are allocated across various national priorities.
- We spend too much on hard power and almost nothing on soft power.

Global Policy Failure II
Failure to Impact on Policymaker Wisdom

- Policymakers are loosely-educated and often dismiss the value of global knowledge.
- Intelligence is most valuable to the public interest when it constantly educates policymakers in a compelling manner.

Global Policy Failure III
Failure to Win Public Support for Intelligence

- Intelligence is not taught in schools and there is no public appreciation for its vital contributions.
- We must establish a public discipline of intelligence across the seven tribes and in the public eye.

Global Acquisitions Failure I
Failure to Impact on What We Buy

Examples
- Aviation temperatures
- Cross-country mobility
- Line of sight distances
- Bridge loading limits
- Ports (-), Airheads (+)
- C4I anti-Internet/open
- OOTW assets (MP etc.)

- US military buys what contractors want to sell, not what we need.
- Strategic generalizations about the real world have no impact on procurement.
- US ignores allied interoperability and affordability needs.

Global Acquisitions Failure II
Failure to Impact on Private Sector IT

- Failed to legislate stable transparent Application Program Interfaces (API).
- Failed to define generic functionalities for joint development.
- Failed to define an agile security architecture.

Global Acquisitions Failure III
Failure to Provide for Intelligence

- US mobility, weapons, and C4I systems do not program funds for the acquisition and delivery of necessary data.
- Intelligence is treated as a "free" good.
- Commanders "assume" intelligence will be provided when needed.

239

OSS.NET®
Global Operations Failure I
Cannot Do Wide Area Surveillance

- US satellites optimized for finding Soviet missile silos
- Air-breather options never had the processing system created to do near real time change detection.
- Still a labor intensive "hit or miss" activity.

OSS.NET®
Global Operations Failure II
Cannot Do Last Mile

- Can't see under jungle canopy or into city streets
- Can't find single individuals with technology--still a clandestine human endeavor and generally can't do it

OSS.NET®
Global Operations Failure III
Cannot Do Real-Time Change Detection

- Air Operations Plans now require 24+ hours to prepare (US/NATO)
- Sensor to shooter processing is terrible-- and mostly manual
- Have lost ability to do quick reaction strikes-- when the lawyers let us.

OSS.NET®
Philosophical Failure I
National Tribe instead of Global Tribes

- National intelligence tribe has monopolized the money/attention.
- Failed to create generic intelligence discipline with seven tribes.
- Failed to develop regional or global intelligence networks.

OSS.NET®
Philosophical Failure II
Government Secrecy Over Public Sharing

- The new paradigm rewards sharing more than secrecy.
- Secrets are primarily valuable in the context of a rich open source knowledge foundation.
- Cannot have smart spies within dumb nation.

OSS.NET®
Philosophical Failure III
Letting Americans Lead is Wasteful

- American dominance of NATO intelligence is wasteful & dangerous.
- *We* need a European alternative emphasizing commercial security, web-based sharing, multi-cultural approaches, global burden-sharing.

240

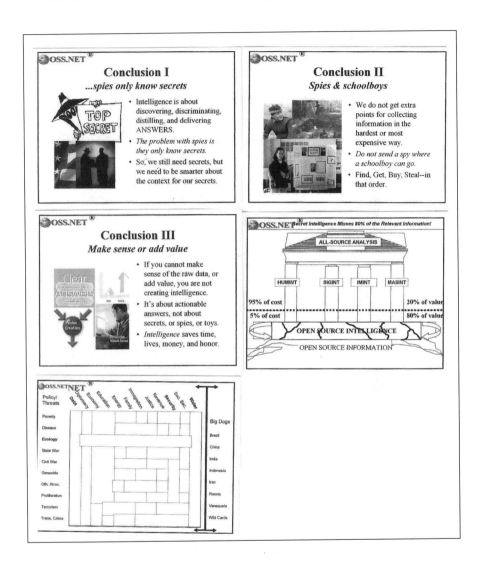

Note: A DVD of the author presenting this briefing at Hackers on Planet Earth 6 is freely available to Members and their staffs, as is a personal briefing by the author at a time and place of the Member's choosing.

Chapter 13
Bin Laden, National Intelligence, and How NOT to Spend the Taxpayer's Treasure[1]

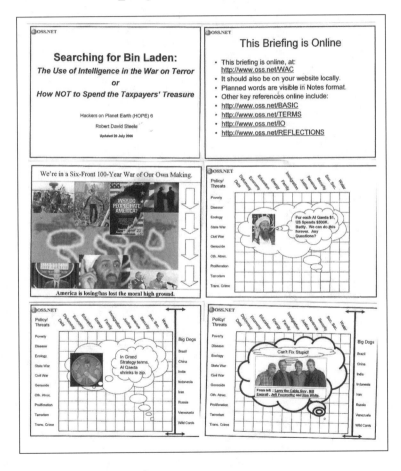

---

[1] This briefing is available in color with words in Notes format at the following URL: http://www.oss.net/HOPE. Read from left to right.

OSS.NET

Plan for the Brief

- Focused only on National Security Budget
- Initial Focus on $60B/Year Spent by IC
- Then Focus on $600B/Year Spent by DoD
- Review Books on Threats and Strategy
- Discuss Needed Reforms in America
- Conclude with Hope: Citizens Party (Non-Rival)

OSS.NET

National Security Writ Small

- Department of Defense - $600B/Year
  - Buys heavy metal military ill-suited to reality
- Department of State –
  - Buys Embassy fortresses and little else
- Department of Justice –
  - Buys heavy-handed ill-focused FBI & suits
- Department of Homeland Security –
  - Buys ill-directed hand-outs and little security

OSS.NET

National Security Writ Large

- Nurture and use <u>all</u> sources of power
- Educated and engaged citizenry
- Competent intelligence
  - Universal coverage (all countries & topics)
  - 24/7 (real time versus one-year "studies")
  - All languages
- Morally sound diplomacy not ideological
- Morally sound capitalism not predatory
- Balanced defense (four threat types)
- Coherent homeland security (engaged citizenry)
- Balanced budget, don't import poverty, export jobs

OSS.NET

Global Intelligence Failure
Breakdown in Collection and Understanding

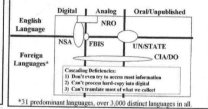

*31 predominant languages, over 3,000 distinct languages in all.

OSS.NET

Global Processing Failure
Breakdown in Exploitation, Dissemination

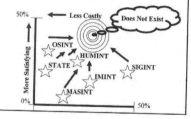

OSS.NET

Threats vs. Sources

Threat		
Threat #1:	Poverty	95%
Threat #2:	Infectious Disease	99%
Threat #3:	Environmental Degradation	90%
Threat #4:	Inter-State Conflict	75%
Threat #5:	Civil War	80%
Threat #6:	Genocide	95%
Threat #7:	Other Large-Scale Atrocities	95%
Threat #8:	Nuclear, bio-chemical weapons	75%
Threat #9:	Terrorism	80%
Threat #10:	Transnational organized crime	80%
Average Importance of "OSINT"		**86%**

244

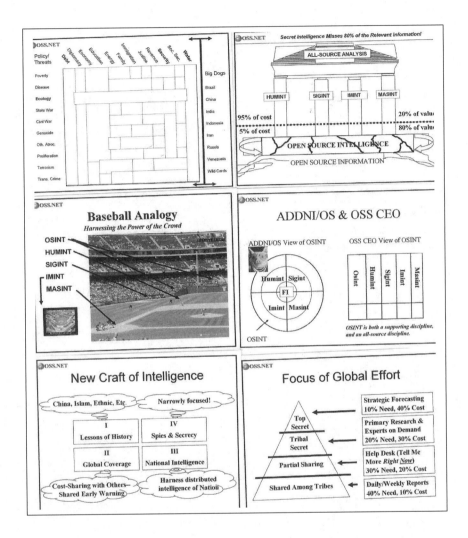

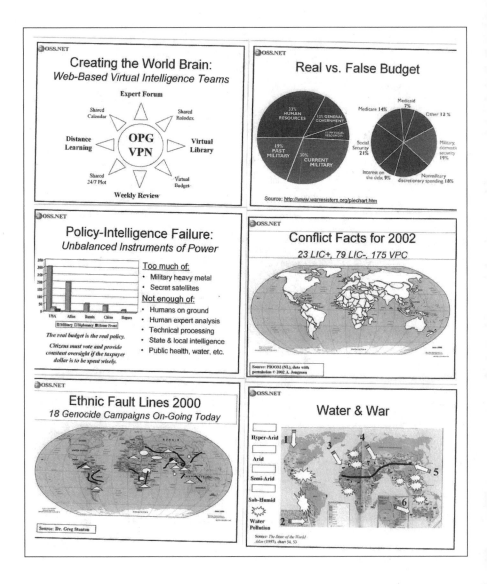

Global Threats to Local Survival

OSS.NET

Complex Emergencies 32 Countries		Water Scarcity & Contaminated Water**	
Refugees/Displaced 66 Countries		Ethnic Conflict 18 Genocides Today**	
Food Security 33 Countries		Resource Wars, Energy Waste & Pollution**	
Modern Plagues* 59 Countries & Rising		Corruption Common 80 Countries	
Child Soldiers 41 Countries		Censorship Very High 62 Countries	

*State of the World Atlas (1997). ** Marq de Villier (Water). John Heidenrich and Greg Stanton (Genocide). Michael Klare et al (Resources), all others from PIOOM Map 2002.

Taxpayer Dollars Focused on Just *10%* of the Threat

OSS.NET

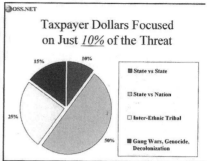

- State vs State
- State vs Nation
- Inter-Ethnic Tribal
- Gang Wars, Genocide, Decolonization

Presidential Trade-Offs
$100 million will buy:

OSS.NET

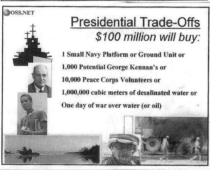

1 Small Navy Platform or Ground Unit or

1,000 Potential George Kennan's or

10,000 Peace Corps Volunteers or

1,000,000 cubic meters of desalinated water or

One day of war over water (or oil)

$1 T/Yr Not Being Leveraged

OSS.NET

- Between interest on the debt, unnecessary military systems, unnecessary secret satellites, and a wide variety of subsidies and tax loopholes, we waste $500B/Year.
- For lack of good economic intelligence and counterintelligence, and ethics at the top, we forego $500B a year in corporate tax contributions to revenue, import-export pricing and insurance fraud, and lost revenues from bandwidth and federally-controlled properties.

Policy-Intelligence Failure
Public is Neither Engaged Nor Informed

OSS.NET

World War III Players

Why This Matters
- Homeland security--"A Nation's best defense is an educated citizenry." (Thomas Jefferson)
- Prosperity--the financial value of ethics, trust, strategic culture
- Global security--the long-term value of public intelligence to multi-cultural policy initiatives, the best pre-emption is moral.

Pelton on Ground Truth

OSS.NET

- Most government and media sources have not actually had eyes on target and boots in the local mud
- You don't have to travel to these places to have them affect home front security
- We simply are not grasping essential ground truths

OSS.NET

Shawcross on Endless Conflict

- Peace operations are as complex and difficult as war operations
- Humanitarian assistance can create black markets and sustain a conflict
- Good will without strength makes things worse

OSS.NET

Kaplan on Frontier of Anarchy

- History, geography, and traveling third class are vital to true understanding
- We are engaged in "a protracted struggle between ourselves and the demons of crime, population pressure, environmental degradation, disease, and culture conflict."

OSS.NET

Heidenrich on Genocide

- 15-18 genocides going on today--scores more over time
- Genocide <u>can</u> be forecast and <u>can</u> be prevented
- Indifference is murder
- Global force needed

OSS.NET

Klare on Resource Wars

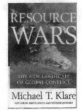

- Energy, Water, Timber, and Minerals will be at the heart of future war
- Ethnic conflict and great power disconnects will compound the challenge
- In this light, corporations are now belligerents and must be treated as such

OSS.NET

de Villiers on Water

- It is the average person, not the corporation, that does the most damage
- Pollution, dams, irrigation, and acquifer mining are all destroying our environment
- We need a national and global water conservation and replenishment strategy.

OSS.NET

Helvarg on Oceans

- Oceans more important than Amazon, should be protected
- Western economic interests are treating oceans as private mines and private cesspools
- Information available from NOAA and UN is not reaching public domain and could help citizen action

Thornton on Industrialized Poison

OSS.NET

- Need new paradigm for controlling bio-chemical threats to society, one focused on probability of risk instead of permission to kill pending proven risk
- "Good science" is code for value-free policy that risks citizens' long-term health for short-term corporate profit

Garrett on Globalized Disease

OSS.NET

- Health of our Nation depends on health of other nations
- Insurance and doctors have helped kill public health (prevention) in favor of hospitals and antibiotics
- We have created resistant forms of disease and may not be able to contain epidemics

Gray on Modern Strategy

OSS.NET

- Technology is not a substitute for strategy
- War is about getting your way, not about combat
- Time matters--use or lose
- Over time strategic culture is more important than arms or money.

Brzezinski on Grand Strategy

OSS.NET

- Europe, Russia, and Eurasian "stans" are the hearth of 21st century opportunity and threat
- Core new players are Turkey and Indonesia
- Iran is more stable, and China less of a threat, that conventional wisdom says
- Geopolitics more important than technology

Kupchan on Failure of Empire

OSS.NET

- Strategic cultures resist incoming information and suffer from "adjustment failure"
- Foreign internal instability merits rapid intervention with strong economic incentives
- Failure to intervene early will lead to emergence of aggressors that are difficult to defeat once out of the box.

Shultz et al on Complexity

OSS.NET

- "Most policymakers do not fully realize the dynamics of the world we live in." (Graham Fuller)
- History and culture are vital to security policy
- Non-military operations are as important as military operations at all times

OSS.NET

Cimbala on Friction

- Friction is real and is destroying our ability to match ends with means
- We don't have a strategy; we don't try to understand the strategies of others; we do not have unity of effort across the diplomatic-defense-justice continuum

OSS.NET

Revolutions *Not* Technical

- Concepts, not technology, are revolutionary
- Best revolutions are actually incremental and simple
- Technology is not a substitute for strategy
- Current & planned arsenal distantly related to real needs

OSS.NET

O'Hanlon on Aid Spending

- We spend half as much on aid as do most of the other developed countries
- Foreign aid in its current form is not preventing conflicts
- Best investment world-wide is in education of women, this cascades across issue areas

OSS.NET

Oakley on Police Peace Operations

- Failed states present us with a global problem that requires an international law enforcement reserve
- UN police often cannot read or drive a car and do not have doctrine
- Constabulary forces are different from small war forces

OSS.NET

Bowden on Manhunts

- Timing is everything--we let the thugs amass billions before we go after them
- We are weak in tactical intelligence against non-traditional (e.g. individual) targets, especially in cities
- It can be done--but is almost impossible to do well if host state is in chaos

OSS.NET

Warfare in the Third World

- Subjective factors including pain threshhold determinant
- Training absorption much more important that arms supplies
- Third World combat is both unconventional and never ending...

250

OSS.NET

Third World War

- Spreading insecurity is directly related to protracted conflict among societal groups
- Incompetent interventions make matters much worse
- Violence <u>can</u> be predicted
- Once begun, the violent will not listen to reason...

OSS.NET

Clark on Modern War

GENERAL WESLEY K. CLARK
WAGING MODERN WAR

- White House does not listen to early warning
- Army doesn't do mountains, tries not to use Apaches etc.
- Air Force doesn't do strategic mobility, needs 24 hours to redirect TACAIR
- Technology loses to weather, lacks intelligence

OSS.NET

Smart Holistic Strategy

- End state must be legitimate governments everywhere
- Ultimate investment is educational, both at home and abroad
- Must do inter-agency holistic planning, apply <u>all</u> the instruments of national power <u>all</u> the time

OSS.NET

The Tunnels of Cu Chi

THE TUNNELS OF CU CHI
Tom Mangold & John Penycate

- Never underestimate the enemy

OSS.NET

New Strategy: 1 + iii:
Need better balance

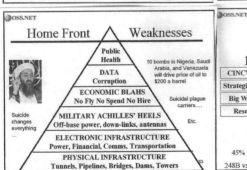

1	i	i	i
CINCWAR	CINCSOLIC	CINCPEACE	CINCHOME
Strategic NBC	Small Wars	State/USIA	Intelligence
Big War(s)	Constabulary	Peace Corps	Border Patrol
Reserve	Ground Truth	Economic Aid	Port Security
	Reserve	Environment	Electronic
		Peace Navy	Public Health
45%	20%	20%	15%
248B vs. 550B	110B vs 20B	110B vs. 20B	82B vs. 36B

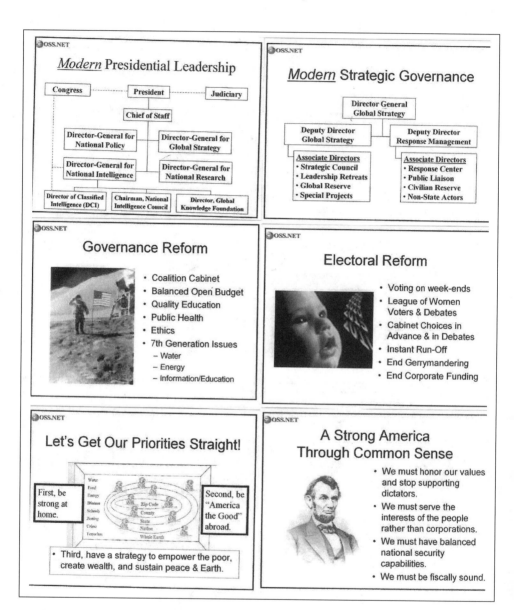

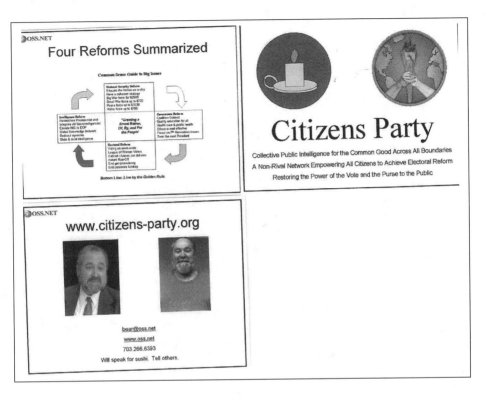

Note: A DVD of the author presenting this briefing at Hackers on Planet Earth 6 is freely available to Members and their staffs, as is a personal briefing by the author at a time and place of the Member's choosing.

Epilogue

Thomas Jefferson said it best: "A Nation's best defense is an educated citizenry." The sad truth of the matter is that Alvin Toffler is correct when he says that his greatest concern is the collapse of all of our institutions. From the New York Times being ineffective to the various religions becoming corrupt, to Congress losing sight of its responsibility as the FIRST branch of government, to the Executive being allowed by Congress to dismiss the policy process in favor of closed inner circles and their perceptions, to the end of the nuclear family and the end of cohesive communities bonded by a national language and the rich pluralistic traditions of a Nation that stands for the freedom to speak out, the freedom to dissent—these all bode ill for the future of the Republic.

Congress has a unique opportunity, either in September or upon its return—but most beneficially for all incumbents seeking re-election—in September—to enact legislation that provides for **public intelligence in the public interest.**

Congress should not under-estimate the Collective Intelligence of the Nation, nor should Congress underestimate the aroused fury of the people as they learn of the mistakes if not the deceptions of the past. The public now has a digital memory, and the public now has a body of activists committed to "the whole truth and nothing but the truth." The days of top-down back-room decisions are over. America is migrating toward a bottom-up "show me" consensual form of governance, and Congress would do well to be attentive to the new opportunities for enhancing public intelligence in support of public policy.

Every aspect of the Smart Nation Act has been thought about and discussed by the top experts in the field. Some bureaucrats will oppose it for selfish reasons, seeking to protect budget share. They are like the Army cavalry generals who accepted the motor truck as a faster means of getting horses and mules to the battlefield. Open Source Intelligence (OSINT), public intelligence, will contribute directly to intelligence reform, to acquisition reform, and to governance reform. Congress has a chance to make a difference, quickly. A Smart Nation Act will both harness and unleash the Collective Intelligence of the Nation, and the world, for the eternal benefit of the United States of America. *St.*

Appendix: The Other Books

	***ON INTELLIGENCE: Spies and Secrecy in an Open World*** Foreword by Senator David Boren (D-OK) Basic reference work providing in extreme detail an examination of all that is wrong with secret intelligence, and how to make it right.
	***THE NEW CRAFT OF INTELLIGENCE: Personal, Public, & Political*** Foreword by Senator Pat Roberts (R-KS) Discusses in detail both global reality and the "new rules" of intelligence.
	***INFORMATION OPERATIONS: All Information, All Languages, All the Time*** Foreword by Congressman Rob Simmons (R-CT-02) Discusses operational challenges, information challenges, and provides both a strategic concept for global IO and multinational information sharing, and a requirements statement for the next generation of intelligence and information sharing capabilities.
	***PEACEKEEPING INTELLIGENCE: Emerging Concepts for the Future*** Foreword by Dame Pauline Neville-Jones, UK Seminal work in the field (edited), combining real-world experiences of practioners, lessons learned from academic studies, a peacekeeping intelligence leadership digest, and historical "best in class" articles on peacekeeping intelligence.

Forthcoming Books

Information Metrics, by Thomas J. Berkholtz

Commercial Intelligence, by Mats Bjore (Sweden)